HOLOCAUST EDUCATION

CHALLENGES FOR THE FUTURE

The National Catholic Center for Holocaust Education, Seton Hill University

The National Catholic Center for Holocaust Education (NCCHE) was established on the campus of Seton Hill University in 1987. Seton Hill initiated this national Catholic movement toward Holocaust studies in response to the urging of Pope John Paul II to recognize the significance of the Shoah, the Holocaust, and to "promote the necessary historical and religious studies on this event which concerns the whole of humanity today." The NCCHE has as its primary purpose the dissemination of scholarship on the root causes of antisemitism, its relation to the Holocaust, and the implications of both from the Catholic perspective for today's world. Toward this end, the Center is committed to equipping scholars, especially those at Catholic institutions, to enter into serious discussion on the causes of antisemitism and the Holocaust; shaping appropriate curricular responses at Catholic institutions and other educational sites; sustaining Seton Hill's Catholic Institute for Holocaust Studies in Israel through a cooperative program with Yad Vashem, the Isaac Jacob Institute for Religious Law, and the Hebrew University; encouraging scholarship and research through conferences, publications, workshops for educators, and similar activities; sponsoring local events on the Holocaust and related topics in the university and the community; and enhancing Catholic-Jewish relations.

HOLOCAUST EDUCATION

CHALLENGES FOR THE FUTURE

Carol Rittner, R.S.M.
Editor

Tara Ronda
Managing Editor

HOLOCAUST EDUCATION
CHALLENGES FOR THE FUTURE

Editor, Carol Rittner, R.S.M.
Managing Editor, Tara Ronda

Published in the United States by
Seton Hill University
National Catholic Center for Holocaust Education
1 Seton Hill Drive
Greensburg, Pennsylvania 15601-1599
724-830-1033
ncche@setonhill.edu
http://ncche.setonhill.edu

ISBN 978-0-9830571-1-6

Funding from The Ethel LeFrak Holocaust Education Conference Endowment made possible both The Ethel LeFrak Holocaust Education Conference and publication of The Ethel LeFrak Holocaust Education Conference Proceedings.

The papers contained in this publication express the opinions of the individual authors and do not necessarily represent the views of the National Catholic Center for Holocaust Education or Seton Hill University.

Cover: *Camp,* 1992
By Samuel Bak. Image Courtesy of Pucker Gallery. Used with Permission

Design and artwork by Glen Powell Graphic Design
Printed by Laurel Valley Graphics, Inc., Latrobe, Pennsylvania 15650

Dedicated to

Dr. JoAnne Woodyard Boyle
President of Seton Hill University
1987 – 2013

" . . . we are in this world to do good . . ."

-- Primo Levi, "Lorenzo's Return" in *Moments of Reprieve*

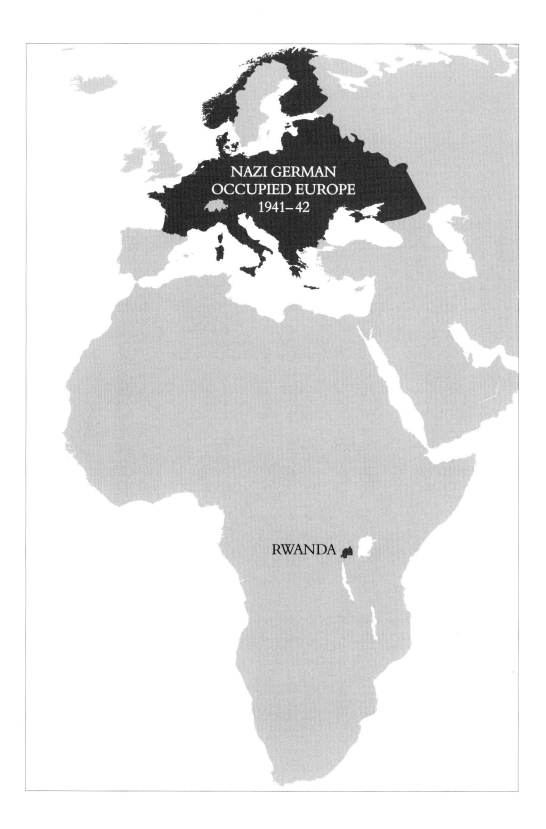

NAZI GERMAN
OCCUPIED EUROPE
1941–42

RWANDA

Table of Contents

Part III: Genocide in Rwanda (1994)

Part IV: The Ethel LeFrak Outstanding Student Scholar Essays

Commemoration, *2001 by Samuel Bak*
Image Courtesy of Pucker Gallery

PART I:
INTRODUCTION

Holocaust Education: Challenges for the Future

. . . .

Carol Rittner, R.S.M.

Distinguished Professor of Holocaust & Genocide Studies and
Dr. Marsha Radicoff Grossman Professor of Holocaust Studies,
The Richard Stockton College of New Jersey, Galloway, NJ

There are many challenges when it comes to Holocaust education, particularly in our "fast moving, changing world, where technology can dictate political, economic, and social changes."[1] But it seems to me that few challenges are more daunting for educators than trying to teach about the response of the Christian churches to the persecution and murder of the Jews in Germany and elsewhere during the Nazi Third Reich, World War II, and the Holocaust. Why? Because it is a complicated topic and does not lend itself to simple black and white answers. What do I mean? For starters, one should not speak about the response of "the Church" to the persecution of the Jews as if there were only one church in Germany, because, in fact, there was not just *one* Christian church in Germany – or elsewhere in Nazi-occupied Europe – but multiple Christian churches divided into different *denominations*, all of which had their own doctrines, practices, authorities, and governing structures.

Christian Churches

There were, for example, Roman Catholic and Protestant Churches. While the Roman Catholic Church was fairly uniform relative to how it was organized and governed and what it believed and taught, Protestant Churches had various structures, doctrines, and beliefs. Protestants included the German Evangelical Church, among whose number were the three major theological traditions that had emerged from the Reformation: Lutheran, Reformed, and United. There were also smaller so-called "free" Protestant churches, such as Methodist and Baptist churches, and then there were the Jehovah's Witnesses, Seventh Day Adventists, and Christian Scientists, among others.

During the Nazi era, among the Protestants, one could find churches that were part of the "German Christian" (*Deutsche Christen*) movement, a politically powerful minority group of pro-Nazi Christians and churches headed by Bishop Ludwig Müller, appointed by Hitler himself to lead the movement. There were also churches that were part of the "Confessing Church," which consisted of 6,000 Protestant pastors who opposed Hitler and the Nazis when it came to the so-called "Aryan paragraph," which required Christian pastors to be dismissed from their pastorates if they had a Jewish ancestral background. While the Confessing Church "insisted upon the churches' freedom from state control in religious matters," it "signaled little opposition to Nazi anti-Semitism."[2] Included in the Confessing Church were such luminaries as Dietrich Bonhoeffer and Martin Niemoeller, among others.

The differences among and between these Christian churches are not insignificant, and anyone trying to teach about the response of the Christian churches to the persecution of the Jews in Germany during the Holocaust must make sure that they keep an *–es* attached to the word **church**. Too often, in my experience, I have found that many teachers forget that it was not **just** the Roman Catholic Church that failed to speak out or help the Jews during the Holocaust, but other Christian churches, as well. Thus, one must make an effort to learn something about the differences between and among these churches in Germany and throughout Nazi German-occupied Europe during World War II and the Holocaust if one is going to try to sort out, understand, and teach about the response of the churches to the persecution of the Jews.

Another thing one has to keep in mind is the contradictory fact – and this applies to all the churches – that Christianity, "a religion of love that taught its members the highest moral principles for acting well. Love your neighbor. Seek peace. Help those in need. Sympathize with and raise up the oppressed. Do to others as you would have them do to you," **also** taught its members that Jews were "Christ-killers, children of the devil, desecrators and defilers of all goodness, responsible for an enormous range of human calamities and suffering." And "this hatred […] led Christians, over the course of almost two millennia, to commit many grave crimes and injuries against Jews, including mass murder."[3] It is with such knowledge, as well as a clear understanding of this contradictory context, that teachers must try to find their way through a complicated labyrinth when teaching about the response of the Christian churches to the persecution and murder of Jews during the Holocaust.

Theology and History

Post-Holocaust Christianity, notably the Roman Catholic Church – but other Christian churches as well – has expressed remorse, clearly and repeatedly, for Christian mistreatment of the Jewish people over the course of nearly two millennia. After World War II and the Holocaust, many Christian churches reformed their characterization and understanding of Jews and Judaism. They incorporated their new understanding into their teaching and preaching, into their biblical commentaries and theological textbooks.[4] Still, those of us who teach about the Holocaust, whether in high school or at the college and university level, have to recognize that there remains a fair amount of ignorance about and prejudice toward Jews and Judaism among some Christians – and among others, too, including Muslims.

In teaching about the Holocaust, we have to deal with the underside of Christian theology and history – that is, with 1,500 years of anti-Judaism in Christian theology – and we have to do so in a way that is historically accurate, theologically correct, and religiously sensitive. We have to teach about these issues in a manner that will enable students – of whatever religious tradition, or none – to be open to the questions and non-defensive about the "answers" regarding anti-Judaism in Christian theology and antisemitism in human history.

We must do so in order to help our students understand how some Christian beliefs and practices prepared the seed ground that helped make possible the persecution and murder of the Jews of Germany and German-occupied Europe during World War II and the Holocaust. And all the while, we also have to acknowledge that there were some Christians and even some Christian churches who resisted the Nazis because they were not disabled by centuries of anti-Jewish teaching and preaching or by antisemitic views and attitudes in church and society.

As Father Kevin Spicer, C.S.C., has said, when dealing with the response of the Christian churches during the Holocaust, nothing is black and white. Rather, there are various shades of grey.[5] There were Christians and Christian churches who resisted the Nazis, and there were Christians and Christian churches who wholeheartedly embraced the Nazis and their agenda to rid the world of Jews and other "undesirables," and there were Christians, even some few Christian churches – Catholic and Protestant – who tried to hide and help Jews and who paid with their lives for doing so.

The Challenge of the Exception

In Germany, "[t]hroughout the period of Nazi rule […] the German Protestant and Catholic churches, their governing bodies, their bishops, and most of their theologians watched the suffering that Germans inflicted on the Jews in silence." There were no explicit public words "of sympathy for the Jews, no explicit public condemnation[s] or protest[s] against their persecution issued from any authoritative figures within the churches or from any of the ecclesiastical offices. Only a few lowly pastors and priests spoke out or rather, cried out forlornly their sympathy with the Jews."[6]

We must not forget these few lowly pastors and priests who spoke out in solidarity with the suffering Jews – people like Monsignor Bernhard Lichtenberg of Berlin's St. Hedwig's Roman Catholic Cathedral, who openly and publicly said a daily prayer for the Jews. He eventually was arrested by the Gestapo and died on his way to Dachau. Or people like Dr. Gertrud Luckner, neither a priest nor a pastor, but a Catholic laywoman who worked for *Caritas* and tried to create a Catholic network to rescue Jews. The Gestapo arrested her and sent her to Ravensbrück concentration camp in 1943. She survived and after the war dedicated herself to repairing and improving Catholic-Jewish relations in Germany. But what we must remember is that the few in the Christian churches in Germany who helped were the exception, not the rule.

In occupied Europe, there was a relatively small number of Christian churches that tried to help the Jews during the Holocaust. The Danish Lutheran Church, for example, issued a pastoral letter in October 1943 expressing solidarity with the Jews. There was also the Bulgarian Orthodox Christian Church, whose Metropolitan in Sofia spoke out for the Jews in "old" Bulgaria. In other parts of occupied Europe, there were men like Catholic Bishop Jules-Gérard Saliège in France, Metropolitan Andrei Szeptyckyj of the Uniate Catholic Church in Ukraine, and Protestant Christians like André and Magda Trocmé in La Chambon, France, as well as a few other Protestant and Catholic clergy who spoke out and tried to help the Jews. But theirs were lonely voices and individual actions. They were not strong enough to stem the tide of evil engulfing the Jews of Germany and other parts of Europe during the Holocaust.

These few people are the *challenge of the exception*. We should ask ourselves what religious beliefs enabled them to recognize the evil and to resist the Nazis in Germany and elsewhere in occupied Europe? What enabled them to speak up or act on behalf of the Jews who were being persecuted, hunted down, and murdered during the Holocaust?

What Made the Difference?

We know what motivated the Nazis and their collaborators: racist ideology, anti-Jewish theological concepts, antisemitism, and hatred of "the other." But what motivated those few Christian churches and those few lowly pastors and priests, Christian laymen and women who tried to help the Jews? As the Protestant Evangelical Christian scholar David Rausch writes,

> The historian is overwhelmed with the question, what made the difference? What made the difference between the few who helped the Jewish people during their dreadful persecution and the multitude who

turned their backs on them? […] What is that moral kernel within our psychological, mental, or religious makeup that makes some react differently from the multitude in the face of prejudice, scapegoating, caricature, oppression, and outright physical violence to a race or religious group different from their own?

That is a difficult question in light of the Holocaust, as its study reveals that only a few Evangelicals, a few Protestants, a few Catholics, a few Orthodox, a few agnostics, and a few atheists (and not necessarily in that order) helped the Jewish people during their persecution.[7]

I have read many books about what beliefs motivated Christians – both churches and individuals – to respond to the persecution of the Jews during the Nazi era, World War II, and the Holocaust, but in my view, none is more powerful than this belief: "Do unto others as you would have them do to you" (Matt. 7:12). If the Christian churches and their people in Nazi Germany and elsewhere in "Christian" Europe had taken that teaching of Jesus to heart and put it into practice, we would not be considering the few, whether individual Protestant or Catholic churches or individual Protestant or Catholic Christians, who resisted the Nazis and tried to help Jews during the Holocaust, but the many who helped and hid Jews during the Holocaust.

The Few and the Many
As Sister Gemma Del Duca has said, "The study of the Holocaust has much to teach about the danger of dictatorship, about the necessity to be guided by religious, ethical principles and universal human values, and about the difficulty and importance of maintaining human dignity in extreme situations."[8] The challenge for all of us, whether teachers or students, is to learn from our study of the Holocaust and other genocides, too.

The essays in *Holocaust Education: Challenges for the Future* are intended to educate and encourage students and others who may be "in extreme situations" to see, judge, and act on behalf of those whose lives are in danger. In other words, studying about the Holocaust should encourage the few who will help become the many who will help. *That* is the challenge of Holocaust education, now and into the future.

Notes

1. See further Gemma Del Duca, S.C., The Ethel LeFrak Holocaust Education Conference Brochure, p. 2.
2. Richard L. Rubenstein and John K. Roth, *Approaches to Auschwitz: The Holocaust and Its Legacy*, rev. ed. (Louisville, KY: Westminster John Knox Press, 2003), p. 259.
3. Daniel Jonah Goldhagen, *A Moral Reckoning: The Role of the Catholic Church in the Holocaust and Its Unfulfilled Duty of Repair* (New York: Alfred A. Knopf, 2002), p. 3.

4. See further, for example, Mary C. Boys, *Has God Only One Blessing? Judaism as a Source of Christian Self-Understanding* (New York: Paulist Press, 2000), and John Connelly, *From Enemy to Brother: The Revolution in Catholic Teaching on the Jews, 1933-1965* (Cambridge, MA: Harvard University Press, 2012).
5. Personal email to me, June 2012.
6. Daniel Jonah Goldhagen, *Hitler's Willing Executioners: Ordinary Germans and the Holocaust* (New York: Alfred A. Knopf, 1996), pp. 436-437.
7. David Rausch, "Hard Questions Asked by the Holocaust," *The Holocaust and the Christian World*, eds. Carol Rittner, Stephen Smith, and Irena Steinfeldt (London, UK: Kuperad, 2000), p. 11.
8. Del Duca, p. 2.

Vatican II and Jewish-Christian Relations: The Legacy and the Challenges Ahead

John T. Pawlikowski, O.S.M.

*Professor of Social Ethics; Director, Catholic-Jewish Studies Program,
Catholic Theological Union, Chicago, IL*

There is no question that chapter four of *Nostra Aetate* ("In Our Time"), Vatican II's statement on interreligious relations, has profoundly impacted Catholic-Jewish relations and also influenced Christian-Jewish relations. The Canadian theologian Gregory Baum, who served as an expert at Vatican II and was involved with the early stages of the text, has termed chapter four the most radical transformation of the ordinary magisterium of the church to emerge from Vatican II.[1] After arguing for centuries that the Jews were responsible for the death of Christ, and as a consequence were ejected from any further covenantal relationship with God, the Roman Catholic Church at Vatican II proclaimed the continuity of the Jewish covenant while rejecting the notion of collective Jewish responsibility for the events on Calvary. It should be noted that the American Catholic hierarchy played a decisive role in shepherding *Nostra Aetate* through the various sessions of the Council until its final approval by an overwhelming margin in October 1965 at the Council's closing session. Without the strong support of the American hierarchy, this document may well have fallen by the wayside in the face of strong attacks from important sectors of the Curia and episcopal delegations.[2]

A person who should not be forgotten in this process is the late Msgr. George Higgins of Chicago, who worked for the Conference of Bishops in Washington and who played a crucial behind-the-scenes role in garnering support within the American episcopacy present at the Council. This also holds true for Fr. Thomas

Stransky, C.S.P., who worked closely with Cardinal Augustine Bea, S.J., in framing the text of chapter four in a way that was acceptable to the body of bishops. Hopefully, Fr. Stransky will complete his reflections on the development of *Nostra Aetate*, a project that has occupied his attention for some years, within the near future. These reflections will prove immensely useful in understanding the dynamics behind the final text.

My focus in this essay will essentially be on Catholic-Jewish relations. Given the diverse nature of Protestant Christianity and the downturn in the influence of ecumenical Protestant coalitions such as the World Council of Churches and the National Council of Churches, one would need to examine developments in each particular denomination, an impossibility for a presentation such as this. As for the Christian Orthodox community, regrettably only a few minor attentions in its understanding of Judaism have occurred.

Nostra Aetate's Impact

The first impact of *Nostra Aetate* was to be seen in the area of textbooks. The pioneering work of the late Sister Rose Thering, O.P., at St. Louis University on the most widely used Catholic textbooks at the primary- and secondary-school levels was given a heightened status with the passage of *Nostra Aetate*. In fact, Sister Thering's study, along with two other studies at St. Louis University on literature and social studies textbooks, were brought to the Second Vatican Council by the late Rabbi Marc Tannenbaum, an official Jewish observer at the Council, and played an important role in convincing the American bishops to support *Nostra Aetate*.[3] Soon after the close of Vatican II, the Office of Ecumenical and Interreligious Affairs at the Catholic Bishops' Conference in Washington, D.C., brought together representatives from the major Catholic textbook publishers to emphasize the need to incorporate *Nostra Aetate*'s new constructive vision of the Church's relationship with the Jewish people into their publications. This challenge was accepted by the publishers in a significant way. Subsequent studies by Dr. Eugene J. Fisher in the seventies[4] and Dr. Philip Cunningham in the early nineties[4] confirmed that the basic distortions of Jews and Judaism present in the pre-conciliar texts had been removed, replaced by a far more positive outlook on the Church's links with the Jewish religion.

Let me add here that the St. Louis studies were part of a tri-faith examination of textbooks coordinated by the American Jewish Committee that included a similar analysis of Protestant and Jewish educational materials. The results from the Protestant studies were quite similar to the Catholic results. As for the Jewish texts, their primary sin was omission of anything on Christianity rather than outright distortion. One short follow-up study on Protestant texts showed some backsliding within certain materials. There has never been a follow-up to the original Jewish study, nor did the original study receive the circulation of the Catholic and Protestant ones. I would strongly propose that appropriate leaders in each religious community undertake a new analysis of their textbooks in terms of Jewish-Christian relations. Such studies would prove very beneficial in identifying issues that require further clarification and development in their own educational materials.

Subsequent to the major rewriting of textbooks, a series of other positive developments have transpired. On the American scene, Dr. M. Christine Athans, B.V.M., offers a comprehensive overview of these developments in an essay in the *U.S. Catholic Historian*.[6] Permit me to summarize a few of the most important ones.

The changes introduced into Catholic educational materials, as well as *Nostra Aetate* itself, were influenced by the beginnings of a revolution in biblical interpretation that began prior to the Council. That revolution affected the Christian understanding of the Old Testament as well as the portrait of Jesus and his teachings. *Nostra Aetate* and the 1985 Vatican *Notes*, along with leading Catholic figures like Cardinals Carlo Martini, S.J., and Joseph Bernardin, were able to present a vision of Jesus in which he was seen as deeply rooted, in a positive sense, in many of the Jewish teachings of his time. Cardinal Martini, a noted biblical scholar in his own right, has written that "Without a sincere feeling for the Jewish world and a direct experience of it, one cannot fully understand Christianity. Jesus is fully Jewish, the apostles are Jewish, and one cannot doubt their attachment to the renditions of their forefathers."[7]

And, in some Christian circles, the Old Testament was even undergoing a name change to "Hebrew Scriptures," "First Testament," or "Tanach" and, more importantly, there was a basic perspectival shift in the Christian view of the first part of the Church's sacred scriptures. The Hebrew Scriptures, my preferred term, were no longer being seen as primarily a prelude or foil for enhanced New Testament teachings, but rather as a source of continuing revelation and spirituality for Christians, as indeed they had been for Jesus himself. The prevalent view that Jewish scholars of the Tanach had nothing to teach Christians because the Old Testament could be authentically interpreted only in the light of the New Testament was falling by the wayside.

The dominant approach to New Testament exegesis associated with the German scholar Rudolph Bultmann that had fundamentally dissociated Jesus from his Jewish roots was breaking down, being replaced with an approach that underlines the importance of knowing the Jewish religious context of Jesus' day for an authentic interpretation of His message. Exegetes were now placing Jesus and the early church squarely within a Jewish setting, undercutting the view put forth by many of their predecessors such as Gerhard Kittel and Martin Noth, who expressed a commonplace view in Bultmann's widely read volumes, *History of Israel* and *The Laws of the Pentateuch and Other Studies:* "Jesus himself [...] no longer formed part of the history of Israel. In him the history of Israel was the process of his rejection and condemnation by the Jerusalem religious community [...] Hereafter the history of Israel moved quickly to its end."[8] The new outlook on Jesus and the early Church has impacted several important official Catholic documents, such as the 1985 Vatican *Notes* and the 2001 Pontifical Biblical Commission's 200-page monograph on how Jews and their Scriptures are seen in the New Testament.

Christian Biblical Interpretation

In the years that have followed the original repositioning of the Christian perspectives on the linkage between Judaism and Christianity in terms of the sacred scripture, we have witnessed even more dramatic developments in the world of biblical interpretation. These developments are often collated under the heading of the "Parting of the Ways" scholarship.[9] Cardinal Joseph Bernardin gave his personal support to this line of biblical interpretation in several of his writings on Catholic-Jewish relations.[10]

The "Parting of the Ways" movement has many voices with diverse perspectives. However, one finds coalescence on several key points: (1) The separation between church and synagogue was a slow, drawn-out process that took at least a century or more in most places and even longer in certain regions. Some scholars, such as David Boyarin, see the Council of Nicea in 325 C.E. as the decisive point of rupture. (2) There was no clear-cut Christian identity in the first century. Most believers of Jesus and his message continued to regard themselves as part of the Jewish community and engaged in various forms of Jewish religious practice. (3) The apostle Paul was not inherently opposed to the continuation of the Jewish Torah tradition and may, in fact, have personally remained to some degree a practicing Jew even after his "conversion" to Christ. (4) The supposed conflict between Jesus and the Pharisees and Jesus and "the Jews" in John's gospel were largely internal battles among various groups of Jews who had accepted Christ and his teachings in different ways and were vying for the dominance of their various perspectives.

This revolution in biblical interpretation has become widespread in Christian scholarship and also is emerging to a degree in contemporary Jewish scholarship. Regrettably, however, it has hardly penetrated into other areas of Christian theology, including systematic, ethics, and liturgy (including the texts of Christian hymns).[11] Such integration remains one of the most important challenges still before us in terms of Christian-Jewish relations. Pope John Paul II spoke on numerous occasions of a deep-seated bond between Jews and Christians at the very level of their basic identities.[12] But, on the whole, neither Christian nor Jewish scholars have picked up and developed this theme, and it has received virtually no attention in the official inter-institutional dialogues.

There are a few exceptions to this continuing neglect of the revolution in biblical scholarship in other areas of scholarly interpretation. On the Christian side, I would point to the recent publication of the work of a group of American and European

Christian scholars (with Jewish consultants) titled *Christ Jesus and the Jewish People Today: New Explorations of Theological Interrelationships*.[13] The work of this four-year project, which enjoyed the full support of Cardinal Walter Kasper and in which he personally participated, focused around the central question, "How can we affirm the continuity of the Jewish covenant and continue to maintain a universal significance for the work of Christ?" While this project has hardly provided a consensus answer to this mega-question, it has moved Christian thought in the right direction in the continuing exploration of this most fundamental issue for Christian theology. The new book edited by Eugene Korn and Robert Jensen titled *Covenant and Hope* is another important contribution to this effort.[14]

Jewish Scholarship

On the Jewish side, we have seen a few promising developments of late. *Dabru Emet*, the Jewish document on Christianity, while not delving into theology in any depth, certainly removed some of the boulders that have blocked Jewish scholars from undertaking a theological re-evaluation of Christianity beyond the classical "idolatry" understanding. Individual Jewish scholars such as Elliot Wolfson, who has spoken of an "incarnational" notion in parts of the Jewish mystical literature in Jesus' day,[15] and Benjamin Sommer, who has written about a certain "divine embodiment" in Jewish and other religious documents from the ancient world, are two examples.[16]

By far the most radical stab at a Jewish theological approach to Christianity has come very recently from Daniel Boyarin, who has been on the cutting edge of Christian-Jewish scholarship for some years. In his latest volume, *The Jewish Gospels: The Story of the Jewish Christ*,[17] Boyarin strongly maintains that all major Christian theological themes find their roots in Jewish teachings of the day. As he sees it, Christology was already a "job description" present in Judaism that was eventually applied to Jesus. That application created some differences between the Jews who in no way accepted Jesus and his teachings and those who opted for some association with his perspective. But the latter group was still included in the wide Jewish tent of the day. It was not until the Council of Nicea, as was mentioned earlier, that the Christian-Jewish option was shut down for those in the Church. While Boyarin may have not yet fully proven his thesis, it is one that neither Christian nor Jewish theologians can ignore. If it prevails, it would cause major splits in the traditional theological wall between Judaism and Christianity on issues such as Incarnation and Trinitarianism.

Other Scholarly Approaches

Soon after the passage of *Nostra Aetate*, several Catholic and Protestant scholars began to explore ways in which the conciliar vision and the new biblical scholarship could be incorporated into systematic theology. They included people such as Monika Hellwig, Paul van Buren, Clemens Thoma, and others. Many, if not most, are now deceased and their replacements have been slow in coming. I myself have been part of this process with my books *Christ in the Light of the Christian-Jewish Dialogue* and *Jewish and the Theology of Israel*.[18] I have further amplified my perspective in a major essay in the *Irish Theological Quarterly* and in two contributions to edited volumes that take up questions related to Paul and Judaism.[19]

I cannot lay out my theological model in its entirety in this essay. Suffice it to say that it is basically grounded in an incarnational theological perspective rather than a messianic Christology, or what I would term a "blood Christology," in which the emphasis is placed on Christ's salvific sacrificial blood-letting on Calvary. The "blood Christology," I might add, was popularized in Mel Gibson's highly controversial film *The Passion of Christ*, which regrettably received support in certain ecclesiastical circles despite the strong criticism it received from a host of biblical and other scholars. In my vision, what became far more transparent through Jesus' ministry and death on Calvary was the profound intimacy between humanity and divinity, with Christ as the central point of linkage, an intimacy that ultimately makes possible human salvation and divine-human reconciliation. But in the process of coming into this new understanding, which if Jewish scholars like Boyarin are to be believed has roots in the Jewish tradition of the day, the Church significantly severed itself from the original revelation through the Jewish people that we need to regain in a positive way as an integral part of Christian identity. We also will need to continue to explore what resonance such an understanding of a God-Man Messiah might have in Jewish thought, something that, as I have already indicated, a few Jewish scholars have begun to investigate.

In the lengthy process of separation, Christianity lost sight of the original revelatory vision associated with the Sinai covenant, a revelation that the late A. Roy Eckardt insisted was in principle as crucial for an authentic Christian identity as the revelation in and through the Christ event. Hence, we need to envision the Christian-Jewish relationship in terms of two distinctive, but not totally distinct, paths that will converge, as Cardinal Walter Kasper has stressed, only in the eschatological age. These paths must be seen as "parallel," replacing the classical vision of a "linear" relationship between the two faith communities. As Christianity became an essentially Gentile religion without much appreciation of its Jewish roots and saw its theology translated into Greek philosophical categories and language, it lost an important revelatory dimension rooted in Torah that Jesus himself manifested and that Paul struggled to maintain even though it was a struggle he would eventually lose, thanks in part to the author of *Acts*. Thus, Judaism preserves a distinctive revelation rooted in history and in creation, something that R. Kendall Soulen has correctly identified as the hallmark of the Jewish covenantal religion.[20] Christians will need to recover this Jewish revelation as part of eschatological completeness.

Some Challenges

The Christian and Jewish revelatory paths cannot be merged all that easily. That is why I speak of "distinctive paths" within a single covenantal framework. In the pre-eschatological age, I see them continuing to play off each other, both "blessed" by God (to embrace the term used by Mary Boys) until the end of days. This represents a far-from-complete model, but I think it answers some of the outstanding questions. Certainly we shall have to continue its development, including whether there is a possibility of opening up this essentially inclusivist Christian-Jewish relationship to a wider pluralistic model without endangering the specificity of the Christian-Jewish relationship. Any expansion on the trilateral model must include the fundamental changes in the Church's understanding of the Christian-Jewish relationship.

A further challenge facing us in the theological realm is the integration of the new vision of the Church's linkage with the Jewish people with Asian, Latino/Latina, and feminist theologies. There have been some efforts along this line by scholars such as Jean Pierre Ruiz, Carmen Nanko-Fernandez, and Peter Phan. But, by and large, the new perception of Christian-Jewish relations has remained foreign to these theologies.

While I have already written of a certain stagnation in the development of a new theological model for the Christian-Jewish relationship in comparison to the years immediately following the approval of *Nostra Aetate*, there also have been instances of backsliding. A prominent voice in this regard was Cardinal Avery Dulles, S.J., who shocked many participants in the 2005 commemorative conference in Washington for the fortieth anniversary of the conciliar document by saying he was unsure Vatican II had declared the continuity of the Jewish covenant after Christ and insisting that we must take far more seriously the passages in Hebrews that depict the Jewish covenant as terminated after Christ.[21] Others, following a similar mindset, have insisted that *Nostra Aetate* carries no theological significance but is merely a "pastoral" statement. I strongly reject both views. The affirmation of Jewish covenantal continuity in *Nostra Aetate* was upheld by Pope John Paul II in several of his speeches, and such an affirmation directly undercuts important segments of classical Christological thinking in the Church. So it cannot be construed as merely a "pastoral" statement, whatever "pastoral" might actually mean for those who propose it. Cardinal Walter Kasper, in private statements to Rabbi David Rossen and to the biblical scholar Joseph Sievers from the Biblicum in Rome, has insisted that Cardinal Dulles' view was not the official view of the Catholic Church as such and claimed that Pope Benedict XVI's address at the synagogue in Rome represented a definitive rejection of Dulles' thesis. It would have proved helpful if Kasper had gone public with this assessment.

Another theological issue that has come to the surface once more in recent years is that of mission to the Jews. Evangelization has become a central theme of Pope Benedict XVI's papacy and no exception seems to be made with respect to the Jews even though concrete efforts in this regard have been only minimal. In June 2009, the American bishops caused a stir in Catholic-Jewish relations when they issued a critique of an earlier study document called "Reflections on Covenant and Mission," which had argued against any organized efforts to convert Jews. This was a position that Cardinal Walter Kasper had supported. In their document, the American bishops tied dialogue and evangelization together, causing an uproar from all sectors of the Jewish leadership. It was one of the rare moments in which there was an agreement and concrete action among all the main religious bodies in the Jewish community. As President of the United States Conference of Catholic Bishops at the time, Cardinal Francis George gathered together a small committee of five bishops. The original text was revised so that evangelization and dialogue were uncoupled, but the revised document never addressed the larger issue of mission to the Jews. Hence, I felt the Jewish leadership let the bishops off the hook far too easily.

But the issue remains on the table. British theologian Gavin D'Costa, who has been involved in dialogue for a considerable number of years, published an article in the renowned journal *Theological Studies*[22] based on a lecture he had delivered at the University of Bristol. In this piece, D'Costa argues for maintenance of a Christian mission to the Jews. In large part, his argument is based on his acceptance of the claim introduced earlier that papal and Catholic Church statements on Catholic-Jewish relations are merely pastoral with no deep-seated theological implications. While I would concur with D'Costa that the issue of Jewish evangelization is far from fully clarified in current Catholicism, I would equally stress that the basic thrust found in the numerous documents that have come forth since the Council decidedly move in the direction of removing Jews from the list of prospective converts. This does not exclude the possibility of individual conversion in either direction but does remove any mandate for targeted efforts toward the Jewish community.

Jewish-Christian Relations and Liturgy

Theology, it must be said, is not conveyed only through books and lectures. It also reaches the members of the Christian community through worship. In fact, that may be its most significant medium of transmission. Regrettably, not much has happened in the area of liturgy in terms of Christian-Jewish relations. We have witnessed some efforts to improve preaching, particularly in Holy Week, an effort that received institutional support in the 1985 Vatican *Notes* and in a document originally issued by 1988 in the U.S. Bishops' Committee on Liturgy working closely with the Bishops' Secretariat for Ecumenical and Interreligious Affairs. That document offers reflection on how the vision of *Nostra Aetate* should be implemented in the various liturgical seasons.[23] The problem is that this document is little known in the preaching world. Now may be the time to bring it back to life, as it will be included in a new collection of post-Vatican II documents on the liturgy to be published by Liturgy Training

Publications of the Archdiocese of Chicago. While preaching is surely a vital area of concern, there is also a need to examine the very structure of the liturgy (e.g., the Advent season), as well as the language found in hymns.[24]

Centrality of the Holocaust

I cannot ignore the continuing importance of the study of the Holocaust. While the 1998 Vatican statement on the Shoah, *We Remember*[25] was far from perfect, it was nonetheless an important recognition of the continuing significance of the Holocaust for the Christian community and beyond. The ongoing activities of the National Center at Seton Hill University have made an indispensable contribution in focusing Catholic attention on this central event in modern history. That work must continue in earnest. The Holocaust is not merely an historical event of fifty years ago or more. The issues it brought to the surface remain central features of contemporary society. In my many talks and writings, including at previous conferences at Seton Hill, I have spelled out some of the ongoing implications of the Holocaust for contemporary questions such as human rights.[26]

Some in the scholarly and educational communities are now submerging the study of the Holocaust into the wider focus on genocide. In theory, I have no particular problem with tying the Holocaust more directly to other examples of genocide such as Rwanda and Cambodia. But I remain firm in my contention that in any such widening of the field, the Holocaust must be kept as the central reality. The Holocaust was not merely one genocide among many; it was the premier genocide because of the comprehensive ideology in which it had its roots, an ideology that had both sacred and secular dimensions at its core. As an ethicist, I also lament the fact that so few of my colleagues in the field have included the Holocaust in any significant way in their contemporary reflections. To that end, I did deliver an address on the continuing significance of the Holocaust for Christian ethics both at the Social Ethics Institute at the University of Vienna and at the second global gathering of Catholic ethicists in Trent, Italy, in August 2010. The latter presentation has recently been published in the journal *Political Theology*.[27]

It would be my sincere hope, my plea that Christian social ethicists begin to take far more seriously than they have to date the continuing significance of the Holocaust for their work. The Shoah remains a persistent challenge for any discussion of public ethics as well as the Church's moral responsibility and self-definition. We owe a profound debt of gratitude to Cardinal Edward Idris Cassidy, who managed to overcome serious internal obstacles and finally put the document *We Remember* on the table for the Catholic community.

Palestinian-Israeli Relationship

I come now to my final major issue and the one that is causing increasingly deep divisions between Christians and Jews, as well as internally within each faith community. That issue, of course, is the continuing Palestinian-Israeli relationship. It can be described as the 800-pound gorilla in the dialogue. For many years, those of us who frequently addressed Jewish audiences would affirm that the inevitable question raised by someone from the audience at such events was, "When will the Vatican recognize Israel?" The process of coming to the point when we could respond "now" was very incremental, spanning well over a decade until the signing of the accords between the Holy See and the State of Israel in December 1993. Some in the Christian community tried to downplay the significance of this agreement, arguing it was merely political. But, in fact, it was far more than that. It put a final lid on the coffin of the theological tradition that had argued that Jews could never again have a homeland of their own as a consequence of their rejection of Christ. The agreement also committed both signatories to a concerted effort to eradicate any remaining vestiges of antisemitism in contemporary society.[28]

But the Fundamental Agreement hardly settled all outstanding issues, even in Catholic-Jewish relations, let alone Jewish relations with the wider Christian community. The Fundamental Agreement still requires a resolution of certain specific policies that have proven contentious, though there is some hope now that agreement may be reached. On the wider front, new issues have arisen that make some previous points of contention pale in significance. I speak primarily of the growing effort, mostly led by segments of Protestant denominations such as the Presbyterians, Anglicans, and the United Church of Canada, to endorse divestment from Israel and the boycott of its goods.

In addition, we have seen the release of the Palestinian Christian *Kairos Declaration* modeled after the *Kairos South Africa Agreement*, which has considerable Catholic Palestinian support even though no current Catholic bishop in the area is an actual signatory. On the Jewish side, the enhanced embrace of John Hagee's United for Israel by leading governmental figures and the support given this Christian evangelical group by the so-called "Christian caucus" in the Israeli Knesset have furthered the growing tension.

The problem as I see it is the ever-increasing polarization on the questions involved. I have never supported the boycott/divestment approach and never will. Other Christian leaders are just as adamant in their endorsement of this process, often simply referred to as BDS. The challenge before us is how we break through the stalemate and begin to defuse some of the tension. Those who continue to support Israel often do it in a way that mitigates any criticism of concrete Israeli policies. Those who stand with the Palestinians reserve their criticisms for Israel alone and make no critique of specific Palestinian actions.

I believe the time is at hand to try to create a new conversation. The International Council of Christians and Jews has developed two projects that move in the right direction, in my judgment. The first is an off-the-record conversation with the people responsible for the *Kairos Declaration*. The other is a multi-year project that commenced this past August at the Catholic University of Leuven (Belgium) and brings together a group of Christian and Jewish scholars from the United States, several European countries, Israel, and Australia around the guiding question, "What understandings might this group of Jews and Christians develop that could serve as resources for constructive dialogue about Israeli-Palestinian issues?" No one imagines that this effort will by itself break through the current impasse, but hopefully it will develop a construct for productive discussions in other settings. Somehow, we must try to create a conversation between Christians and Jews on the Israeli-Palestinian issue. Otherwise, there is real danger that all the goodwill and reconciliation we have reached since the passage of *Nostra Aetate* and the issuance of similar Protestant documents, as well as *Dabru Emet* on the Jewish side, may collapse.

The projected conversations will need to focus both on immediate problems such as acts of terrorism as well as Jewish attacks on Palestinians and on Christian institutions. But there is also need to explore the more ideological and even theological questions involved in the current conflict such as Christian Zionism, the biblical notion of land and its role in redemption, and a theology of belonging that would involve mutual recognition by all three major religious communities in the region of the inherent right of the other two to reside in the area. None of this will prove easy, but we cannot shrink from the challenge.

Some Questions

I would like to propose to you some questions that I have presented to the *Promise, Land, and Hope* group as a way of beginning a discussion on this very difficult topic: (1) Is there any possibility for an academic embrace of Christian Zionism? Or is Christian Zionism inherently opposed to a just solution for Israel/Palestine? If Christian Zionism cannot be embraced, how do we react to those who embrace it in the name of the Bible and to international Jewish leaders and politicians in Israel who embrace it as the most "authentic" Christian approach? (2) Is the land tradition in the Hebrew Scriptures a perspective that remains valid in the contemporary era? (3) Is there any retention of the biblical land tradition in the New Testament? (4) Does the land tradition play an authentic role in eschatological visioning? (5) Is there a basic universalizing aspect to Christianity that renders the land tradition less important for Christianity than for Judaism? Is there any legitimate sense in which Christianity does retain a "landed" dimension? (6) If Christianity embraces the Jewish covenant and considers itself integrated in some way in that original, ongoing covenant, does this demand that the biblical land tradition must be central to its own covenantal identity? (7) If the biblical land tradition and the quest for justice clash at some point, as some would contend, which takes priority for Christians?

These are certainly not all the questions that need attention, but putting them on the table in a clear and honest way can help towards the creation of the understanding we require to chip away at the polarization that currently marks any consideration of the Israeli-Palestinian issue.

Conclusion

I would like to re-emphasize that we have come a very long way in transforming the Christian-Jewish relationship since *Nostra Aetate*. It is one of the most remarkable interreligious transformations history has ever witnessed. We should never lose sight of that as we reflect on what still needs to be done. To say, however, that some stagnation and backsliding have not set in would be dishonest. One area I have not mentioned thus far is the role of women in the inter-institutional dialogues. They have been increasingly marginalized, and fault for this lies equally with Christian and Jewish leaders. Such marginalization is totally unacceptable in this time of women's rise to equal status in global society. Let us end it without further delay.

The last fifty years has certainly seen the planting of important seeds for the permanent creation of a transformed Christian-Jewish relationship. Whether those seeds mature into the full reality of such a relationship or whether they experience a drought depends on us. As the 2009 Berlin document from the International Council of Christians put it, this is a time for *recommitment* that involves central tasks for both religious communities.[29]

Questions

1. *How does seeing Jesus in His Jewish context affect your understanding of Him as the source of your Christian faith?*

2. *How does the new picture of the Common Era affect your understanding of the Jewish-Christian relationship?*

3. *In light of the new presentation of the Christian-Jewish relationship in the first century, how would you explain a response to the question of who killed Jesus to some individual or audience?*

Bibliography

Boyarin, Daniel. *The Jewish Gospels: The Story of the Jewish Christ*. Foreword by Jack Miles. New York: The New Press, 2012.

Connelly, John. *From Enemy to Brother: The Revolution in Catholic Teaching on the Jews, 1933-1965*. Cambridge, MA: Harvard University Press, 2012.

Cunningham, Philip A. et al. *Christ Jesus and the Jewish People Today: New Explorations of Theological Interrelationships*. Grand Rapids, MI: William B. Eerdmans Publishing Co., 2011.

Fisher, Eugene J. and Leon Klenicki, eds. *The Saint for Shalom: How Pope John Paul II Transformed Catholic-Jewish Relations*. New York: Anti-Defamation League & Crossroad, 2011.

Jacoby, Oren, director. *Sister Rose's Passion* (Film). Storyville Films, 2004.

Kronish, Amy and Eli Tal-El, directors. *I am Joseph Your Brother* (Film and Study Guide). Interreligious Coordinating Council in Israel & U.S. Council of Catholic Bishops, 2001.

Pawlikowski, John Thaddeus, "The Significance of Catholic-Jewish Dialogue and Holocaust Studies for Catholic Ethics." *Political Theology* 13.4 (2012): 444-457.

Notes

1. Gregory Baum, "The Social Context of American Catholic Theology," *Proceedings of the Annual Meetings of the Catholic Theological Society of America*, 1986, 41: 87.
2. For the text of the groundbreaking Episcopal statement in support of the schema on the Jews at Vatican II, cf. the *Dialogika* page on the website of the Council of Centers for Christian-Jewish Relations, www.ccjr.us.
3. For the summary and reflections on these findings, cf. John T. Pawlikowski, O.S.M., *Catechetics and Prejudice: How Catholic Teaching Materials View Jews, Protestants and Racial Minorities* (New York: Paulist, 1973).
4. Eugene J. Fisher, *Faith without Prejudice: Rebuilding Christian Attitudes toward Judaism*, revised and expanded ed. (New York: The American Interfaith Institute and Crossroad, 1993). (Original Edition, 1977).
5. Philip Cunningham, *Education for Shalom: Religion Textbooks and the Enhancement of the Catholic and Jewish Relationship* (Collegeville, MN: The Liturgical Press, 1994).
6. For a comprehensive history of Catholic-Jewish Relations in the United States, cf. M. Christine Athans, "Courtesy, Confrontation, Cooperation, Jewish-Christian/Catholic Relations in the United States," *U.S. Catholic Historian*, Spring 2010, 28: 107-134.
7. Carlo Maria Martini, S.J., "Christianity and Judaism: A Historical and Theological Overview," *Jews and Christians: Exploring the Present, Past, and Future*, ed. James H. Charlesworth (New York: Crossroad, 1990), p. 19.
8. Martin Noth, *The Laws in the Pentateuch and Other Studies* (Edinburgh, UK: Oliver and Boyd, 1966).
9. Examples of the "Parting of the Ways" scholarship include the following: Adam H. Becker and Annette Yoshiro Reed, eds., *The Ways That Never Parted: Jews and Christians in Late Antiquity and the Middle Ages*, Texts and Studies in Judaism 95 (Tubingen: Mohr Stiebeck, 2003); Reimund Bieringer and Didier Pollefeyt, eds., *Paul and Judaism: Crosscurrents in Pauline Exegesis and the Study of Christian-Jewish Relations* (London, UK: T & T Clark International, 2012); Anthony J. Saldarini, "Jews and Christians in the First Two Centuries: The Changing Paradigm," *Shofar*, 1992, 10: 32-43.
10. Cardinal Joseph Bernardin, *A Blessing to Each Other: Cardinal Joseph Bernardin and Jewish-Catholic Dialogue* (Chicago: Liturgy Training Publications, 1996).
11. National Conference of Catholic Bishops, Bishops' Committee on the Liturgy, *God's Mercy Endures Forever: Guidelines on the Presentation of Jews and Judaism in Catholic Preaching* (Washington, DC: United States Catholic Conference, 1988).
12. John T. Pawlikowski, O.S.M., *Pope John Paul II on Christian-Jewish Relations: His Legacy, Our Challenges*, The Inaugural Annual John Paul II Lecture on Christian-Jewish Relations, March 1, 2012 (Boston, MA: Boston College, Center for Christian-Jewish Learning). Also cf. Eugene J. Fisher and Leon Klenicki, eds.,

Pope John Paul II: Spiritual Pilgrimage: Texts on Jews and Judaism, 1979-1995 (New York: Anti-Defamation League & Crossroad, 1995). For a somewhat updated version of this volume, cf. Eugene J. Fisher and Leon Klenicki, eds., *The Saint for Shalom: How Pope John Paul II Transformed Catholic-Jewish Relations* (New York: Anti-Defamation League & Crossroad, 2011).

13. Philip A. Cunningham, Joseph Sievers et al., eds., *Christ Jesus and the Jewish People Today*, Foreword by Cardinal Walter Kasper (Grand Rapids, MI: William B. Eerdmans Publishing Company, 2011).

14. Robert W. Jenson and Eugene B. Korn, eds., *Covenant and Hope: Christian and Jewish Reflections* (Grand Rapids, MI: William B. Eerdmans Publishing Company, 2012).

15. Elliot Wolfson, "Gazing Beneath the Veil: Apocalyptic Envisioning the End," *Reflections on Revelation and Tradition: Jews and Christians in Conversation*, eds. John T. Pawlikowski and Hayim Gore Perelmuter, eds. (Franklin, WI: Sheed & Ward, 2000), pp. 77-103.

16. Benjamin D. Sommer, *The Bodies of God and the World of Ancient Israel* (Cambridge, UK: Cambridge University Press, 2012).

17. Daniel Boyarin, *The Jewish Gospels: The Story of the Jewish Christ*, Foreword by Jack Miles (New York: The New Press, 2012).

18. Cf. John T. Pawlikowski, O.S.M., *Christ in the Light of the Christian-Jewish Dialogue*, Reprinted Edition (Eugene, OR: Wipf and Stock, 2001); *Jesus and the Theology of Israel* (Wilmington, DE: Michael Glazier, 1989).

19. Cf. John T. Pawlikowski, O.S.M., "Christology and the Jewish-Christian Dialogue: A Personal Theological Journey," *Irish Theological Quarterly*, 2007, 72: 147-167. "Re-thinking Pauline Theology: Can It Undergird a Positive Christian-Jewish Relationship?" *Justification According to Paul: Exegetical and Theological Perspectives*, ed. Ondrej Prostrednik (Bratislava, Slovakia: Comenius University, 2012), pp. 231-240.

20. R. Kendal Soulen, *The God of Israel and Christian Theology* (Minneapolis, MN: Fortress, 1996).

21. Avery Cardinal Dulles, "Evangelization and the Jews," with a response by Mary C. Boys, Philip A. Cunningham, and John T. Pawlikowski, *America*, October 2002, 187 (12): 8-16; "The Covenant With Israel," *First Things*, November 2005, 22.

22. Gavin G. D'Costa, "What Does the Catholic Church Teach about Mission to the Jewish People?" with responses by Edward Kessler and John T. Pawlikowski, O.S.M., *Theological Studies*, September 2012, 73 (3): 590-640.

23. Cf. Note #11 and John T. Pawlikowski and James A. Wilde, *When Catholics Speak about Jews* (Chicago, IL: Liturgy Training Publications, 1987).

24. One liturgist who has taken the challenge of Christian-Jewish Relations seriously is Liam Tracey, O.S.M. Cf. "The Affirmation of Jewish Covenantal Vitality and the Church's Liturgical Life," *Christ Jesus and the Jewish People Today: New Explorations of Theological Interrelationships*, eds. Philip J. Cunningham et al. (Grand Rapids, MI: William B. Eerdmans Publishing Co., 2011), pp. 268-286.

25. Judith H. Banki and John T. Pawlikowski, O.S.M., *Ethics in the Shadow of the Holocaust: Christian and Jewish Perspectives* (Franklin, WI: Sheed & Ward, 2001).

26. John T. Pawlikowski, "Catholicism and Human Rights in the Light of the Shoah," *Learn, Teach, Prevent: Holocaust Education in the 21st Century*," ed. Carol Rittner, R.S.M. (Greensburg, PA: Seton Hill University, 2010), pp. 67-78.

27. Cf. John T. Pawlikowski, "The Significance of Catholic-Jewish Dialogue and Holocaust Studies for Catholic Ethics," *Political Theology*, 2012, 13 (4): 444-457.

28. For more on the significance of the Fundamental Agreement, cf. Eugene J. Fisher and Leon Klenicki, eds., *A Challenge Long Delayed: The Diplomatic Exchange between the Holy See and the State of Israel* (New York: Anti-Defamation League, 1996).

29. *A Time for Recommitment* (Sankt Augustin/Berlin, GE: Konrad Adenauer Stifting, 2009).

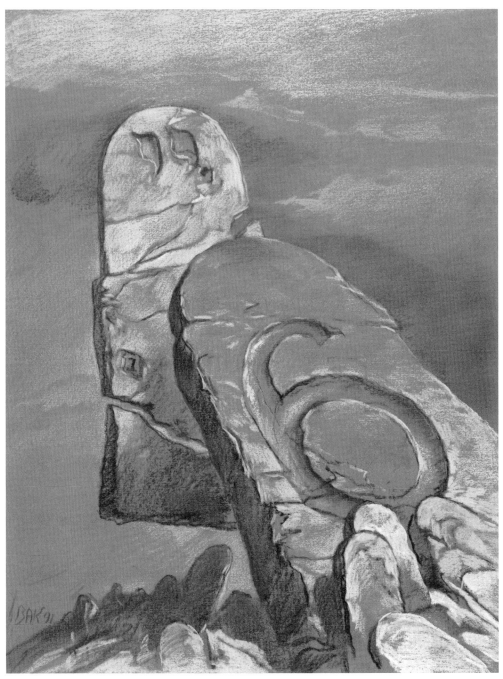

The Number, *1991 by Samuel Bak*
Image Courtesy of Pucker Gallery

"You Shall Not Murder": Ethics, Holocaust Education, and Religion

■ ■ ■ ■ ■ ■ ■ ■ ■ ■ ■

John K. Roth

Edward J. Sexton Professor Emeritus of Philosophy and
Founding Director of the Center for the Study of the Holocaust, Genocide,
and Human Rights, Claremont McKenna College, Claremont, CA

"You shall not murder." Exodus 20:13

In a prolific and magisterial career, the Jewish artist Samuel Bak (b. 1933) has drawn on his experience as a victim and survivor of the Holocaust to assess the damage done by that catastrophe and to weigh how best to live in what he calls "a world that cries out for repair."[1] A moving example of his work is a 1991 painting called "The Number."[2] It depicts two stone tablets tipping and falling into barren space, a cemetery-like abyss. The tablets themselves suggest signs of death. In the background, cracked and breaking apart, one of the two is inscribed with Hebrew letters that refer to God. In the foreground, the second tablet bears the number 6. Recalling the sixth of the Ten Commandments – "You shall not murder" – Bak's portrayal makes one wonder: In a post-Holocaust world, what remains of the Sixth Commandment?[3] Has murder silenced God's voice and destroyed its credibility? The responses that individual persons and human communities make to those questions, which profoundly pertain to ethics, Holocaust education, and religion, are decisive in "a world that cries out for repair."

With Bak's "The Number" as its point of departure, this essay explores how the most important challenges linked to Holocaust education in the twenty-first century pivot around the commandment, "You shall not murder," and its implications for interreligious understanding and action in particular. To contextualize my approach to these issues, I need to add that in late 2012, the University of Washington Press published *Encountering the Stranger: A Jewish-Christian-Muslim Trialogue*, a volume that the philosopher Leonard Grob and I have edited. The contributors include eighteen scholars, six from each of the Abrahamic traditions, with women and men in the international mix. The book's chapters have been crafted in ways that engage each writer in conversation with other contributors. A distinctive feature of the book is that the Holocaust and its aftereffects informed the engagement and reflection, a process that was significantly advanced by an invitation from the United States Holocaust Memorial Museum (USHMM). Thanks especially to Victoria Barnett, the staff director for the USHMM's Committee on Ethics, Religion, and the Holocaust, the contributors to *Encountering the Stranger* met seminar-style at the Museum in Washington, D.C. Drawing on some of my writing for *Encountering the Stranger*, this essay's four parts begin by recalling moments in our writing group's encounters with the Holocaust.

Know Before Whom You Stand

While exploring the permanent exhibition at the USHMM, sixteen of the contributors to *Encountering the Stranger* stood before the remnants of a Torah ark from the synagogue in the German town of Nentershausen. Desecrated but not destroyed completely in the November 1938 pogroms collectively called *Kristallnacht*, this Torah ark is honored within the museum, which is appropriate because the *Aron ha-Kodesh* (the Holy Ark), as it is called in Hebrew, occupies a special, sacred space in every synagogue.[4] It does so because the ark houses scrolls, precious possessions for each and every Jewish community, that contain inscriptions of the Pentateuch, the Five Books of Moses – Genesis, Exodus, Leviticus, Numbers, and Deuteronomy – the most important parts of the Hebrew Bible (*Tanakh*).

Visitors to the USHMM are not told what happened to the Torah scrolls that were once safely kept in the ark of the Nentershausen synagogue. It is not far-fetched, however, to think that those scrolls, like so many others during the years of the Holocaust, were mutilated and burned. So, as one stands before the Torah ark at the USHMM, an absence can be felt. Disrespect for and defacing of the Other, as the scarred and empty Torah ark suggests, would silence – if it could – scripture that proclaims one God to be the creator of the world and human life (Genesis 1-2); tells the story of Abraham, whose faith gave birth to Judaism, Christianity, and Islam (Genesis 11-25); and affirms that "you shall love your neighbor as yourself" (Leviticus 19:18).

Absence and silence can be intensified as one stands before the Nentershausen Torah ark at the USHMM because, while the Torah scrolls from the Nentershausen ark are missing, Hebrew writing on its lintel, a supporting beam or mantel above the ark's doors, is not. Like many Torah arks, the one at Nentershausen had an inscription taken from the Talmud (Berachot 28b), the authoritative rabbinical commentary on the Torah: *Da lifnei mi attah omeyd* – Know before Whom you stand. These words, which call one to attention and accountability, to reverence and awe before God, the source and sustainer of life, did not escape the notice of those who plundered the Nentershausen synagogue in November 1938, for an unknown assailant attacked them in a violent attempt to silence their voice, erase their authority, and eradicate their credibility. Their scarred condition bears witness to shameless arrogance even as the wounded words provide a fragile and poignant, if not forlorn, judgment against the hubris and hatred that divide humankind.[5]

When the contributors to *Encountering the Stranger* reconvened for discussion after exploring the USHMM's permanent exhibition, the trialogue concentrated for a time on the Torah ark from Nentershausen. We came to feel that the ark had addressed us through the words on its lintel: Know before Whom you stand. Differences in our religious traditions meant that our experiences were not identical during and after the time when we faced those words, but all of us agreed that the encounter with the desecrated Torah ark and its scarred inscription made us deeply aware of concerns we shared. Whether our identities were Jewish, Christian, or Muslim, we all could feel the loss, including the denial of freedom to practice one's religion that would be ours if places and writings sacred in our own traditions were so horrifically disrespected and profaned. We could also feel abhorrence for any person or community identified with our own tradition who would stoop to such atrocity, an experience that made us mindful of our accountability and responsibility for the traditions that are ours.

As we took stock at the USHMM, focusing our attention and trialogue on renewed and deepened awareness that we stand responsible before God, our co-religionists, and those who profess faiths related to but different from our own, we were well aware that our work was taking place in a post-9/11 world in which the al-Qaeda attacks on New York's World Trade Center and the Pentagon in Washington, D.C., had exacerbated suspicion about Islam and hostility toward Muslims. We scarcely could have anticipated, however, the upsurge of such suspicion and hostility that erupted in the summer and autumn of 2010, when plans for the construction of an Islamic cultural center and mosque near "Ground Zero" in New York City became so highly charged and volatile that the answer to the question, "Is America Islamophobic?" – the cover of *Time* magazine raised it explicitly on August 30, 2010 – arguably was yes.

If genuine trialogue among Jews, Christians, and Muslims was not conspicuous by its absence during the summer and autumn of 2010, too often its place was replaced by strident, intolerant, religiously and politically partisan, and belligerent voices, which were epitomized by that of Terry Jones, an obscure Christian pastor from Gainesville, Florida. His "Burn a Koran Day" campaign was thwarted only after American political and military leaders intervened with warnings that Jones's plans would seriously inflame much of the Muslim world. Even that intervention, however, was insufficient to deter Jones completely. On March 20, 2011, he publicly burned the Qur'an. Within days, news of that provocation swept through Afghanistan, leading to demonstrations and violence that left more than twenty people dead, including several United Nations employees, and about 150 wounded.

More recently, another test for interreligious understanding and trialogue in the United States loomed large when two pressure cooker bombs exploded near the finish line of the Boston Marathon on April 15, 2013. Murdering three persons, including an 8-year-old boy, and seriously wounding 140 others, the bombing allegedly was carried out by Tamerlan Tsarnaev, 26, and his brother Dzhokhar Tsarnaev, 19, whose links to militant Islam, among other factors, complicated already difficult issues about American immigration policy.

No Ethical Injunction Is More Important

No ethical injunction is more important than "You shall not murder." Human civilization depends on it. So does the value of religion, including Judaism, Christianity, and Islam. In one way or another, all three of these traditions affirm that murder is wrong. It violates God's commandment.

Christianity, my religious tradition, emphasizes the Ten Commandments, especially as they are stated in Exodus 20 within the Hebrew Bible. Yet, Christians – individually and collectively – have often disobeyed the Sixth Commandment, the one that says, "You shall not murder." Indeed, Christians have even incited and committed murder in God's name. Jews and Muslims have been victims of that crime. When it comes to murder, there is much need for Christian repentance and atonement.

The facts stated above have many implications for me. How, for example, should I respond to Christianity's violations of the commandment against murder? Where does Christianity's sometimes murderous history allow me – require me – to stand when it comes to dialogue with Jews and Muslims? Are those traditions innocent when judged by the Sixth Commandment? What if all three, in their own particular, distinctive, and non-equivalent ways, are guilty of violating the Sixth Commandment? How can and should "trialogue" go forward in response to the possibility that murder must be faced by all three of these traditions? Is it possible, crucial even, for Jews, Christians, and Muslims to explore whether God's injunction against murder might provide a foundation for trialogue that could benefit these traditions individually, in relation to each other, and in ways that might bring about changes that would make it at least less necessary for us to speak of ours as "the age of genocide"?

Here it is worth noting that, according to the biblical scholar David Flusser, the Christian New Testament "does not use the term 'Ten Commandments' even once," but the injunction against murder is emphasized in multiple instances, especially by Jesus in ways that are thoroughly consistent with the Jewish tradition that He observed.[6] In Matthew 19:16-22, Mark 10:17-22, and Luke 18:18-23, for example, Jesus stresses the importance of obeying God's commandments and explicitly condemns murder. Paul does the same in Romans 13:9, adding that the Sixth Commandment, along with those prohibiting adultery and theft, "are summed up in this word, 'Love your neighbor as yourself.'"

Flusser's observation about the Christian New Testament may be appropriate for the Qur'an as well. If the latter does not use the term "Ten Commandments," it prohibits murder both explicitly and implicitly. Representative passages such as the following bear witness to that claim: (1) "Whoever kill[s] a human being, except as a punishment for murder or other villainy in the land, shall be looked upon as though he had killed all mankind" (5:32); (2) "You shall not kill – for that is forbidden by God – except for a just cause" (6:151); (3) "Do not kill except for a just cause (manslaughter is forbidden by Him)" (25:68).[7] These texts use *kill* more than *murder*. If qualifications such as "except for a just cause" surround the former, as they often do in Jewish and Christian interpretations as well, at least an implied imperative against murder exists in these texts. That imperative is without qualification – unless, of course, one argues that an instance of murder is really an instance of justifiable killing and thus not murder at all. All three of the traditions have employed such dubious reasoning when it suited them, a fact that complicates but by no means invalidates the injunction against murder. It is in this fraught area that some of the most crucial aspects of contemporary Jewish-Christian-Muslim trialogue are to be found, particularly as violence rages in the Middle East and elsewhere, improvised explosive devices (IEDs) and suicide bombers deal death, drones strike, and problematic claims about the "justice" of what are murderous actions are sounded on all sides of conflicts in which Jews, Christians, and Muslims are deeply affected, embedded, and implicated.

Here it is important to underscore that interreligious discussion focused on the Sixth Commandment will be complicated by the fact that in specific times and places, one tradition and its members may be deeply and distinctively implicated in murder, while others have such responsibility to a lesser extent or not at all. Both within and among the Abrahamic traditions, these differences must be identified and acknowledged, their meanings probed and their reverberations assessed. During the Holocaust and in the Rwandan genocide, for example, Christianity and Christians had immense involvement in and distinctive responsibility for the devastation. More recently, the *Washington Post* editorialist Michael Gerson rightly criticized Mahmoud Ahmadinejad and other Iranian Muslims for inciting genocide with deadly rhetoric by repeatedly insisting that Israel must be "wiped off the map."[8] Just as Christians struggle to be accountable for Christianity's complicity in genocide, Muslims need to rein in the murderous violence currently advocated or unleashed from within that tradition, and Jews should keep testing Israeli governmental and military policies in light of the Sixth Commandment as well. The necessary soul-searching requires self-study and self-criticism from within each tradition, but when such inquiry is carried on inter-religiously – in contexts where the soul-searching is mutually encouraged and supported – inquiry may go deeper, honesty may be more profound, and openness to constructive change may be increased. The possibilities and prospects for such work are themselves matters that need discussion within and among the Abrahamic traditions. To the extent that multi-faceted soul-searching can develop, chances remain to salvage the Sixth Commandment from the fate that "The Number," Samuel Bak's painting referenced at the outset, foresees and fears even in its resistance against that oblivion.

As Bak's art suggests, hopes for such salvage and for the interreligious trialogue that could help to promote it must remain guarded. To some extent, the Sixth Commandment has had a braking effect on humankind's propensity for violence. Unfortunately, a frank historical appraisal leads to the conclusion that the most distinctive quality about the Sixth Commandment is the extent to which it has been violated – disregarded, dismissed, and disrespected. Coupled with those characteristics, one must add that the Sixth Commandment has never been backed sufficiently by credible sanctions, divine or human, that would ensure full respect for and obedience to it.[9]

"What have you done?" God asked Cain after he murdered Abel. In the early twenty-first century, Jews, Christians, and Muslims alike need to hear God putting that question to them with particular reference to murder and other forms of killing as well. In more ways than one, such hearing is not easy. The slaughter-bench of history, to use Hegel's phrase, calls into question the functional status of the Sixth Commandment. A commandment that is not obeyed may still be a commandment, but its functional status depends on obedience and credible sanctions against disobedience.

An injunction that is not heeded lacks credibility. When Nazi Germany, supported by many German Christians, unleashed the Holocaust, the force of the imperative "You shall not murder" was impugned to the degree that millions of Jews were slaughtered. It took the violence of a massive world war, which left tens of millions more corpses in its wake, before the Third Reich was crushed and the Holocaust's genocidal killing centers were shut down. At least in the three major monotheistic traditions, God is the source and the ultimate vindicator of the Sixth Commandment. If God is not acknowledged and obeyed, His existence is not necessarily eliminated, but His authority is curtailed. And if God's authority lacks credibility, then the nature of God's existence is affected, too. How has the Sixth Commandment functioned and fared in history? Two of the words that must be used in response to that question are *poorly* and *badly*. Unless Jews, Christians, and Muslims find ways to work together and reverse that situation, human civilization itself is imperiled more than ever.

The Sixth Commandment will continue to be the imperative that is the most necessary, although not sufficient, condition for human civilization. No less clear is the fact that this commandment will continue to be violated, often immensely and with a large measure of impunity. Furthermore, the God who prohibits murder is also the One who will do relatively little, if anything, to stop human beings from committing homicide or genocide.

The Jewish philosopher Emmanuel Levinas, who lost much of his family in the Holocaust, insisted that "You shall not murder" means nothing less than "You shall defend the life of the other."[10] The Sixth Commandment and the task that Levinas rightly identifies as following from it show that nothing human, natural, or divine guarantees respect for either of those imperatives, but nothing is more important than making them a key responsibility in Jewish-Christian-Muslim understanding, for they remain as fundamental as they are in jeopardy, as vitally important as they are threatened by humankind's murderous destructiveness and indifference.

What May the Dead Have to Say?
The commandment against murder remains, disrespected and impotent though it often is. If that injunction is not at the heart of ethics in all three of the Abrahamic traditions, their moral stature is bereft and suspect. To my mind, the point of Jewish-Christian-Muslim trialogue is much more ethical than theological. Granted, ethical and theological perspectives are often related and even inseparable, but they are not identical. Ethical relationships, characterized by caring for one another, are what trialogue most needs to achieve. At the core of those relationships stands the commandment and commitment not to murder one another. I doubt that trialogical discussion about God, important though it can be, is likely to advance this cause much beyond a basic agreement that murder is wrong.

What may be more helpful, but I expect only by a little, is discussion that clarifies what is included or excluded in the concept of murder. The problem here is that the human propensity for rationalization and self-righteousness will try to justify killing as non-murder, thus explaining murder away, while at the same time indicting opponents as murderers when their actions attack one's own people. If agreement that murder is wrong can serve as a basis for Jewish-Christian-Muslim trialogue, that agreement will need to get beyond rationalization, self-righteousness, and every other impulse that finds "them" murderous but never "us." In various ways, times, and places – past, present, and probably yet to come – Jews, Christians, and Muslims have committed murder, not in the same degree or measure or even in equivalent ways, but with enough bloodshed to say that none of the three traditions is innocent of murder.

Killing acts can be accidental and unintentional. Killing acts of that kind are not murder, nor are they carried out in self-defense or to protect others from life-threatening violence. But those qualifications still leave murder taking an immense toll, not only in individual homicidal acts but also in terrorist attacks, the denotation of IEDs, war crimes, crimes against humanity, and genocide. Typically, murderous actions require an intention to inflict or cause death, often including premeditation and careful planning. Importantly, intent ought not to be construed too narrowly lest murderous acts be falsely denied and swept away by the defining strokes of self-serving pens. Where murder is concerned, particularly the mass murder associated with terrorist attacks, war crimes, and crimes against humanity, intent should not be restricted to premeditation and careful planning. Room should also be left for indictments based on considered judgments that there are good reasons to think that the actions a person or group has carried out or is undertaking were/are likely to inflict death in ways that exceed reasonable understandings of self-defense or the protection of others against life-threatening violence. No one-size-fits-all rationale exists to decide these cases, or even to define the terms that are unavoidably in play within such judgments. For that reason, I suggest a different approach that might make the injunction against murder a more credible and fruitful basis for Jewish-Christian-Muslim trialogue. This approach concentrates neither on God nor on concepts, but on the dead.

So many of the dead are dead not because they lived to a ripe old age or even because disease, untimely though it may have been, ended their lives. So many of the dead – children, women, and men; both the young and the old – are dead because they were murdered. If most of the murdered do not have their lives stolen by what we typically mean by homicide, neither are they killed as enemy combatants in warfare nor are they the unfortunate civilian casualties of euphemistic "collateral damage" during military operations, a category that unethically washes murder away. The murdered ones include the innocent – a real and valid category, notwithstanding ideologies that make all victims "guilty" – especially in recent times the innocent slaughtered in rocket attacks, drone launches, and air strikes, wiped out by suicide bombings and IEDs, annihilated in mass shootings, starved to death, butchered in hundreds of lethal ways. Those unjustly robbed of life by human decisions and human actions are the ones we need especially to see and to heed. But if we settle for calling these dead *victims*, we misplace where key aspects of the emphasis need to be placed. By speaking of victims, we rightly call attention to the victimizers, to the murderers. By speaking only of victims, however, we obscure the faces of the dead and the humanity of the murdered, those who, in George Steiner's words, have been "done to death."[11]

"Try to look," wrote the Auschwitz survivor Charlotte Delbo, "just try and see."[12] She wanted people to see the defaced faces of the dead (especially the murdered dead), to discern what those faces say about right and wrong, to take to heart how the humanity of the dead – even, indeed especially, in their silence – resounds the imperative against murder. Another French voice, that of the Catholic priest Patrick Desbois, echoes Delbo's. Desbois's mission has been to help us – Jews, Christians, Muslims, and more – to remember the humanity of more than 1.5 million Jews who were shot to death at hundreds of extermination sites in eastern Europe during the Holocaust. They were murdered by Germans and their collaborators – baptized Christians undoubtedly and overwhelmingly among them – and then left to rot in unmarked mass graves that scar the earth in Ukraine, Belarus, and Russia long after the Holocaust. By interviewing hundreds of witnesses who did see the dead, Desbois says that he seeks "to establish the truth and justice." Surely, fidelity to the injunction against murder is inseparable from that task.[13]

Some of the interviews conducted in 1946 by the American psychologist David P. Boder are among the earliest with persons who survived the Holocaust. Using the wire recording technology that was state-of-the-art at the time, Boder interviewed "about seventy people, representing nearly all creeds and nationalities in the DP [displaced persons] installations in the American Zone." He recorded 120 hours of testimony, which was translated, he said, "to keep the material as near to the text of the original narratives as the most elementary rules of grammar would permit."[14] Eight of these interviews were published by the University of Illinois Press in 1949. The last one contains the testimony given in Munich by a man named Jack Matzner on September 26, 1946.

Born in Wiesbaden, Germany, Matzner, 42 when the interview took place, was a Jew of Polish descent. Deported from Germany to Poland in 1938, he illegally returned to Germany for a time, and then he and his family were reunited in Antwerp, Belgium. On May 14, 1940, soon after the Germans occupied Belgium, Matzner went to France. Eventually arrested, he was deported to the East. The account he gave to Boder after surviving "fifty-five months of concentration camps" included episodes that were deeply embedded in his memory (200).

On one occasion in 1945, Matzner was inside Germany as a slave laborer for the Heinkel Aviation Industries. He reports that his captors beat him and then imprisoned him in a flooded cellar with "about ninety or ninety-five people," many of whom were already in water that was "chest high." Matzner's account to Boder continued as follows:

> Those who were lying there were already dead. And those who were standing had arranged the bodies of the dead in such a manner that they could stand or sit on them. Otherwise the ones who were still living

would also have drowned. I did the same thing. I found myself a place at the wall. I dragged two bodies which were under the water and arranged them against the wall, and I sat on them. And so I remained in the water, counting from that morning, exactly two days and two nights (217).

Boder interviewed Matzner, but perhaps with those frozen and drowned Jews from Matzner's account in mind – to say nothing of the millions who had been starved and beaten to death, shot, or gassed – he ended the introduction to his book with these words: "The verbatim records presented in this book make uneasy reading. And yet," he added, "they are not the grimmest stories that could be told – I did not interview the dead" (xix). That last thought-provoking phrase – "I did not interview the dead" – became his book's title.

If we see the dead, if we listen carefully, thoughtfully, for what they "say," the humanity of their mutilated bodies, the screams that cry out in silence, demand "You shall not murder." How could they not? No divine or human voice can speak with more authority, more passion and urgency, than that. Neither the figurative face of God nor the face of the actual living can exceed what the faces of the murdered ones tell us about the fragile preciousness of the gift of human life. If we cannot heed what the murdered ones say, Jewish-Christian-Muslim trialogue will fall short of its potential for good.

As noted earlier, during the development of *Encountering the Stranger*, the contributors were privileged to meet for discussion at the United States Holocaust Memorial Museum in Washington, D.C. During our time together, I think we saw and heard some of the murdered ones. When we looked into each other's eyes, when we listened to each other's voices, when we considered what we ought to say, and later what we ought to write as we revised the essays that we shared at the Museum and that now form the contents of *Encountering the Stranger*, our encounters with the dead made a difference. The murdered ones made us see, I believe, not only how the injunction against murder can be a basis for Jewish-Christian-Muslim trialogue, but also why it must be.

Carry On, Carry On

The legendary Irish musician Tommy Sands has shown for decades that seemingly fragile and powerless realities – for example, his guitar and voice singing songs he recalls from the past or writes for the present and future – can be resilient sources of encouragement and strength, inspiring commitment to deepen understanding, cultivate respect, and heal discord. Two hallmarks of his music, which played important parts in the peace process that calmed the violent "troubles" long separating Protestants and Catholics in Northern Ireland, are persistence and inclusion.

"Carry on," says one of Sands's famous songs, "carry on, / You can hear the people singing, / Carry on, carry on, / Till peace will come again."[15] Traditional Irish music, and Sands's versions of it are no exception, is scarcely triumphal. It assumes no guarantees that what is right and good will prevail. Seeing and remembering the murdered dead, lamenting the wounding and loss of life, yearning for conditions that preserve and sustain the existence and good that people share, this music carries on by summoning resistance against the joy-robbing afflictions produced by disrespect for and exclusion of the other. Absent persistence that refuses to stop combating the causes of injustice and suffering, what Sands calls "the lonely years of sorrow" are likely to go on and on, leaving immense waste and no peace in their wake.[16]

Signs of Sands's persistence were visible during the summer of 2010 when he and his multi-talented musical family accepted Leonard Grob's invitation to visit the Stephen S. Weinstein Holocaust Symposium, the eighth in a biennial series at Wroxton College in England. Many of the contributors to *Encountering the Stranger* are members of this symposium, which was the source from which that particular Jewish-Christian-Muslim trialogue evolved. Sands and his family had recently returned to the United Kingdom after bringing their music and testimony to embattled Israelis and Palestinians, whose prospects for peaceful coexistence remain so fraught that even a Tommy Sands might have been deterred from trying to improve them. Far from being deterred, however, Sands and his family took their fragile instruments, their seemingly powerless music, and carried on by offering visions of alternatives that invited Israelis and Palestinians to join him in song and in creative politics, too.

As Sands made clear to the Weinstein Holocaust Symposium, the alternatives he envisions emphasize inclusiveness, and his understanding of inclusiveness places a premium on hospitality, on welcoming the stranger, indeed on turning strangers into friends. "Let the circle be wide round the fireside," Sands sings, "and we'll soon make room for you / Let your heart have no fear / There are no strangers here / Just friends that you never knew."[17]

Are such sentiments more than feel-good wishful thinking? Perhaps not, and yet when Sands and his family sing this song, skepticism and cynicism can be laid to rest, if only momentarily. It is worth noting, too, that the contributors to *Encountering the Stranger* were once just that – strangers who came from religious traditions that have harbored and often intensified fear of each other. Some of us contributors – Jews and Christians – were strangers when we first met at the Wroxton symposia initially organized by Leonard Grob and Henry Knight in 1996. Friendship grew and its circle expanded to include the Muslim contributors to that book – some of them strangers to each other as well as to their Jewish and Christian partners before they accepted the risky invitation to engage in trialogue and found friendship in that process. This small but expanding circle confirmed that Sands's vision – "There are no strangers here / Just friends that you never knew" – could be much more than sentimental, feel-good, wishful thinking.

As the trialogue unfolded, it became increasingly clear that the goal for our small circle and for the interreligious understanding needed so much in our twenty-first century world is one and the same. In Sands's words, that goal is to "make room for you," to meet and treat each other well. Translated into the terms of interreligious relations, this goal means that Jews, Christians, and Muslims need to show hospitality to one another, and nothing is more fundamental to that hospitality than pluralism, which at its core entails that religious differences are more than "tolerated" or even "respected," but are also welcomed. Even that way of putting the point, however, remains too abstract, for the key is that religiously different persons and communities need to welcome one another. For that to happen, people and communities often have to change internally and in relation to each other. Such work is easier said than done. It requires setting aside the exclusive and all-too-often violence-prone conviction that my way is right and yours is not; it entails embracing Tommy Sands's precarious but truthful insight that closing "our eyes to the other side" makes us "just half of what we could be."[18]

No one-size-fits-all approach grasps what the hospitality of pluralism entails. For the three Abrahamic traditions, for the individuals and communities in which those traditions live, the hospitality of religious pluralism always must be attentive to needs, responsibilities, and opportunities that reflect the particularity and specificity of time and circumstance. Yet in those details, the shared, persistent, and inclusive goal of the hospitality of pluralism is to create and sustain welcoming conditions so that "There are no strangers here / Just friends that you never knew." Hospitality extended to the other, what Tommy Sands calls making "room for you," is at the heart of ethics in the Abrahamic faiths. In *Encountering the Stranger*, the Muslim scholar Khaleel Mohammed emphasizes how that teaching is and must be normative in Islam, using that point to criticize his tradition when it comes up short. The hospitality of pluralism is supported whenever the Abrahamic traditions are self-reflective in that way.

The hospitality of religious pluralism entails a profound and humane humility that can help turn strangers into friends. Jews, Christians, and Muslims can and should care deeply about their traditions and about how to make them the best they can be. They can even say that for them it would not really be thinkable to embrace another tradition as one's own. But at the same time, the hospitality of pluralism requires recognition that neither *my* way nor *your* way is *the* way.

All religious traditions – individually and even collectively – are incomplete, fallible, in need of correction and revision as they encounter one another, probe themselves, and expand their horizons. To cite Tommy Sands once more, the Abrahamic traditions, each and all, need to see that if they close their eyes to the other side, they are just half of what they could be. But if these traditions open themselves in hospitality to one another, they will come closer to what shows itself to be right, good, and truly awesome – the "beyond," the divine, that each seeks and can find, at least in part, even while its fullness eludes our human grasp, as it must. If responsibilities of this kind become more pronounced and widespread, it will be at least less necessary for us to speak of ours as "the age of genocide," because the commandment "You shall not murder" is better observed and not destined to be the shattered and abandoned number 6 in Samuel Bak's poignant painting.

Questions

1. *Do you agree that no ethical injunction is more important than "You shall not murder"? Why?*

2. *Is there a difference between killing and murder? If so, how should that difference be understood?*

3. *How can education about the Holocaust and other genocides make a difference when the threat of mass murder is confronted?*

4. *Imagine that you are speaking with a person whose religious outlook or tradition is different from your own. How might you begin to have a dialogue about murder with her or him? What difficulties or dangers would be important to avoid or engage? Where do you think the discussion might lead?*

5. *How can religions best be encouraged to be accountable for their complicity in mass murder?*

6. *In the twenty-first century, what are the most important steps that Jews, Christians, and Muslims — individually and together — can take against murder, especially mass murder?*

Bibliography

Berger, Alan L., ed. *Trialogue and Terror: Judaism, Christianity, and Islam after 9/11*. Eugene, OR: Wipf and Stock, 2012.

Grob, Leonard and John K. Roth, eds. *Anguished Hope: Holocaust Scholars Confront the Palestinian-Israeli Conflict*. Grand Rapids, MI: William B. Eerdmans, 2008.

Hayes, Peter and John K. Roth, eds. *The Oxford Handbook of Holocaust Studies.* Oxford, UK: Oxford University Press, 2010.

Roth, John K. *Ethics during and after the Holocaust: In the Shadow of Birkenau.* New York: Palgrave Macmillan, 2005.

Volf, Miroslav, ed. *Do We Worship the Same God? Jews, Christians, and Muslims in Dialogue.* Grand Rapids, MI: William B. Eerdmans, 2012.

Notes

1. See Samuel Bak, "Facing My Own History and My Story with *Facing History and Ourselves," Illuminations: The Art of Samuel Bak* (Brookline, MA: Facing History and Ourselves, 2010), pp. 2-4.
2. For helpful commentary on this Bak painting, consult the podcast by Lawrence L. Langer, available with an online copy of the painting at: http://www.facinghistory.org/print/3351.
3. Different traditions number the Ten Commandments differently. Jews and many Protestant Christians, for example, take "You shall not murder" to be the Sixth Commandment. For Catholics and Lutherans, that injunction is the Fifth Commandment.
4. Authorized and incited by Nazi leaders when a minor German official died after an assassination attempt by a young Jew named Herschel Grynszpan, the antisemitic riots of *Kristallnacht* ("crystal night") targeted Jewish communities throughout Germany and Austria on November 9-10, 1938. Sometimes these November pogroms are referred to as the "Night of Broken Glass" because the wreckage included so many smashed windows that the replacement value reached more than two million dollars in the cash equivalent at the time. The onslaught was far more devastating than that. A great many Germans, their religious heritage and identity overwhelmingly Christian, were involved and implicated in the widespread carnage. While their friends and neighbors watched, the perpetrators looted and wrecked Jewish homes and businesses, torched hundreds of synagogues while intentionally inactive fire brigades stood by, desecrated cemeteries, killed scores of Jews, and terrorized virtually every Jew in the Third Reich. In the aftermath, some 30,000 Jewish men were arrested and sent to concentration camps at Dachau, Buchenwald, and Sachsenhausen. The November pogroms of 1938 showed that no Jew could ever expect to live a normal life in Nazi Germany.
5. For insightful discussion of the significance of the Torah ark at USHMM, one that helped to inform the reflections here, see Henry F. Knight, "Before Whom Do We Stand?" *Shofar*, 28 (3): 116-34. One of the contributors to *Encountering the Stranger*, Knight particularly called attention to the Torah ark at USHMM when our trialogue took place there.
6. David Flusser, "The Decalogue in the New Testament," *The Ten Commandments in History and Tradition*, eds. Ben-Zion Segal and Gershon Levi (Jerusalem: Magnes Press, 1990), p. 221.
7. The quotations from the Qur'an are from N. J. Dawood's translation, *The Koran: With Parallel Arabic Text* (New York: Penguin Books, 1990).
8. See Michael Gerson, "Iran's Incitement to Genocide," which appeared in the *Washington Post* on April 4, 2013, and is available online at: http://www.washingtonpost.com/opinions/michael-gerson-irans-hate-speech-is-an-incitement-to-genocide/2013/04/04/2686e7a8-9ca1-11e2-9a79-eb5280c81c63_story.html. This article provides links to document the uses of language that Gerson identifies as incitements to genocide. Under the United Nations 1948 Convention on the Prevention and Punishment of the Crime of Genocide, "direct and public incitement to commit genocide" is a punishable act. Also pertinent in this context is Alvin H. Rosenfeld, ed., *Resurgent Antisemitism: Global Perspectives* (Bloomington, IN: Indiana University Press, 2013). This 500-page volume documents multiple sources and ways in which anti-Jewish and anti-Israeli hostility remains relentless and virulent in the twenty-first century.
9. If there is life beyond death, God's judgment may provide sanctions that condemn murder beyond all doubt and without remainder. Unfortunately, that result comes too late to be effective in history, for neither the murdered nor their murderers have returned to tell what God may have done with them. Nor has God made that situation crystal clear. Meanwhile, within history, murder is sometimes punished, but not with sufficiently credible deterring impact. History's mounds of murdered dead grow larger and larger.
10. Emmanuel Levinas, "In the Name of the Other," *Is It Righteous to Be? Interviews with Emmanuel Levinas*, ed. Jill Robbins & trans. Maureen V. Gedney (Stanford, CA: Stanford University Press, 2001), p. 192.

11. George Steiner, *Language and Silence: Essays on Language, Literature, and the Inhuman* (New York: Atheneum, 1967), p. 157. I am indebted to Paul C. Santilli for this reference. On the importance of encountering the face of the dead, especially the murdered dead, Santilli's thought influences mine. See especially Paul C. Santilli, "Philosophy's Obligation to the Human Being in the Aftermath of Genocide," *Genocide and Human Rights: A Philosophical Guide*, ed. John K. Roth (New York: Palgrave Macmillan, 2005), pp. 220-32.

12. Charlotte Delbo, *Auschwitz and After*, trans. Rosette C. Lamont (New Haven, CT: Yale University Press, 1995), pp. 84-86.

13. See Patrick Desbois, *The Holocaust by Bullets: A Priest's Journey to Uncover the Truth behind the Murder of 1.5 Million Jews* (New York: Palgrave Macmillan, 2008). For more information about Desbois and his findings, see http://www.yahadinunum.org. See also Maria Danilova and Randy Herschaft, "Ukraine Slaughter Was Opening Salvo of Nazis' Final Solution," *Seattle Times*, 1 February 2009: A10. The Desbois quotation is taken from their Associated Press article. Desbois heads *Yahad-In Unum* (Hebrew and Latin for "together"), an association of Catholics and Jews that seeks reconciliation between their traditions. Its web site is noted above.

14. David P. Boder, *I Did Not Interview the Dead* (Urbana, IL: University of Illinois Press, 1949), p. xiii. Subsequent page references to Boder's book appear within parentheses.

15. For more detail on Tommy Sands, see his autobiography, *The Songman: A Journey in Irish Music* (Dublin: Lilliput Press, 2005). See pp. 252-57 for Sands's commentary on the lyric quoted here.

16. See Sands, *The Songman*, p. 256.

17. Although Sands indicates that he did not record "Let the Circle Be Wide" until 2009, he notes that he has sung this "song of welcome" repeatedly and around the world. See the comments by Sands that accompany his album *Let the Circle Be Wide* (West Chester, PA: Appleseed Recordings, 2009).

18. The quotation is from Sands's "Let the Circle Be Wide."

PART II:
GENOCIDE IN EUROPE
(1939 – 1945)

"Never Again":
An Unfinished Agenda[1]

- - - - - - - - - - -

Irving Greenberg

Rabbi, Scholar, Author, New York, NY

It has been 80 years since Adolf Hitler and the Nazis launched their "Thousand Year Reich," and 70 years since World War II ended and the total assault on the Jews of Europe came to a halt. But we are still struggling to try to understand how in the heartland of Europe, the central domain of Christendom for more than a millennium, in the core zone of modernity and democracy, an attack on human life and dignity could have been pursued basically unchecked and carried out so successfully for 12 years.

The Holocaust has become the most widely researched, studied, and documented crime of all time. That, however, has not stopped countries, leaders of world religions, and others from denying that it ever happened, or in some way trying to trivialize or dismiss this terrible event we have come to call the Holocaust.

A Comfortable Life Shattered

In 1961, my comfortable life was shattered as the result of my first full-throated encounter with the catastrophe of the Holocaust. Ever since then, I have tried to grasp, even in a limited way, the staggering extent of the cruelty, suffering, and degradation that preceded and accompanied the murder of the Jews. The work of Father Patrick Desbois helped me see that in Ukraine and elsewhere, more were killed as the result of the systematic shooting to death of men, women, and children than I had initially realized, even after many years of study and research about the Holocaust.[2] To round up, transport, then gas and eliminate 6 million Jews in the ghettos and killing camps of Nazi-occupied Europe was no small feat. It required a highly organized effort on the part of the Germans and their collaborators. The victims had no way of fighting back because all the power was on one side. This resulted in one-sided cruelty, mockery, and sadistic violence against the Jewish victims – men, women, and children.

In the early 1960s, I tried to introduce a course in Holocaust Studies at Yeshiva University in New York City. Yeshiva is an educational institution with Jewish sponsorship that is committed to integrating Jewish culture and civilization into its educational programs. One of its goals is to train rabbis. My proposal to introduce a course on the Holocaust was opposed by the dean, who said that such a course was not "academic." In fact, he asked me to bring him evidence of other respectable universities that would allow such a course. After a lot of research, I found only two institutions: Brandeis University and Harvard Divinity School. The dean dismissed Brandeis because it was Jewish and Harvard Divinity because the course was being taught by an adjunct professor, Erich Goldhagen.

Despite initial opposition from some sources, today courses about the Holocaust are now widely taught in colleges and universities all over the USA and beyond. In the late 1990s, the government of Sweden, for example, set up a Commission to study teaching about the Holocaust, and they have led the effort to spread such education across the European community. This is all in addition to the many films about the Holocaust, such as *Schindler's List*, that are shown in movie theaters across the country. There also has been a remarkable spread of Holocaust commemorations in many communities in the USA and Europe. Then there is the work being done through the United Nations (UN), which for years has been a hotbed of antisemitism and anti-Zionism. The UN established Auschwitz Liberation Day, a day on which the Holocaust is commemorated at United Nations headquarters in New York City.

There also is the work that was done by President Jimmy Carter's Commission on the Holocaust. In 1979, when the Commission was going to recommend that a Holocaust museum be created on the mall in Washington, D.C., one of the most highly placed Jews in American government pleaded with us not to do it. Why? Because it would be a mistake, he said, to make such a recommendation to the President of the United States. Americans would not be interested. It might even stir up antisemitism among the American population. Today, we can see just how mistaken that highly placed government official was, for the United States Holocaust Memorial Museum (USHMM), which opened in April 1993, is the third most visited museum on the mall. And, interestingly enough, 80% of the visitors to the Holocaust Museum are not Jewish.

Developments in Christian-Jewish Relations and Understanding

In the late 1960s, during the Six Day War (June 5-10, 1967) when it appeared that a repetition of the Shoah might occur in the Middle East, the Holocaust burst into public consciousness and spread among people in many parts of the world. During these years, discussion of the Holocaust became critical to dialogue between Jews and Christians, and it had an amazing impact, particularly on the Roman Catholic Church. Some of this had started earlier, in 1958, with the election of Angelo Cardinal Roncalli as Pope of the Roman Catholic Church. During World War II, Roncalli had served as Papal Nuncio in Turkey. When he was elected pope, Roncalli took the name of John XXIII. He convened Vatican II (1962-1965), and he urged the Catholic bishops of the world to work on the document that eventually resulted in *Nostra Aetate* ("In Our Time"), the Vatican II decree that opened the door to a series of advances in Jewish-Catholic dialogue, including Pope John Paul II's remarkable visit to Israel and Yad Vashem in March 2000. All of this helped encourage the development of official positive statements over the years that were issued by the Vatican and by various Catholic bishops' conferences in Europe, the Americas, the UK, and Australia that encourage and support dialogue and cooperation between the Catholic Church at all levels and the Jewish people.

While there have been attempts, particularly under Pope Benedict XVI, to roll back the advances in understanding and cooperation between Catholics and Jews, two popes, John XXIII and John Paul II, lent their considerable weight to helping to change attitudes and teachings about Jews and Judaism in the Catholic Church. Despite having a conservative agenda in other areas, Pope John Paul II repeatedly affirmed the dignity of Judaism, repeatedly spoke out about and affirmed the Covenant between God and the Jewish people, saying that it had never been revoked. It was Pope John Paul II who visited the synagogue in Rome in April 1986, where he called the Jewish people "our elder brothers" and condemned persecution and displays of antisemitism "at any time and by anyone." These were extraordinary gestures on the part of the Catholic Church.

We have to remember the enormous transformation that has taken place over the years within Christianity. For nearly two millennia, Christians had created a privileged sanctuary of hatred within their gospel of love. Jews and Judaism itself were one area within this gospel of love where it was respectable, even sacred, to allow such hatred. Up until Vatican II (1962-1965), as far as Roman Catholics were concerned, the Jewish people were unfaithful, blind, and hard-hearted because they had not "recognized" Jesus as the promised messiah. The New Testament replaced the Old Testament, and Christians replaced Jews as the "New People of God," faithful to a "New Covenant" established through Jesus with God. Jews were to be despised, cast out of societies, condemned. For Christians, Judaism had no right to exist.

Over the centuries, devastating images developed in the Christian psyche: Jews were "children of the devil," their places of worship were "synagogues of Satan," and their matzo was baked with the blood of slaughtered Christian children. This poison was injected deep into Western culture. In literature and art, in social and economic life, Jews became uncanny, demonic, beyond the human pale. It was this status accorded to Jews and Judaism within Christianity that later metastasized into Nazi racial hatred of the Jews in the 20th century. Nazi antisemitism fed on anti-Jewish images and stereotypes that had its roots deep within Christian teaching and preaching of contempt for Jews and Judaism.

Still, there were some great Christians – Catholic and Protestant – who were determined to end Christianity as a source of hatred for Jews and Judaism. They worked tirelessly over the years to change the attitudes of Christians toward Jews and Judaism, particularly within the Catholic Church, but also within the other Christian churches. I am thinking, for example, of Franklin Littell, Roy and Alice Eckhardt, Eugene Fisher, Sister Rose Thering, Father John Pawlikowski, and so many others, both living and dead. These scholars helped bring about a transformation within Christian doctrine, teaching, and preaching about Jews and Judaism, and this transformation was supported and encouraged by the remarkable leadership of Roman Catholic Christians like Pope John XXIII before and during Vatican II and by Pope John Paul II after Vatican II until his death.

The American Lutheran Church also underwent a significant transformation in terms of its attitudes, teaching, and preaching about Jews and Judaism. I am thinking, for example, about the fact that the Church apologized for Martin Luther's unbridled antisemitism, even though Luther remains the foundation, the cornerstone, the nurturing force of Lutheranism. What they have done is extraordinary. Being self-reflective about your own religious tradition, having the willingness to apologize for harm done, and having the spiritual strength to acknowledge and check the element of evil and destructiveness within a sacred tradition is a remarkable achievement.

The process for Jews to rethink their relationship with Christians and Christianity in light of these developments within various Christian denominations has been slower. It has taken time for Jews to recognize that Christianity is a world religion that on its own terms also has had a remarkable encounter with the divine. In 2000, the National Jewish Scholars Project, facilitated by the Institute for Christian and Jewish Studies in Baltimore, issued a document entitled *Dabru Emet: A Jewish Statement on Christians and Christianity*.[3] By spring 2001, more than 225 leading Jewish scholars and theologians from around the world had signed *Dabru Emet*.

Scholarly Approaches to Studying the Holocaust

Over the years, various scholarly approaches to the Holocaust have emerged. One that stands out is the ongoing debate between *intentionalists* and *functionalists*. This is the debate between those who emphasize that the total destruction of the Jews was intended by Hitler and the Nazis from the very beginning (the *intentionalists*) and those who insist that it was far more improvised, developing and metastasizing at various inflection points, such as in September 1939 with the outbreak of World War II and in June 1942 with Nazi Germany's invasion of the Soviet Union (the *functionalists*).

Over the years, scholars also have raised various questions: What were the issues involved in the actual killing of peoples? Was it ideology that motivated people, or was it, as with the German army, a matter of obeying orders and meeting the expectations of peers that was key to the murders? Consider, for example, the men in Reserve Battalion 101 that Christopher Browning profiles in his book *Ordinary Men*.[4] He shows how the men who carried out mass murder were not motivated by ideology but by the orders of their superior officers and the expectations of their peers.

Another debate that has gotten stronger over the years is that between those I call *individualists*, who focus on the central role of national racial hostility, animosity, and hatred of the Jews, and those I call *universalists*, who focus on eliminating everyone from minority populations to so-called "surplus populations." In addition, there is the ongoing discussion about antisemitism. Were these issues the driving forces, or were there issues of economic utility? Who profited from the Jews being eliminated and sent away? Related to all these debates has been a particular focus on the roles of bureaucracy and technology. Zygmunt Bauman's influential book *Modernity and the Holocaust*[5] emphasizes that some of the central institutions of modern life – technology and bureaucracy – are important forces that account not only for the Holocaust, but have to be dealt with in the future if we are to avoid such things as the Holocaust happening again.

Helen Fein's work has had a significant influence on me, particularly her book *Accounting for Genocide*,[6] which is now almost three-and-a-half decades old. She brought together statistics about the death and survival rates of Jews in various German-occupied countries during World War II and the Holocaust. The difference in Jewish survival in the various European countries was enormous, ranging from 95 percent surviving in Denmark to 90 percent dead in Poland, Latvia, and Lithuania. She asked a simple, fundamental question: What accounted for the wide variation in rates of Jewish survival?

Clearly the difference lay not in Jewish behavior, neither passive nor armed resistance. Armed resistance for the Jews was a decision about how to die, not how to live. The disparity between the power of the Nazi-armed forces and the relative powerlessness of the Jewish armed resistance was enormous. It was not Nazi behavior that made the critical difference, because it was murderous everywhere. The single critical difference, argues Fein, was the behavior of the bystanders. The more bystanders there were who resisted, the greater was the chance that Jews would survive.

Some years ago, a Jewish survivor from Denmark told me that he and his family had been evacuated by the Danish resistance from Copenhagen in 1943 when the Germans began their round-up of the Jews. He told me that the most amazing thing for him was when he came back home nearly three years later and the apartment where his family had lived and which they had been forced to leave overnight was untouched. It had been completely protected all those years. No one had moved into it or stolen anything from it.

Contrast the Danish story with that of Lithuania, where the population was virulently antisemitic and where the killing of Jews was happening even before Nazi Germany's army arrived on the scene. After the Germans came with their killing squads, they often turned to the Lithuanians for help. Many served as auxiliaries in the killing squads. Ninety percent of the Jews in Lithuania did not survive. To this day, there are strong elements in Lithuania who insist that the Jews were Bolsheviks – communists – who deserved what they got from the Nazis.

According to Fein, the most highly correlated factor in Jewish survival or non-survival in a German-occupied country during World War II and the Holocaust was the strength or weakness of pre-war antisemitic political parties. If there were successful pre-war antisemitic parties in a country, it meant that antisemitism was endemic in the population, that antisemitism had become routine enough, respectable enough, for it to be turned to successful political advantage. That was the measure of the non-Jewish population's attitude toward Jews in an area, region, or country in German-occupied Europe during World War II and the Holocaust. Such antisemitic attitudes always worked against the Jews and for the Nazis.

An Unfinished Agenda

Let me just say a few words about what, in my view, remains to be done when it comes to teaching and studying about the Shoah, the Holocaust. We need to continue studying the role of bystanders during the Holocaust, and other genocides as well. We need to follow-up and extend the work of scholars like Helen Fein, who did so much to bring to our attention the impact of bystanders on the survival and non-survival of Jews during the Nazi era. We need to explore and extend the work of Victoria Barnett, whose book *Bystanders: Conscience and Complicity during the Holocaust*[7] has added to our understanding of the role of bystanders during the Holocaust. We need more study and research about the righteous gentiles who tried to help and save Jews during the Holocaust. We need to continue, expand, and complement the work of scholars like Eva Fogelman,[8] Nechama Tec,[9] and Mordecai Paldiel[10] who have helped us to understand better what motivated and enabled non-Jews in Nazi-occupied Europe to risk their lives – and often the lives of their families – to help Jews during the Holocaust.

Of course what happened during the Holocaust needs to be studied and taught, but what is needed even more is to rouse the world's conscience, if it has one. We must try to understand the evil in order to work to change the conditions that made it possible; what is needed are not apologies, not reparations, but a renewed respect for human beings.

Both Jews *and* Christians believe that human beings are made in the image and likeness of God (see Genesis 1:27). The Nazis degraded, demeaned, and denied victims their dignity and humanity. The overall purpose of the Nazis was to make their victims into beings of no value, to make the death of their victims seem routine, not shocking, to the killers. All of this was done over the course of days, months, even years, not in a fit of temper or with a loss of sudden control, but steadily, routinely. At the heart of the Nazis' cruelty toward Jews and others during the Third Reich, World War II, and the Holocaust was nothing short of the defacing of the image of God.

For me, the central question the Holocaust raises is nothing less than, "How can we prevent this from happening to anyone ever again?" All the education, all the public awareness about the Holocaust will have failed if we do not find a way to translate moral teaching into institutional changes so that not just individuals, but governments as well, understand they have a serious responsibility to act to prevent genocide – against anyone at any time anywhere. Thus far, we have not been too successful at doing this, because as you know, there have been several genocides since 1945, despite much greater awareness of the Holocaust.

The legislation that set up the U.S. Holocaust Memorial Museum included a special provision for a Committee on Conscience because from the beginning, Elie Wiesel – all of us on the President's Commission – understood that it wasn't enough simply to remember the Holocaust, or even its so-called lessons. What was needed was to create a committee or functional institution that would alert the government and the public to the danger of an impending genocide so that the American public would exercise the political will to move the American government to do something concrete to stop the killing. Unfortunately, neither the U.S. Holocaust Memorial Museum nor its Committee on Conscience has been very successful in carrying out this mandate, despite their many efforts in this regard. We have more work to do.

Cambodia, the former Yugoslavia, Rwanda, Darfur, and Sudan. These are places where mass atrocity crimes, even genocide, went on for extended periods of time. Yet the governments of the West, the governments of the most democratic countries in the world, failed to stop these outrages or came in very late to try to do something. In all these cases, the political institutions concluded that the cost of intervention was too high, that they had to deal with the political protectors of the perpetrators of genocide such as in Cambodia in the 1970s, where China stood behind the Khmer Rouge, or in Rwanda in the 1990s, where at the time, President Bill Clinton concluded that the will of the American people would not support another military intervention. The fact that serious, even responsible, political figures understood that it was politically unwise or unprofitable to make an intervention in these and other places is a measure of how far we have to go if we are really serious about preventing or stopping another genocide.

Many, many people, both in this country and in other countries beyond our borders, have been faithful to an agenda of Holocaust education. They have continued to develop and strengthen the dialogue between Jews and Christians, despite setbacks from time-to-time. They have developed Holocaust courses in colleges and universities, curricula for middle schools and high schools, and annual Holocaust commemorations at the local, state, and national levels. They have reached millions of people by organizing conferences and seminars, journals and on-line publications about the Holocaust. All of this should be recognized and celebrated even though we still have more work to do. Far from surrendering to the continuing persistence of hatred in the world, let us do our best to show that the capacity for renewal through love is stronger than hatred, stronger than death. That is the ultimate unfinished agenda of Holocaust education.

Questions

1. *To what extent do you think the new, more positive teaching and understanding about Jews and Judaism is filtering down "to the people in the pews?" What evidence can you cite to support your answer?*

2. *Identify a statement, other than* Nostra Aetate, *issued by the Roman Catholic Church that encourages better understanding between Jews and Catholics. What are three (3) suggestions it makes to further that understanding?*

3. *What does the document* Dabru Emet *have to say about Christianity and the Holocaust? How would you explain* Dabru Emet *to a Jewish audience? How would you explain it to a Christian audience?*

4. *What do you see as the "unfinished agenda" when it comes to Holocaust education? Be concrete and specific in your response.*

Bibliography

Connelly, John. *From Enemy to Brother: The Revolution in Catholic Teaching on the Jews, 1933-1965*. Cambridge, MA: Harvard University Press, 2012.

Frymer-Kensky, Tikva, David Novak, Peter Ochs, David Fox Sandmel, and Michael A. Signer, eds. *Christianity in Jewish Terms*. Boulder, CO: Westview Press, 2000.

Living in the Image of God: Jewish Teachings to Perfect the World - Conversations with Irving Greenberg as conducted by Shalom Friedman. Northvale, NJ: Jason Aronson, Inc., 1998.

O'Malley, John. *What Happened at Vatican II?* Cambridge, MA: Belknap Press of Harvard University Press, 2010.

Rittner, Carol, Stephen D. Smith, and Irena Steinfeldt, eds. *The Holocaust and the Christian World: Reflections on the Past, Challenges for the Future*. New York: Continuum, 2000.

Notes

1. Rabbi Greenberg's essay was edited by Dr. Carol Rittner, R.S.M. and is based on his October 21, 2012, keynote presentation at Seton Hill University.
2. Patrick Desbois, *The Holocaust by Bullets: A Priest's Journey to Uncover the Truth behind the Murder of 1.5 Million Jews* (New York: Palgrave Macmillan, 2009).
3. Institute for Christian-Jewish Studies, http://www.icjs.org/.
4. Christopher R. Browning, *Ordinary Men: Reserve Police Battalion 101 and the Final Solution in Poland* (New York: HarperCollins, 1992).
5. Zygmunt Baumen, *The Holocaust and Modernity* (Ithaca, NY: Cornell University Press, 2001).
6. Helen Fein, *Accounting for Genocide: National Responses and Jewish Victimization during the Holocaust* (Chicago, IL: University of Chicago Press, 1984).
7. See further, Victoria J. Barnett, *Bystanders: Conscience and Complicity during the Holocaust* (Westport, CT: Praeger, 1999).
8. Eva Fogelman, *Conscience and Courage: Rescuers of Jews during the Holocaust* (New York: Anchor Books Doubleday, 1994).
9. Nechama Tec, *When Light Pierced the Darkness: Christian Rescue of Jews in Nazi-Occupied Poland* (New York: Oxford University Press, 1987).
10. Mordecai Paldiel, *The Righteous Among the Nations: Rescuers of Jews during the Holocaust* (New York: Harper, 2007).

Teaching about the Holocaust in the 21st Century

. . . .

Yehuda Bauer

Professor Emeritus of History and Holocaust Studies at the Avraham Harman Institute of Contemporary Jewry at the Hebrew University of Jerusalem and Academic Advisor to Yad Vashem, Jerusalem, Israel

The problem of teaching about the Holocaust in the 21st century immediately raises the question of how relevant the topic is to the students who listen to you. After all, World War II ended in 1945. That is nearly 70 years ago. The first question a student will ask is, "What does all this have to do with me?" The answer is that what happened to the Jews is something that could happen to any group – not in the same way, not in the same environment, and not under the same conditions, but it could happen nonetheless. In fact, similar things have been happening since the Holocaust and, therefore, to avoid such things happening in the future is the main purpose of teaching about the Holocaust today – especially to non-Jewish audiences.

Rescuers

One of the basic things you have to realize, however, is that one cannot teach students, whether younger students or adults, only about sheer horror. Such teaching won't be accepted. It will be rejected for very obvious reasons: people do not want to be put into a situation of total despair, of total hopelessness, which, as we know, was the situation of the Jews in Europe under the Nazis. We also have to remember that there were rescuers during the Holocaust, and we have to teach about them, too. They were a very small minority, but they are the ones who provide us with a way out of all the despair and hopelessness.

The rescuers show that there were choices: that people could follow the policy of the murderers – betray their neighbors, be totally indifferent to the fate of their neighbors – or they could resist by trying to help or rescue the people who were being persecuted and, ultimately, murdered. Sometimes these choices were very complicated, but recognizing that people had choices enables us to teach about the Holocaust. Rescuers help us realize that some people had to act, not only against the Nazis, the Germans, and the armed collaborators, but often against their own neighbors – those non-Jews who would betray both the rescuers and the people they were hiding and trying to help.

Remember, it was not easy to help Jews. There were economic considerations, for example. Keeping somebody in hiding required a lot of money and sacrifices on the part of those who were trying to help. How would they be able to provide the wherewithal that people needed? From where would they get the money? Not only food was needed, but sometimes medicine also was needed, not to mention a place to stay. Sometimes people were hidden in holes dug in fields, or they were hidden in holes dug under pig sties. In other words, trying to help someone or some few during World War II and the Holocaust was an extremely complicated matter, not simple at all.

What Caused the Holocaust?

In teaching about the Holocaust, one has to ask what caused the Holocaust. It was not caused by the intervention of some supreme being. It was not caused by God or by Satan. The Holocaust was caused by human beings. When we deal with mass violence, specifically with genocide, with the intent and action to annihilate human groups as such, in whole or in part, we are addressing a common human trait. The problem is not that killing children and defenseless adults is inhuman. The problem is that these acts, including sadism, torture, and the like, are very human indeed.

What today we call genocide is the intention to annihilate groups of humans, whatever they are, wherever they are, whether ethnic, national, racial, economic, social, political, or religious groups. And that has been with the human race since its very beginning, since it emerged in East Africa some 150,000 to 200,000 years ago. In 2010, two burial grounds of human beings were uncovered, one in a place called Talheim in Southern Germany, and one in a place called Scheltz in Austria. These burial sites are from Neolithic times, from about 10,000 B.C. These human groups very clearly had been murdered by other human groups, because in those mass graves were found the stone implements with which these people had been killed. In those mass graves, there were men, women, children, and babies. In other words, a group was killed. And throughout ancient history, medieval history, modern history, there have been attempts to annihilate groups as such.[1]

The Holocaust: An Extreme Case?

What the Nazis did was, in effect, the *extreme* case of genocide. Why do I say extreme case? In what way is the Holocaust more extreme than, let us say, the attempted annihilation of all the Tutsi in Rwanda in 1994? Or in what way is the Holocaust more extreme than what is going on today in Sudan, in the area of Darfur and now also on the borders between South and North Sudan? And what about what happened in other places between 1945 and today in Cambodia, China, and other places?

Why do I say the Holocaust was the most extreme case of genocide? Not because of the number of victims. More people died in the Maoist so-called "Leap Forward" in China, where perhaps 15 million or more Chinese peasants died, and more people have died in other similar mass violence and murders. Also, it is not the percentage of Jews murdered – of the 17 million Jews existing worldwide in 1939, close to six million (about one-third of the total population) were killed or died as a result of Nazi policies during the Holocaust. A higher proportion of Armenians in Ottoman Turkey during World War I died during the Armenian genocide. A higher proportion of the Tutsi, as related to all the Tutsi in Rwanda, died there in 1994. So, it's not the number and it's not the proportion. And it's not the brutality, because the suffering of the victims is the same in all cases – literally, in all cases. So if it's not the suffering, not the number, and not the proportion, what is it?

A Global Concept

The idea to kill all the Jews developed in stages with the Nazis – the idea to kill every single person with three or four Jewish grandparents, not only in Germany or in Europe, but quite literally all over the world, is unprecedented. No such thing had ever happened before in human history, at least not as far as I'm aware. The Nazi idea to kill all Jews was a *global* concept. It was to be a *global* annihilation of a people.

This global concept was motivated by ideology, and the ideology that accompanied the Nazi idea had nothing to do with real life. Contrary to Nazi assertions, the Jews did not control the German economy, direct any army, possess any territory, or have a united political organization of any kind. No political united body representing German Jewry had ever existed. The first such body was established by the Jews in September 1933 in response to the Nazi rise to power, because they needed someone to represent them in the new situation that had arisen in Germany.

Hitler, the Nazis, and the Jews

Hitler and the Nazis accused the Jews of illusionary, delusionary things. First and foremost, the Jews were accused of creating a conspiracy to control the world. This supposedly Jewish world conspiracy can actually be found in the teaching of the Church Fathers in the first three and four centuries of the Common Era, the period when Judaism and Christianity fought each other for supremacy in the pagan world of the Roman Empire until Christianity won out. During that period, Jews were accused of having killed Jesus, although everyone now knows that the Romans had killed him. But in order to be on the good side of the Romans, the Church Fathers created an ideology that accused the Jews and not the Romans of killing Jesus. What was their rationale? It was said that the Jews were possessed by Satan. What is it that Satan wanted? Satan wanted to control the world. So what did the Jews want? The Jews wanted to control the world. That libel exists to this day.

During the Middle Ages, the Jews were also accused of the so-called "blood libel," that is, of using the blood of Christian children to create matzos (unleavened bread) for Pesach (Passover). This accusation derives from a certain type of theology that demeaned and damned Jews. Hitler and the Nazis adapted and adopted such theological ideas, although they rejected Christianity.

Another factor contributing to the marginalization and persecution of the Jews was the secularization of European society. People turned against the Christian Churches. Much of European society adopted the antisemitism of the Christian Churches, but without the protection Christianity traditionally had given the Jews. Christianity had never actually advocated for or acted in order to annihilate the Jewish people. In fact, if you look at the famous 5th-century book by St. Augustine of Hippo, *De Civitate Dei* (*City of God*), the Jews are accused of everything under the sun – but the answer is not to kill them. The answer is to suppress them, to discriminate against them, and so on, but not to kill them. Why? Because Jews have souls, and killing a Jew would be a mortal sin.

The Nazis accused the Jews of corrupting German society, when, in fact, throughout history, Jews had been some of the pioneers of German literature, philosophy, and art; they had also sacrificed more than their share for the Fatherland during World War I. The Nazis and their supporters did not go after the Jews because they wanted their property. Initially, they wanted to drive the Jews out of Germany, then they wanted to take their property, and only later did they want to kill them. The Roma were in a similar situation, but the Roma were persecuted by Germans generally, and by the Nazis particularly, not as an existential threat as the Jews were considered to be, but because they were considered a nuisance. However, there was never a Nazi intent to kill all the Roma – in fact, there was **an explicit decision not to do so**.[2]

The accusations against the Jews, what we call Nazi antisemitism, were purely ideological, with no pragmatic elements in them. Hitler and the Nazis' central accusation against the Jews was of a supposed Jewish conspiracy to rule the world, as I have already mentioned, to replace the existing strata of world and government leaders by so-called international Jewry in order to install Bolshevik rule in the world. This theory was pure Nazi fantasy, but it was also a real belief. It was the basic motivation to unleash the war – World War II – that was supposed to prevent that apocalyptic danger.

Many historians argue, however, that the structure of German society led to an impasse, the solution to which was found in the murder of the Jews, with antisemitic ideology only in the background. There can be no doubt that structural, economic, and social problems, as well as political and military exigencies, significantly contributed to the development of the genocide of the Jews. But structures do not kill. People kill people, and they have to be motivated to do so.

The Holocaust

As educators, you need to be aware that the Holocaust was not pre-planned; it was pre-figured. In other words, the kind of ideology that I have tried to summarize briefly was a preparation, the kind of controlling idea that led to the murder of the Jews of Europe, but it took place in stages. Hitler and the Nazis decided, not right at the beginning, but in stages, to kill every person with three or four Jewish grandparents everywhere in the world if they could. There is no historical precedent for such a policy decided upon by a political apparatus and directed towards the extermination of every single individual of the targeted group as defined by the perpetrator that the state bureaucracy could find.

As late as January 30, 1939 – the war did not break out until September 1939 – in a major speech to the German Reichstag (parliament), Hitler threatened the Jewish race with annihilation:

> Today I will once more be a prophet: If the international Jewish financiers in and outside Europe should succeed in plunging the nations once more into a world war, then the result will not be the Bolshevization of the earth, and thus the victory of Jewry, but the annihilation of the Jewish race of Europe.[3]

Hitler's remark came as a total surprise to the people who were listening to him because nothing yet had been prepared. In fact, as late as May 1940, Heinrich Himmler, the head of the SS and the person who would be responsible a year later for the mass murder of the Jews, wrote in a memorandum to Hitler that the annihilation of a people was un-German, Bolshevik, and **unacceptable**.[4]

In May 1940, there was still no planning. It was only with the invasion of the Soviet Union in June 1941 that the annihilation started consensually. By that time, the ideology had penetrated to such a degree that it was accepted, and the conclusion from it was to kill the Jews. Before June 1941, the idea had been to deport the Jews to Madagascar in Africa or elsewhere. Six months before the invasion of the Soviet Union, when the Nazis already knew that they were going to attack the Soviet Union, the idea was to deport all the Jews to the Arctic regions of the U.S.S.R., where they would die of cold and starvation. That idea spread: If we do that in the occupied

Soviet Union, then why not in Poland? Why not in Western Europe? Why not everywhere where it is possible to do so? In fact, five months after the invasion of the Soviet Union, on November 28, 1941, Hitler himself told Hajj Amin al-Husseini, the grand mufti of Jerusalem, that once Nazi Germany won the war, they would turn to all the countries in the world to solve the Jewish problem.[5]

In this environment of Nazi-occupied Europe, what was the relationship of Jews to the non-Jews around them? As I have already indicated, the vast majority of the peoples amongst whom the Jews were living were scared or indifferent. Many collaborated with the Germans, but some also tried to help the Jews. Denmark, for example, had a small number of Jews; in 1943, during the German occupation of that tiny country, an overwhelming majority of the population aided in helping the Jews escape from Denmark into neutral Sweden. In Serbia, where the Serbian police collaborated with the Germans in hunting down Jews to kill them, the overwhelming majority of Serb peasants were quite willing to help Jews. The Jews who survived there were rescued by these peasants. The same also applies to the Bulgarians. The Bulgarian military, police, and government were responsible for the mass murder of Jews *outside* of Bulgaria in areas controlled by the Bulgarian Army during the war. But *inside* Bulgaria, there was an odd coalition between the Bulgarian Orthodox Church, the underground Communist Party, the underground Socialist Party, liberals, and even some important members of the ruling Fascist Party. They opposed sending the Jews to their death; thus, the Jews were not sent on trains and trucks to extermination camps. And then, of course, we also have the case of Albania, where there were very few Jews, but they were helped by Albanians, who were Muslims. These cases and others, of both individuals and groups, show that it was possible to choose to try to help Jews during World War II and the Holocaust.[6]

The Irrationality of the Nazis

During the Holocaust, the Nazis killed the very people who were working for them while they were working for them. For example, the Lodz ghetto in Poland was, in fact, a vast concentration camp, a slave labor camp filled with sweatshops. Jews were starving. They had to work impossible hours to produce goods, mainly for the German army. One estimate is that up to 9% of certain necessities – uniforms, boots, and all kinds of woolen and metal accessories that the German army needed – were produced in the sweatshops of the Lodz ghetto. Obviously, it was in the interest of the Germans to keep this ghetto going in order to get what they needed. In the end, however, the Germans destroyed the ghetto, explicitly saying that economical considerations should not count because the Jews had to disappear, meaning they had to be killed. The Nazis and their collaborators murdered even the specialists whom they had kept alive for awhile out of rational considerations. So, you see, the Germans acted against their own interests. They killed people who were working for them.

This concept was not medieval. It was something completely new; to kill the people who work for you had no precedent.

The Christian Churches

What about the Christian Churches, you may ask? One cannot speak about the singular *attitude* of the Catholic Church, but rather you must talk about *attitudes* in the plural. Those attitudes ranged from active collaboration in the killing of Jews to actively helping Jews. In Hungary, for example, there is the case of Cardinal József Mindszenty, who after the war became a martyr under the Communist regime that had persecuted him. In 1944, however, he celebrated a Mass thanking God for having removed the Jews from Hungary.[7] Then there is the case of the Primate of the German Catholic Church, Cardinal Adolf Bertram, who it is said (but this is disputed) ordered Mass to be celebrated in memory of Adolf Hitler on May 5, 1945, one week after Hitler had committed suicide and three days before the end of the war.[8]

The other side of the story is that of Catholic priests who were killed by the Germans for trying to help Jews. This applies to a number of priests in Northern Italy, as well as to some in Germany who were sent to Dachau and killed because they spoke out against the murder of the Jews. For example, Monsignor Bernhard Lichtenberg, a priest in Berlin, was arrested by the Nazis for publically praying for the Jews and died on his way to Dachau. Father Rupert Mayer was a Jesuit priest in Munich who was persecuted by the Nazis for speaking out for the Jews. In France, Jules-Géraud Saliège, the Catholic Archbishop of Toulouse, worked with the Jewish underground to save Jewish children. And then there were the nuns, like Margit Szlachta in Hungary and others in Poland, Belgium, Italy, and elsewhere. All these helped Jews, and some died trying to do so. So, you see, you can't really generalize. I would argue – whether you agree with me or not, I don't know – that it was not theology but the character of the person and the kind of education he or she had received that helped make the difference in the choices these priests and nuns made.

What about Pope Pius XII (Eugenio Pacelli), the head of the Catholic Church from 1939 to 1958? Contrary to some writers, I'm quite convinced that Pius was not an antisemite. He was a member of a Roman aristocracy that regarded the Jews with suspicion and contempt, but also with sympathy and some kind of feeling. When it came to the point of clearly condemning what the Nazis were doing to the Jews, he faltered, although he had all the information needed to know what was happening to them. The fact is, he refused to mention the Jews in his famous 1942 Christmas radio message, in which he said that hundreds of thousands of people had died because of their beliefs and their origins (*stirpe*), but he refused to explicitly mention Jews either then or later.

Some documents seem to show that he or some people very close to him approved the rescue of Jews in at least two convents in Rome that we know of; he did not initiate such action, though – he just did not try to stop it. Pius XII wanted to remain neutral. He was afraid of German action against the Vatican if he spoke out in favor of the Jews. He was, after all, the Vicar of Christ on earth. His major task was to prevent the Catholic Church from coming to harm. And, for him and for so many in the Roman Catholic Church, the *major* enemy wasn't Nazism but Soviet Bolshevism. Nazis were certainly bad. Pius opposed Nazism privately in his letters and so on, but he would not attack the Nazis publicly because Nazis, after all, fought against Bolshevism.[9]

Archbishop Angelo Roncalli, the Vatican Nuncio to Turkey who later became Pope John XXIII, Pius XII's successor as Head of the Catholic Church, was actively involved in rescuing Jews by issuing false baptismal certificates. There were others who tried to do the same thing, issue false documents to help Jews, but there were still others, like some clerics in the Balkans and the Baltic countries, who actively supported Nazi policies against the Jews. This is the Catholic Church, complex and complicated, not simplistically clear.

The Protestant Churches are equally complicated. The Huguenots in France rescued Jews en masse, one might say, as did the Lutherans in Denmark and the Lutheran minority in Slovakia. Then, there was the Christian Orthodox majority in Volhynia, which was part of Ukraine, who actively supported the Germans. The Lutherans in Germany, by an overwhelming majority, also actively supported the Germans.

In my view, so much regarding a person's attitudes towards the Jews depended on economic and political conditions and not just on theological ideas, although they certainly contributed to how people thought and acted. Still, one could say that how people treated the Jews, whether with indifference, hostility, or sympathy, depended very largely on individuals and the choices they made. And despite what one may say, people clearly could make choices – not easy ones, not safe ones, but they could make choices about the Nazis, the Jews, themselves, and their families.

The Challenge

Now, can you teach all that? I doubt it, and yet you have to. First, however, you have to teach yourselves, which means you have to study constantly and continuously. And all the while you have to distill from your study whatever you can in order to give your students one major thing: the desire to learn more, to know more, to study more. Hillel, a famous Jewish sage from the 2nd century BCE, after having said that the core of the Jewish teaching was to not do unto others that which you would not want to be done to you, added, "And now go and learn." If you do that, I think you will have some measure of success in teaching your students in the 21st century about the Holocaust.

Questions

1. What are some of the challenges facing teachers in the 21st century who want to teach students about the Holocaust?

2. Is it legitimate to speak about the Holocaust as the most extreme case of genocide? Why or why not?

3. Most people know the names of leading Nazis who implemented policies and practices aimed at murdering the Jews of Europe during the Holocaust, but who are some of the people who tried to thwart the Nazi attempt to do so? What did they do, and why should we teach about them?

4. In what way can one say that the story of the Christian Churches during the Holocaust is a complicated one? Give some examples.

Bibliography

Bauer, Yehuda, with the assistance of Nili Keren. *A History of the Holocaust*, rev. ed. Danbury, CT: Franklin Watts, 2002.

Browning, Christopher R., with a contribution by Jürgen Matthäus. *The Origins of the Final Solution: The Evolution of Nazi Jewish Policy 1939-1942*. London: William Heinemann, 2004.

Crowe, David M. *The Holocaust: Roots, History, and Aftermath*. Boulder, CO: Westview Press, 2007.

Harran, Marilyn et al. *The Holocaust Chronicle: A History in Words and Pictures*. Lincolnwood, IL: Publications International, Ltd., 2000.

Rubenstein, Richard L. and John K. Roth. *Approaches to Auschwitz: The Holocaust and Its Legacy*, rev. ed. Louisville, KY: Westminster John Knox Press, 2003.

Zuccotti, Susan. *Under His Very Windows: The Vatican and the Holocaust in Italy*. New Haven, CT: Yale University Press, 2002.

Notes

1. See further, Richard L. Rubenstein and John K. Roth, *Approaches to Auschwitz: The Holocaust and Its Legacy*, rev. ed. (Louisville, KY: Westminster John Knox Press, 2003), especially "Part One: Holocaust Origins," pp. 23-117.

2. *"Keine Vernichtung der Zigeuner"* ("No annihilation of the Gypsies"), Himmler's note in his appointment diary for April 20, 1942 (Hitler's birthday), after consultation with Hitler and Reinhard Heydrich, the head of the RSHA, the main Nazi police organ; in *Der Dienstkalender Heinrich Himmlers, 1941/42* (Hamburg: Christians, 1999), p. 405.

3. See further, "Excerpts from Adolf Hitler's Speech to the Reichstag, January 30, 1939," *Witness to the Holocaust: An Illustrated Documentary History of the Holocaust in the Words of Its Victims, Perpetrators and Bystanders*, ed. Michael Bernebaum (New York: HarperCollins, 1997), p. 161.

4. Himmler Memorandum to Hitler, May 25, 1940, Nuremberg Trial Documents, IMT NO-1880.

5. Klaus-Michael Mallmann/Martin Cüppers, *Halbmond und Hakenkreuz: Das "Dritte Reich," die Araber und Palästina* (Ludwigsburg: Wissenschaftliche Buchgesellschaft, 2006), p. 107: *"Deutschland (ist) entschlossen, Zug um Zug eine europäische Nation nach der anderen zur Lösung des Judenproblems aufzufordern und im gegebenen Augenblick (sich) mit einem gleichen Appell auch an aussereuropäische Völker zu wenden"* ("Germany is determined to demand the solution of the Jewish question from one after the other of all European states, and at the right moment to turn with the same appeal to non-European nations").

6. Sixty-three Albanians were given the title of Righteous by Yad Vashem; Iael Nidam-Orvieto and Irena Steinfeldt, "The Rescue of Jews in Albania through the Perspective of the Yad Vashem Files of the Righteous Among the Nations" (Jerusalem: Yad Vashem, 2012). More cases are slowly coming to light. Parts of only one Jewish family (out of about 200) in Albania were caught by the Germans.

7. Randolph L. Braham, *The Politics of Genocide: The Holocaust in Hungary, Vol. 2* (Detroit, MI: Wayne State University Press, 2000), p. 1047-8.

8. John Cornwell, *Hitler's Pope: The Secret History of Pius XII* (New York: Viking, 1999), p. 317, quoting Carlo Falconi, The Silence of Pius XII (London, UK: Faber, 1970); Bertram ordered "to hold a solemn Requiem in memory of the Führer and all those members of the Wehrmacht who have fallen in the struggle for our German Fatherland." See also, Saul Friedländer, *Die Jahre der Vernichtung: Das Dritte Reich und die Juden 1939-1945*, (Munich, GE: C.H. Beck, 2006), p. 691, quoting Klaus Scholder, *Ein Requiem für Hitler*, (Berlin, GE, 1988), p. 236, f. However, Ronald S. Rychlak, in "First Things," vol. 124, June/July 2002, pp. 37-54, says that the order to hold the Requiem Mass of May 1 or 2, 1945, was never sent out.

9. Cornwell, *Hitler's Pope*; David Bankier, Dan Michman, Iael Nidam-Orvieto, eds., *Pius XII and the Holocaust: Current State of Research* (Jerusalem: Yad Vashem, 2013).

Response to Yehuda Bauer

. . . .

Carol Rittner, R.S.M.

*Distinguished Professor of Holocaust & Genocide Studies and
Dr. Marsha Radicoff Grossman Professor of Holocaust Studies,
The Richard Stockton College of New Jersey, Galloway, NJ*

Some years ago, I read a short article written by Yehuda Bauer entitled, "Holocaust education is the key to preventing genocide in the future."[1] In this presentation, Professor Bauer does not argue that the key to preventing genocide is Holocaust education. Perhaps that is because in the seventeen years since he wrote that essay, Professor Bauer has been sobered by the genocides or genocidal events that have occurred in all too many places around the world: Chechnya, Guatemala, Congo, and Darfur, to name just a few places.

Over the past two decades, we have watched with horror as long-smoldering ethnic resentments in Europe morphed into a viciousness we haven't seen since World War II and the Holocaust ended. On television and in newspapers in this country and around the world, we have seen concentration camps once again in the heart of Europe, refugees fleeing for their lives. In Sarajevo, on CNN and Sky News, we saw – in real time – civilians threading their way through burned-out streets, trying to avoid sniper fire from armed military thugs perched in the hills surrounding that once bustling, multicultural, sophisticated city. We have seen snipers picking off innocent men, women, and children for sport.

Yes, I can understand why I did not hear Yehuda Bauer say, "Holocaust education is the key to preventing genocide in the future." What, then, did I hear him say?

One thing I heard Professor Bauer say is that in teaching about the Holocaust – teaching about any genocide – "One cannot teach pupils of any age just sheer horror."

Why? Because, he argues, "It won't be accepted. It will be rejected for very obvious reasons: a person doesn't want to be put into a position of total despair and total hopelessness […] this is not the way that one can teach anything."[2] What Bauer suggests is that in addition to teaching about the horror of the Holocaust, we should also teach about rescuers, few though they were. Why? Because rescuers show through their actions that "there was a choice: people could either follow the policy of the murderers – betray their neighbors, remain totally indifferent to the fate of their neighbors,"[3] or they could try to help, which brings me to Steven Spielberg.

Steven Spielberg once said that making *Schindler's List* changed his life completely. Why? Because it made him think about "choices," about how people make them and how they affect others. If making *Schindler's List*, a film about a German businessman who saved the lives of more than 1,100 Jews during the Holocaust (1939-1945), had such an effect on Steven Spielberg, I think that Yehuda Bauer is suggesting that learning about rescuers during the Holocaust could also have an effect on us.

Of course, we cannot teach about rescuers untethered to the context within which they acted – World War II and the Holocaust, a deadly dangerous time for Jews and for those who tried to help them. But, what we should keep in mind about the rescuers is the issue of "choice," because it highlights the fact that a person can choose an option when faced with the question, "Whose side am I on?"

We know from survivor testimonies that between 1933 and 1939, while most governments and individuals in Europe and elsewhere looked the other way, tens of thousands, perhaps even millions of people in Nazi Germany were involved in persecuting, harassing, registering, and, after 1939 and the outbreak of World War II and the Holocaust, rounding up, ghettoizing, deporting, transporting, concentrating, and murdering six million Jews in the heart of *Christian* Europe. At the same time, a relatively small number of non-Jews – "small" given the overall population of Europe at the time (approximately 700 million) – found the moral courage to shelter thousands of Jews who were the targets of Nazi hatred and persecution.

During the Holocaust, it was as easy for people to say, "The Jews *are* a problem," as it was to say, "The Jews are not *my* problem." In fact, many people said, "The Jews have nothing to do with me, or mine, or us. I have my own family, myself to worry about." But the righteous, the rescuers, the "upstanders" could not say such things. They could not stand by, they could not join in persecuting and harassing Jews, much less torturing and murdering Jews. The righteous could not turn their backs on the Jewish people who were being hunted down all over Nazi-occupied Europe. The righteous had to act. They had to do something to help the despised, vulnerable, isolated, frightened Jews.

Like the Nazi perpetrators, who were neither devils nor monsters but ordinary human beings, rescuers lived in the same moral sphere as the other 700 million people who walked the footpaths and streets of Europe. They breathed the same air, had the same fears, and faced the same challenges as did other people in German-occupied Europe. It is a mistake to make the perpetrators *other* than what they were – *ordinary* human beings – or to make the righteous *more* than what they were – *ordinary* human beings – for it allows us to say, "I'm not like them. I'm just **an *ordinary* person**, neither a monster (a perpetrator) nor a saint (a rescuer). I am neither capable of killing, like the perpetrators, nor of helping, like the righteous." We must not make either the perpetrators or the rescuers *larger* than life. Rather, we must keep them as what they were: life-size during a time when humanity was diminished. It is important for us to remember this, which is why Elie Wiesel insists, "[W]e must know about these good people who helped Jews during the Holocaust" and "We must learn from them."[4]

Allow me, if you will, to say something else, not because Yehuda Bauer said it or alluded to it, but because I think it is important to think about when teaching about genocide, whichever genocide it may be, and that is this: it may seem obvious, but still, I think teaching about the Holocaust must give attention to moral and ethical questions, not just to facts and figures. Teaching about genocide should strengthen in some way commitment to the moral principle, "Thou shalt not stand idly by when another person, community, or people is suffering" – at least, not if we – *I* – want to retain my humanity. And allow me, if you will, to argue for the kind of education that I think may help encourage commitment to such a moral principle: an education for humanity. What do I mean?

By "an education for humanity," I mean an education that teaches the common humanness of the other, an education that stresses the values of caring and that emphasizes compassion and responsibility, an education that prepares an individual for doing acts of good. And we need legitimate authority – politicians, clergy of all religious persuasions, principals, and parents, among others – to appeal to values of caring, justice, and inclusiveness in their public statements, policies, and, yes, in their personal private lives. Such an education can help to create what the late Protestant Christian theologian Robert McAfee Brown called "a moral society," a society that is not afraid to put the interests of those who are suffering above national self-interest so that metaphorically, or really, we "do not stand idly by when another person, community, or people is suffering."

After the Holocaust, many people who had been part of the vast Nazi machinery of destruction and death found refuge in the excuse, "It wasn't my fault. I'm not responsible. What could I do? I was only following orders. There wasn't anything I could do." Such people, quintessential bystanders and bureaucrats, saw no relationship between what they were doing – or not doing – and the consequences of their action. It was as though those who were responsible, in one way or another, for the decisions and actions that had such dire consequences for Jews and for others, lacked all humanity. They were merely cogs in a bureaucratic wheel, citizens in an impersonal society. In contrast, the decisions and actions of rescuers during the

Holocaust exemplify another kind of behavior, and they constitute a vivid and powerful communal memory bank that has the power to liberate us from that paralyzing excuse, "There isn't anything I can do."

When we teach about the Holocaust, let us heed the voices of those who urge us to remember the atrocities committed by the Nazis and their collaborators against the Jewish people and others during the Holocaust. Let us also, as Professor Yehuda Bauer suggests, teach about rescue, heeding the voices of rescuers who highlight for us both the possibility of individual choice and the strands of human mercy that tie us human beings to one another. If we do that, perhaps we will stand a chance of preventing genocide in the future.

Notes

1. Yehuda Bauer, "Holocaust education is the key to preventing genocide in the future," *The Press of Atlantic City*, 8 November 1995: A11.
2. Ibid.
3. Ibid.
4. Elie Wiesel in Carol Rittner, R.S.M. and Sondra Myers, eds., *The Courage to Care: Rescuers of Jews During the Holocaust* (New York: New York University Press, 1986), p. x.

Response to Yehuda Bauer

. . ■ . ■ . ■ . ■ . ■ . ■ . ■ . ▪ . ▫

John K. Roth

Edward J. Sexton Professor Emeritus of Philosophy and
Founding Director of the Center for the Study of the Holocaust, Genocide,
and Human Rights, Claremont McKenna College, Claremont, CA

Yehuda Bauer's presentation, "Teaching about the Holocaust in the 21st Century," reflects on the relevance of such teaching, a theme that invites elaboration about the meaning of the Holocaust in today's world. Our attempts to grasp the meaning(s) of that catastrophe affect how, what, and why we teach about it.

Dictionaries indicate a variety of ways in which the word *meaning* can be defined, but the one that fits best with this response to Bauer is the idea that *meaning* refers to the sense or significance, the purpose or outcome of something. Using that understanding as the point of departure, consider the following proposition: The meaning of the Holocaust in the world today is *changing*, **contested**, and *catastrophic*.

Regularly, I collect Holocaust-related items that come to my attention in news stories and other communications. Note three of them. First, a fundraising communication from the United States Holocaust Memorial Museum highlights how and why the meaning of the Holocaust in the world today is *changing*. In the letter I have in mind, museum director Sara Bloomfield wrote this sentence: "For a child born today, the Holocaust will be a distant event that he or she will know through the pages of history alone."[1] Unavoidably, the passage of time changes the meaning of events, including the Holocaust. With that passage, events, including the Holocaust, lose their immediacy. It is scarcely unnoticed or surprising that the time is soon coming when no one living will have first-hand experience or eyewitness memory of the time of Nazi Germany's genocide against the Jewish people, let alone direct awareness of specific details about that onslaught.

More and more, the Holocaust will be mediated and represented, so much so that a good question will be, "Is it possible to encounter, to know, to teach about the Holocaust directly, or will our encounters, our knowing, our teaching be about the mediations, the representations, of that history?" Already in years soon after World War II ended, Charlotte Delbo, one of the most eloquent and insightful survivors of Auschwitz, was well aware of a version of the changes and challenges that could not be averted: "Today," she wrote, "people know / have known for several years / that this dot on the map / is Auschwitz / This much they know / as for the rest / they think they know."[2]

Delbo, of course, would admit that today our "knowledge" about the Holocaust, or at least what we think we know about that disaster, is vastly greater than it was in 1946 when she began to write *Auschwitz and After*, her memoir-trilogy. The advances in research not only about the Holocaust itself but also about the conditions and circumstances that led to it—including the long history of antisemitism—and the aftereffects and reverberations of the Shoah affect our understanding of what the term *Holocaust* denotes and connotes. In Holocaust studies, current subfields (for example, a focus on what happened to Jewish women and children during those times) barely existed twenty years ago, but now they do. We seem capable of knowing more and more about the Holocaust; no end to research about the topic is coming. At the same time, this work has an unintended consequence and a paradoxical implication because no one, no institution or person, can undertake, absorb, or comprehend it all, thus leaving us to ask, "What does all of the research, the study, the knowledge about the Holocaust mean? What have we really *learned* from it? How will further changes in the study of the Holocaust affect our grasp of its meaning?"

Many of the changes that affect the meaning(s) of the Holocaust in the world today do so by making the meaning(s) *contested*. In that regard, mull over a statement from Avner Shalev, chairman of Yad Vashem, Israel's Holocaust memorial and museum. In a February 2012 *New York Times* article that discussed Yad Vashem's outreach, which at the time included a ten-day seminar especially for teachers and professors from Taiwan, Shalev was quoted as saying that "this [the Holocaust] is the most complicated phenomenon in human history."[3]

How do we, how should we, receive and respond to a statement like that one? Is the claim that the Holocaust is "the most complicated phenomenon in human history" true, false, some mixture of the two, or perhaps less a factual claim than a way of underwriting a privileged position for the Holocaust, one undergirding the view that no effort should be spared to educate the world about the Holocaust and to advance the "lessons" that are embedded in it?

If Shalev was quoted correctly in the *New York Times* article, it seems that his proposition would have to be contested, if only to ask how one would know and show that the Holocaust is the most complicated phenomenon in human history. The same would be true of any claim that took the form, "the Holocaust is the most _____ phenomenon in human history." Think of the adjectives that could fill the blank in that formula. Terms such as *devastating*, *destructive*, *important*, *unprecedented*, and *unique* would be among them, but any and all of those formulations are contestable.

The fact that the meaning of the Holocaust in today's world is *contested* will not be eliminated by forgoing language that describes the Holocaust as *the most* of "anything" in human history. Of course, it is important and imperative to emphasize that the fact of the Holocaust itself (the genocidal slaughter of millions of European Jews) remains beyond contesting, and yet just what to say about the place and status of that event in human history also remains a question, and what to say is very much contested. How, for instance, should the Holocaust be understood in relation to other genocides? It can be argued that the Holocaust was an instance of genocide or nothing could be, but what kind of genocide was the Holocaust? Is it the most extreme, the worst, of any genocide to date? What snares and delusions await if one is tempted to go there or if one does not make such comparative judgments?

It is no exaggeration to say that the contested meaning of the Holocaust is a matter of life and death, a prospect that takes us to the third dimension of my proposition that the meaning of the Holocaust in today's world is changing, contested, and *catastrophic*. Just as there are multiple ways in which the meaning of the Holocaust is changing and contested, many more than can be identified in these remarks of mine, so too are there varied ways in which the meaning of the Holocaust in today's world can be called catastrophic. To identify one major aspect of what I mean, think about words from an editorial that appeared on the Vatican's internet news site on January 27, 2012, the anniversary of the Holocaust Memorial Day established by the United Nations in 2005, its date coinciding with the liberation of Auschwitz in 1945. Warning against "the risk that people will forget, or even worse, deny the Holocaust," the Vatican editorial underscored that "the memory of the Holocaust is a crucial point of reference in the history of mankind, when we try to understand what is at stake when we speak of the essential dignity of every human person, the universality of human rights, and commitment to their defense." Then the editorial added that the Holocaust is also "a place for the most radical questions about God and about evil."[4]

Many of the important developments in international law emerged in the wake of the Holocaust. One thinks of the United Nations Convention on the Prevention and Punishment of the Crime of Genocide, the Universal Declaration of Human Rights, and the establishment of various international tribunals to prosecute those who commit crimes against humanity. Nothing about the Holocaust, however, guarantees that its meaning will include success in deterring mass atrocity crimes, preventing genocide, or honoring human rights. To the contrary, the Holocaust was catastrophic because it did so much to undermine confidence about ethics, reason, humanitarian progress, and the hope that "never again" would be so much more than the bereft slogan it has become. Furthermore, while the Vatican editorial was correct to point out that the Holocaust raises "radical questions about God and about evil," what about attempts to respond to those questions in convincing ways? The Holocaust is not the only event that does so, but it continues to scar religious and philosophical life. At least, it does so if we let the Holocaust in and do not ignore, forget, preempt, sanitize, or over-instrumentalize it.

The Holocaust assaulted all that human beings hold most dear when we are at our best. Nothing human, natural, or divine guarantees life and respect for those persons and realities, but nothing is more important than our commitment to honor and defend them, for they remain as significant as they are fragile, as meaningful and precious as they are endangered.

Notes

1. The letter is undated, but it reached me in early March 2012.
2. Charlotte Delbo, *Auschwitz and After*, trans. Rosette C. Lamont (New Haven, CT: Yale University Press, 1995), p. 138. The quotation is from *Useless Knowledge*, the second part of the trilogy called *Auschwitz and After*.
3. The statement attributed to Shalev is found in Ethan Bronner, "From Overseas Visitors, a Growing Demand to Study the Holocaust," *New York Times*, 14 February 2012. Available online at http://www.nytimes.com/2012/02/15/world/middleeast/lessons-from-the-holocaust-are-widespread-and-varied.html?_r=1&pagewanted=all
4. The editorial, "Preserve the Memory," by Fr. Lombardi, is available online at: http://www.news.va/en/news/fr-lombardi-editorial-preserve-the-memory.

Response to Yehuda Bauer

James E. Waller

Cohen Professor of Holocaust and Genocide Studies,
Keene State College, Keene, NH

Dr. Bauer's presentation gives us a deep well of material from which to draw, as has his groundbreaking scholarship in Holocaust studies over the years. He is well-recognized, deservedly so, as one of the doyens of Holocaust scholarship and pedagogy. When he addresses us about the problem of teaching about the Holocaust in the 21st century, even the most seasoned teachers in the field should take note.

While there are many avenues I could take in responding to his presentation, I was particularly challenged by his question of how relevant the topic of the Holocaust remains to students. I hold an endowed professorship in Holocaust and genocide studies at the only US institution, Keene State College, to offer an undergraduate major in the field. So, the question Bauer raises of "What does all this have to do with me?" is one frequently asked by students in our courses and, I suspect, in yours as well. As Bauer explains, our students come to recognize that a large part of what the Holocaust has to do with us is rooted in the fact that repetition of genocide continues. Students come to learn that if each of us can begin to see our brothers and sisters in the world community, no matter how far outside our doorstep, as a priority in our values and life choices, then, perhaps, we can ensure that "Never Again" means far more than "never again will Germans kills Jews in Europe in the 1940s."

So, while I agree with Bauer that one of the fundamental reasons for studying the Holocaust lies in avoiding the repetition of such tragedies in the future, I remain perplexed at his insistence, both in this presentation and his other presentations and writings, to characterize the Holocaust as the "most extreme" case of genocide. He asserts that it's not the most extreme because of the number of victims or the percentage of Jews murdered in proportion to the total number of Jews all over the world. And, he claims, it's not the most extreme due to the brutality of suffering, because the suffering of the victims is the same in all cases.

How, then, does he defend the Holocaust as the most extreme case of genocide? His central defense is that the Nazi idea to kill all Jews was a global concept, in his mind, an unprecedented concept that has not been repeated since the Holocaust. He contrasts this, for instance, with the Nazis' explicit decision to kill some, but not all, of the Roma. In the 2006 Meyerhoff Annual Lecture at the US Holocaust Museum, Bauer asserts the same limitation for the Poles – there was never a German plan to kill all of them. Bauer also points out the unprecedented reality that the Nazis killed the very people who were working for them, while they were working for them. He argues that this non-pragmatic reality indicates the centrality of ideology as a motivating concept.

Others far more accredited than I can take issue with Bauer's interpretation of the Nazi intent for the Roma, and there are scholars who certainly do argue for the existence of a Nazi intent to kill not just some, but all of the Roma – and perhaps even all of the Poles. In my own research, I have challenged the role of ideology as a central explanatory mechanism in perpetrator behavior. Both areas of research strike me as something about which reasonable people could disagree.

As a comparative genocide studies teacher-scholar, though, what I am better positioned to raise is the question of why Bauer feels it necessary to defend the Holocaust as the most extreme case of genocide. Comparativists focus on the similarities among, and differences between, episodes of genocide and mass atrocity (including the international crimes of war crimes and crimes against humanity). In studying cases individually, we also look at the historical links of cases to one another. The similarities and differences we uncover are richly instructive on many levels, but very few comparativisits see a need to venture into the "most extreme" discussion. Ranking genocides on extremity isn't a comparative discussion as much as it is a discussion of what one colleague calls "the Olympics of suffering" or a hierarchy of victimization. Designating any genocide as "most extreme" means it's a privileged status category to which none others need apply.

Why does "most extreme" matter to Bauer or to anyone working or teaching in this field? At its most cynical, the use of "most extreme" to describe the Holocaust can smack of a political use of victimization. A colleague in the field, who happens to be Jewish, has expressed to me his fear that some take "never again" as only to mean "never again to the Jews." When one characterizes the Holocaust as "most extreme," it can seem to feed into a notion of privileged suffering – that is, that one victim group's suffering is more "extreme" than another's. Bauer goes to great lengths, both in this presentation and his other work, to assert "the suffering of the victims is the same in all cases – literally, in all cases." Elsewhere, Bauer has even claimed that it is "immoral" to compare sufferings from victims of genocide. How does that assertion stand, though, in the face of his equally insistent characterization of the Holocaust as the "most extreme" case of genocide?

I want to be clear that I've never had the privilege to discuss this question with Dr. Bauer. So, I think it best to respond less to him at this moment and more to the general dynamic that still exists with the field of comparative genocide studies – what place does the Holocaust hold in the field? What is the historical, and contemporary, relationship between comparative genocide studies and the Holocaust? What role does the Holocaust play in comparative genocide studies? What does it mean for the Holocaust to be "de-centered" from comparative genocide studies? What happens if "genocide" becomes the master category rather than "Holocaust?" Does analyzing other genocides, exploring their similarities *and* differences, detract from the uniqueness of the Holocaust?

I join with most others in the field of Holocaust and genocide studies who applaud, Steven Katz's persistence notwithstanding, the demise of the fractious uniqueness versus universal debate in our field. To his credit, over two decades ago Dr. Bauer removed himself from the uniqueness pole of that debate and found ways to understand some of the universal implications of the Holocaust. So, while few people in the field still remain in the terminological prison of "unique" or "universal," quite a few people have substituted words and phrases that still privilege the Holocaust in relation to other cases of genocide. I see compensatory replacements in words such as "unprecedented" and phrases such as "most extreme." For instance, even Timothy Snyder, author of the critically-acclaimed *Bloodlands*, a book that some see (mistakenly so, in my opinion) as a challenge to the memory of the Holocaust, describes the Holocaust as an "unprecedented" crime. As I read it, the usage of "unprecedented" and "most extreme" are the currently accepted covers for the now verboten use of "unique" – same meanings, just different words.

Certainly, it must be recognized that the Holocaust produced a scholarly literature that spawned a comparative discipline. Holocaust studies provided the theoretical frameworks, research strategies, and subject specialists that laid the groundwork for comparative genocide studies. It can also be argued, though, that the field of comparative genocide studies was born in *opposition* to the dominant Holocaust discourse, as an act of scholarly revolt against a Holocaust "establishment" that many perceived to be overly resistant to comparative study and connections with other genocides.

I suggest that, as Alex Alvarez has said, "all genocides are simultaneously unique and analogous." The Holocaust is not, in my opinion, "uniquely unique" in such a way as to stand separate and privileged from other genocides. Such a position certainly has implications for the politicization of the Holocaust as well as for the politicization of genocide. Ultimately, it is assertions like "most extreme," indefensible in my opinion, that hamper the integration of Holocaust studies into the larger field of genocide studies. I believe this is incredibly unfortunate because comparative study can substantially enrich our understanding of the Holocaust; the scope and dimensions of the Holocaust can be better understood in the context of a broader comparative perspective. As just one of many examples, Doris Bergen has described how research into the use of sexual violence and rape as a tool of ethnic cleansing in the former Yugoslavia invigorated a rethinking of the role of sexual violence and rape in the Holocaust.

I find it interesting how we selectively appreciate the power of context. Gerhard Weinberg has been influential in my own work with his strong reminders that the Holocaust cannot be fully understood without placing it in the context of World War II, a contextual necessity that I believe Bauer would embrace as well. When the challenge is raised, though, about placing the Holocaust in the context of genocide studies, too many still refuse that contextual opportunity to deepen our understanding of the Holocaust. Somehow, for some, the Holocaust is perceived to lose its relevance when contextualized, a very mistaken perception in my mind. As a point of fact, I would argue that the Holocaust stands to lose more relevance when it is not contextualized within the broader framework of genocide studies. To not consider the Holocaust in the context of other genocides is to essentially distort it by, as Bauer admitted in his 2006 address, "setting it apart, outside of history." The Holocaust is too important to stand outside of the history of genocide, it must be rooted inside of that history.

Beyond the scholarly and pedagogical issues, however, let me close with a human perspective. Carol, John, and I were given copies of Dr. Bauer's remarks to preview before this conference. It so happened that on the same day I previewed Bauer's presentation, I later had a Skype conversation with a friend from Rwanda. He had lost his parents and several siblings in the 1994 genocide. At the age of thirteen, he became head of the small household that remained when the killings were over. I knew the "most extreme" language in Bauer's presentation had left me unsettled and I was sharing some of my reactions with my friend. He went silent and the internet connection was strong enough for me to see some tears welling in his eyes. I asked him to share his heart with me. He simply said, "Why does someone even ask the question of which genocide is the most extreme?"

My friend is not a scholar or teacher in the field; he's simply a man still trying to find his way to survival. He doesn't want to win the Olympics of suffering and he doesn't even want to run in it. He's just genuinely puzzled at why someone would even ask the question of "most extreme." Why does the question matter? What does it hope to accomplish? Do we think any less of the Holocaust if we remove the "most extreme" moniker? For my Rwandan friend, describing the Holocaust as "most extreme" minimizes his suffering and the losses he has endured. Who would dare say his experiences in the Rwandan genocide are less extreme? But, again, who would even dare ask that question? And why? I was mute then and I remain mute now – I can't explain to my friend, or to myself, why the issue of "most extreme" is even raised and what good purpose it serves for us as teachers and scholars. And Dr. Bauer's presentation, for all its considerable merits, has brought me no closer to an answer.

What Will We Do When the Survivors Are Gone?

Stephen D. Smith

Executive Director of the University of Southern California (USC) Shoah Foundation Institute for Visual History and Education, Los Angeles, CA

What will we do when the survivors are gone? It's a challenging question. Every survivor has a story to tell, says Isaac Goodfriend, a survivor of the Holocaust who has told his own story many times to many different audiences. But let me introduce you to another kind of testimony, one that is visual.

Figure 1

Naomi Blake is an artist and this sculpture is her testimony, although it's not in words. However, it does reveal her soul. Throughout her life, Naomi has made public sculpture in England, including a piece entitled "Abandoned" (see figure 1), which is at the United Kingdom Holocaust Centre in Nottinghamshire, an organization I had the privilege to found. "Abandoned" is eight feet tall and is very typical of her work. What is particularly interesting to me is that the artist, to the best of my knowledge, has not given any oral testimony to the Shoah Foundation or to any other organization for that matter.

I remember talking to Naomi after she created the piece for the Holocaust Centre, and I asked her, "Why did you choose the title 'Abandoned' for this sculpture?" She responded by describing how she arrived at Auschwitz-Birkenau from Hungary along with her ten brothers, sisters, and cousins, and how she went through the first selection. Only she and her sister survived that selection. She had come from a Hasidic home in Budapest, and like so many pious Jews who made that terrible journey to the end of their lives, Naomi did so with piety and belief, only to realize at the end of her journey just how abandoned she was – by God and by human beings.

In creating "Abandoned," she inscribed a protest on the sculpture: "Why do you hide your face? Why do you forget our affliction and oppression?" (Ps. 44:24). In fact, the only words that Holocaust survivor Naomi Blake left behind are these words of protest from the Bible. I was so used to hearing the narratives of survivors in words, on texts, in sounds, and on video, and yet, here was Naomi Blake, a Holocaust survivor, leaving behind a form of testimony that was unexpected to me. The more I thought about her statement, the more I realized that in order to understand the witness, we have to understand the very process of witnessing itself. What does it mean to carve out that sculpture, inscribe those words of scripture, and then stand in front of the world with your act of witness and say, without words, "This is my experience"?

Images

Another witness without words is a painting by Roman Halter (see figure 2), a Holocaust survivor from Poland. More than any other, this painting made me struggle with the question of what we will do when the witnesses of the Holocaust are gone. I've looked at this image many times. It sits on my mantel at home. It is a small but intense image. Originally, I only saw a single face. I did not notice the second face until the day I learned that Roman Halter had died.

Figure 2

That day, I lifted the image in my hands to scan it because I wanted to pay tribute to Roman and his extraordinary life in a lecture I was going to give. As I looked at it more closely, I saw for the first time a mother and child. I thought about Roman and why he had chosen to depict an image of a mother and a child. I thought back over other works he had done, specifically one I had seen hanging in the Imperial War Museum in London; the Madonna and child image, which seemed to represent a combination of the personal and the sacred, maybe even a struggle between the two, was present in many of his works. In his more overt work, he incorporates crucifixes, Chagall-fashion, with the dark, sharp edge of the Holocaust overlaid.

Although Roman Halter was a very close friend of mine, I had never actually listened to his testimony in Shoah Foundation's archive, so I went there to listen to his voice, to hear his testimony. I thought there might be some clues that would illuminate for me why he chose to depict the image of a mother and a child, about the struggle between the personal and the sacred that runs through his work. I went to the archives to find his testimony, but it was not there.

My friend, Roman Halter, who had encouraged me to make sure survivors' testimonies were documented, who had tirelessly gone in and out of schools telling his story to young people, who had given up his work in architecture so he could paint and represent his story through artwork, had not given his oral testimony. He had written a book and he had bequeathed his artwork to the world, but in that moment when I had depended on a particular form of testimony, what I thought was there was not there at all. There was no recourse, no second chance, because Roman Halter, the eyewitness, was gone.

And yet I found that his act of witness was very present. I thought about what it means to have this wealth of witness testimony in all its variety and how we make sense of its multiple voices. Roman Halter and Naomi Blake have both left their testimony, just not on video.

Testimonies in Various Forms

We have witness testimony in many forms – in literature, in books and memoirs, in fiction and non-fiction forms. There is artwork and there are memorials placed by Holocaust survivors around the world; there are paintings and sculptures. Survivors have made documentary films and written family narratives. We have scrapbooks, diaries, and letters. And there are the lasting relationships that Holocaust survivors have developed with young people in high schools, colleges, and universities. This whole wealth of material is available to us in its many forms.

I think the question, "What are we going to do when the survivors are gone?" needs to be restated. The more important questions are, "What are we going to do with this varied witness material bequeathed to us by Holocaust survivors? How are we going to use it to tell their stories in the future?"

There is the lingering impression that Holocaust survivors did not tell their stories, but actually, they did. From the early 1940s on, eyewitnesses were leaving their legacy. The main issue was the lack of audience. In order to bear witness, you have to have two parties: the witness and an audience. The witness cannot witness in a vacuum. There has to be at least some receptivity to the act of witness because witnessing is not for the benefit of the witness – the person giving testimony – but for those who listen to what he or she has to say. After WWII, there was not a high level of receptivity to what survivors had to say. People wanted to get on with their lives and deal with their own losses; they had little time for what happened to others. That was then. This is now.

The USC Shoah Foundation

Over the decades, the act of bearing witness has developed further. As we know, in the 1970s, 80s, and 90s in particular, survivors developed the use of various representational forms to tell their stories. As the video age emerged, video testimony became the dominant testimonial form, which brings me to the University of Southern California's Shoah Foundation. The USC Shoah Foundation's Visual History Archive (VHA) has 52,000 testimonies in 32 languages from 56 countries. It is an archive so vast that if we continuously ran all the testimonies we have in the archive, 24 hours a day every day, it would take 12 years to watch all of them. We at the Shoah Foundation – and all of our colleagues, including many of you – have only just begun to find out what the witnesses have left us in their testimonies. Like any other archive, you have to open the files to find new knowledge. The question for all of us is, "Are we paying lip service to the legacy, or are we trying understand what has been given to us?"

To make access easier, the Shoah Foundation's video archives have been indexed in one-minute segments. For each of those segments, we have described the content using a controlled vocabulary. For example, if you want to know something about *hunger* in *Auschwitz*, you can use those keywords to access video segments in which survivors and others speak about hunger in Auschwitz in given segments of video. Or if you want to know something about how children experienced Auschwitz, you would look up the terms *children* and *Auschwitz*, and our search engines would scroll though our vast archive and identify all of the segments of video testimony about children and Auschwitz.

What this means is that today, researchers can focus in on a given keyword or words and find particular content, thus enabling focused research using this vast trove of video material from witnesses. We at the Foundation are interested in providing access to the Shoah Foundation's 52,000 video testimonies. We want to provide that access to researchers, teachers, scholars, and interested laypeople in a way that is user-friendly, helpful, efficient, and effective.[1]

Bearing Witness

The content of the Visual History Archive (VHA) goes well beyond the provision of historical data. We also are attempting to develop our own literacy to listen more deeply to the personal stories witnesses tell. Let me tell you a brief story to illustrate my point.

Victoria Vincent lived in England. She was a survivor who I got to know early in my interaction with Holocaust survivors. I spent quite a lot of time with her in 1995, going to schools with her and listening to her tell her story to young people. Each day we would go to a high school where she would tell a brief version of her experiences in Milan, Italy, in Auschwitz-Birkenau, and on the death marches. Afterwards, students would ask questions. Most of us have experienced that many times. But I noticed that she always cried at the same point in her testimony.

One day in the car, I asked Victoria Vincent if she would mind trying to explain why she always broke down at the same point in her testimony. I remember saying to her, "It isn't when you are talking about being captured in Milan, and it isn't when you are telling them about being tortured in the detention center. It isn't when you tell them about being deported or about spending five days of hell on a train that ends up in Auschwitz. It isn't when you tell them about the grueling commandos you were put in, and it isn't even when you talk about the typhus, dysentery, or the mass murder of the Hungarian Jews you witnessed. No, you always cry just before you go on the death march. Why? It seems very late in your experience."

"Well," she said, "it's all very simple. The Germans were hanging four girls who had been involved in the uprising in Auschwitz-Birkenau in October 1944 – two in the morning and two in the evening." She told me that she was standing in a row of five women. On one side of her was her sister Olga, from whom she had been separated in Milan, and they had only found each other a year later in Birkenau. "I needed my sister and she needed me. The two of us were kind of a self-help group. On the other side of me was the sister of one of the girls that was being hanged." It was at that moment that she realized the loss and the tearing apart that was occurring in front of her very eyes. She told me, "I had my thick-rimmed glasses on, and I knew that if my glasses got knocked off in the rush for food or the crush of work, I wouldn't get back to my barracks because without my glasses, I'm literally clinically blind. And I knew that at any moment, I could lose them. If I did, I'd be gone."

She told me she was standing there thinking about all of that and about the girls who were being hanged, when she thought to herself, "Maybe I should swap places with the girl who is being hanged because she's strong, she's courageous, and she's achieved something, but I could be gone by nightfall." Then she said, "My heart was beating and pounding in my chest as I tried to summon the courage to step forward and say, 'Take me!' But I couldn't do it. I just couldn't do it because I wanted to live another day."

The remnants of a Christmas tree were still up in the *appellplatz* (roll-call area). The S.S. had put it there, and it had been there over the Christmas holidays. She said, "I was so angry, so frustrated, and I thought to myself, 'How dare you! How dare you!'" She told me that the combination of all those things was just too much for her, just too overwhelming, and that's what brought on the tears every time. But she never made explicit why. I asked her then to tell me why she chose each episode of testimony in her "life history." What I found was a series of short stories with various levels of meaning – family, tradition, resistance, tenacity, loyalty, survival, love, hatred, trust, survival, etc. I began to "read" testimony in a whole new way.

Survivor Testimonies and the Future

I've thought a lot about Victoria Vincent, about what she told me, and about other Holocaust survivor testimonies I've heard. The question I always ask myself – and it's the question we at the USC Shoah Foundation ask ourselves all the time – is, "What do we do with all of this material going into the future?" There are, of course, many ways to address this issue, some technical and others having to do with purpose. I'd like to focus on purpose for a moment.

One question Shoah Foundation interviewers have always been asked to put to those they interview is, "What is your message for the future?" Virtually all of the testimonies in our archive contain a response to this question. What we've discovered based on a random sampling of testimonies is that while interviewees might be talking very specifically about their experiences – Jews under National Socialism, their own experiences as victims of the Nazis, the destruction of their communities by the Nazis and their collaborators, etc. – there is almost always a very universal message about the future. By "universal," I mean that survivors are saying – perhaps to their grandchildren, even to all of us – "Think about your values and choices. Be proud of who you are. Think about the choices you make and how they might impact your world, the world generally."

There are also "instructions" for us about issues like antisemitism in the world and support for the State of Israel, which, as you might imagine, is extremely important to survivors' legacy given what they lived through. In an overwhelming number of testimonies, survivors talk about family, but they also talk about racism in the world today, history, and memory. And they talk about their desire that we use their testimonies in a way that empowers people to think about their role in the world.

The challenges we face at the USC Shoah Foundation revolve around how we can stay true to the purpose behind these testimonies and how we can create resources to deliver what we have to a broader audience.

Resources

At the Shoah Foundation, we have created a number of resources, two of which I want to highlight here. *IWitness* is an online resource created to connect students with the past, engage them in the present, and motivate them to build a better future. There are 2,500 hours of audiovisual testimony in this program for students to access and search using keywords. Students can learn how to search a subject area, learn about the context of a testimony, and create their own projects. What is particularly important about the *IWitness* program is that students can work in a structured and contextualized environment in which they control their learning experience. They become witnesses to the witnesses themselves. Students can then use their own stories to identify their values within the survivors' stories.[2]

Another project we have is called *New Dimensions in Testimony*. In this project, we are taking our own experiences of inviting survivors and witnesses into our classrooms, asking them to tell us about their experiences, then engaging them in conversation. *New Dimensions* allows us to make available to teachers and students film segments in which survivors respond to the various kinds of questions students often ask survivors after listening to them speak about their experiences during World War II and the Holocaust. First, students and teachers view and listen to a short version of a survivor's testimony. Then the viewers ask their questions. For example, they might ask questions for clarification: "Did your sister survive? Did your parents survive? Did you meet other members of your family after liberation?" Or they can ask questions like, "Do you still believe in God after your experience? Do you feel hatred or bitterness after what you've been through? Did you revenge against your tormentors? How do you feel about Germans today? Have you been back to your hometown? What do you feel like today when you see racism in the world? How do you feel when you see genocide happening again?" On the whole, most students do not seek clarification about historical detail, although they do want to have certain kinds of information. What they really want to know is, "What does all of this have to do with me?"

Into the Future

At the USC Shoah Foundation, we hope that schools and universities, museums, and Holocaust centers around the world will use the resources we have as part of their own programs and teaching. We have the kind of resources that can help us stay true to the purpose(s) behind why survivors have told their stories, and we want to share our vast archive with future generations of students and teachers.

The president of the University of Southern California, C.L. Max Nikias, often talks about the classics, which he refers to as the *super texts* of civilization. Those super texts, he reminds his audiences, have been around for centuries, even millennia in the case of Aristotle and Plato. These great works of literature are fundamental to and embedded within our civilization.

I asked him once, "Why is it that an institution like the Shoah Foundation is at a research university like USC?" He said, "Because what you have in the archives, these testimonies of Holocaust survivors, and others, are *super texts*. They don't need to stand the test of time for us to know that these testimonies are *super texts* – **now**."

We have inherited from survivors these testimonies at the USC Shoah Foundation; we have also inherited a responsibility to protect, interpret, and share them with others, and to try to make sense of it all. We have inherited many forms of witness, text and non-narrative forms, all of which we have the responsibility to preserve and share. The answer to the question, "What will we do when the survivors are gone?" is that we will take their legacy, preserve it, make it accessible to the world, and continue to make sense of it for generations to come in order to make the *witnesses' witness* relevant within our world.

Questions

1. *How shall we teach about the Holocaust once the survivors are no longer with us? What shall we do when they are gone?*

2. *What are some of the ways that teachers and students can make use of the vast resources available through the USC Shoah Foundation?*

3. *How do various forms of testimony (narratives, novels, photographs, paintings, sculptures, memorials) bear witness to the Holocaust?*

4. *What are some ways that teachers and students can use various forms of testimony to teach about the Holocaust?*

5. *Is any one form of bearing witness to the Holocaust – or to any genocide – better than any other form? Explain.*

Bibliography

Delbo, Charlotte. *Auschwitz and After*, 2nd ed. New Haven, CT: Yale University Press, 2013.

Langer, Lawrence L. *The Ruins of Memory*. New Haven, CT: Yale University Press, 1993.

Novitch, Miriam. *Spiritual Resistance: Art from the Concentration Camps, 1940-1945*. Philadelphia, PA: Jewish Publication Society, 1981.

Skloot, Robert, ed. *The Theater of the Holocaust, Vols. 1 and 2*. Madison, WI: The University of Wisconsin Press, 1983 and 1999.

Smith, Stephen. *Making Memory: Creating Britain's First Holocaust Center*, 2nd rev. ed. Laxton, UK: Quill Press, 2002.

Volavkova, Hana, ed. *I Never Saw Another Butterfly: Children's Drawings and Poems from the Terezin Concentration Camp, 1942-1944*, 2nd ed. New York: Schocken, 1994.

Notes

1. See further, http://vhaonline.usc.edu.
2. See further, http://iwitness.usc.edu.

Using Videotaped Testimonies of Holocaust Survivors

■ ■ ■ ■ ■ ■ ■ ■ ■ ■ ■

Joanne Weiner Rudof

Archivist, Fortunoff Video Archive for Holocaust Testimonies,
Yale University, New Haven, CT

In a paper entitled "On Holocaust Education," presented in Prague on June 29, 2009, Yehuda Bauer noted the importance of knowing why we teach the Holocaust. He stated that we teach the topic because:

> [It] is a central issue for all of civilization […] because of unprecedented motivations and character, and the global impact it had, and has, as the paradigm of genocide. […] [T]he Holocaust should, in principle, be taught analytically, yet on the other hand also as the story of individuals who were caught up in it. A historian is someone who tells stories. Unless a teacher uses this tool, no impression or effect will result. On the other hand, to just tell stories is counter-productive. Students must be encouraged to investigate the facts, the connections, the contexts.

I would add that teachers also must investigate, learn, and come to know "the facts, the connections, the contexts" prior to embarking on the often-perilous path of teaching this subject.

Popular Culture and the Holocaust

In the United States, most knowledge about the Holocaust comes from popular culture representations, films like *Schindler's List*, *Life Is Beautiful*, and *The Diary of Anne Frank*. While reaching large audiences and briefly raising consciousness about the Holocaust, Omer Bartov reminds us of the problems that occur when these are the only encounters one has with this subject. He notes that "some of the fundamental problems of this genre are that [the stories they tell] may well be viewed by the public as the norm rather than the exception in that universe of industrialized killing."[1]

Bartov further expresses his concern that if a film like *Schindler's List* is the "only version of the Holocaust to which much of the general public […] [is] exposed […] whose authority as a true reconstruction of the past is reinforced by the fact that it is based on an 'authentic' story," it obliterates "the fact that in the real Holocaust, most of the Jews died […] [and] most of the Germans either collaborated or remained passive bystanders."[2] Bartov also expresses how troubling it is that the viewers believe they are "seeing things as they 'actually were.'"[3]

Holocaust Testimonies

Yehuda Bauer says that as teachers, we must first present "the facts, the contexts, the connections," then we must make them real and meaningful and present the stories of individuals. One method to meet this formidable challenge is the use of Holocaust video testimonies. When one watches Holocaust testimonies recorded under ideal circumstances, one can witness memory transforming itself into language. It is quite a different experience from watching a Holocaust-themed fictionalized film or documentary, or reading a memoir, fictional work, textbook, or book resulting from historical research. Many of the aforementioned have value for teaching, expanding our knowledge, and broadening perspective, but some have little value or even negative value.

First-person life stories have been recorded almost from the beginning of human time. Cave drawings are a record of lives lived. In more contemporary times, life stories take many forms: diaries, journals, art, musical compositions, poetry, memoirs, movies, audio, and video recordings. During World War II, some victims of Nazi genocidal and extermination policies were recording their stories as they were occurring. We have, for example, extraordinary diaries, some written by young people, like *The Diary of Dawid Sierakowiak: Five Notebooks from the Łódź Ghetto*. Sierakowiak recorded despair, hopelessness, starvation, and disease, as well as his foreknowledge that they would not survive – and he did not. Like Anne Frank, he was with his family, but unlike what is recorded in her diary, he watched as members of his family died. It would be impossible for even the most sanguine playwright or screenwriter to craft a positive or redemptive message from Sierakowiak's diary.

There are hundreds of such contemporaneous historical documents. More become available every year, as do analyses of these documents, like Samuel Kassow's seminal work *Who Will Write our History: Emanuel Ringelblum, the Warsaw Ghetto, and the Oyneg Shabes Archive*, published five years ago. The members of the *sonnderkommando* in Birkenau [sonnderkommando were groups of Jewish prisoners in the Nazi extermination camps who were forced to work in the gas chambers and crematoria] wrote their accounts and buried them in bottles, some of which were found after the war in the ruins of the crematoria. They became *Megilès Oyshvits*, translated into English from the Hebrew and in 1985, adapted from the original Yiddish as *The Scrolls of Auschwitz* by Ber Mark.

Many survivor accounts were recorded shortly after the war. There are thousands of them in the Warsaw Jewish historical archives. Survivors gathered in *landsmanshaften* and compiled texts, photographs, maps, and drawings published as *yizkor* books, rich sources of life before the war. These *yizkor* books also served as a record of events during and immediately afterwards in hundreds of European cities and towns. The New York Public Library has made their large collection of these available online.[4]

David Pablo Boder traveled to the Displaced Persons (DP) camps in 1946 and, with a newly available wire-to-wire audio recorder, taped the stories of 119 Jews and non-Jews in nine languages. His book, published in 1949, bore the apocryphal title, *I Did Not Interview the Dead*. Survivors never stopped writing, and they never stopped talking, certainly among themselves and often to others when they found empathetic listeners.

Video Testimonies

In 1979, the first video accounts of Holocaust survivors and witnesses were recorded by a local project in New Haven, Connecticut. This grassroots organization videotaped the testimonies of 183 people. These videos were transferred to Yale University in 1981. Today, the collection has grown to 4,500 testimonies, recorded by Yale with the assistance of 36 formally affiliated projects in North America, South America, Europe, and Israel. Many other individuals and institutions also have videotaped Holocaust survivors and witnesses since that first effort in 1979, creating new genres requiring new skills to "read," use, and understand them.

The video accounts vary greatly based on both the methodology of the individual or institution recording them and the individuals involved. Dori Laub, a child survivor of the Holocaust and now a psychiatrist, in partnership with Laurel Vlock, a local New Haven television host, began with four tapings in 1979 at Dr. Laub's office. They started at six in the evening, anticipating they would be done by eight or nine. They finished after one in the morning and were astounded at what had just occurred. They realized that given an empathetic and informed listener, memory welled up and almost overwhelmed all those participating in the recording sessions. They observed that the best format was no format, that allowing the witnesses to tell their stories in their own words, not imposing chronological order, time limits, or questionnaires, resulted in extraordinarily detailed and moving audio-video "documents." Their observations and method were later formalized into a training program. Funding was obtained to expand the program both in New Haven and elsewhere.

At Yale, during preliminary phone conversations with witnesses and in the studio prior to the taping, we make it clear that we want to hear the witnesses' stories the way they would like to tell them. We ask them to imagine they are sitting and looking at a family photo album and to describe the photographs, or we suggest they begin with their earliest memories of home, family, and community. The interviewer tells the survivor that when the camera goes on, the interviewer will state the date, the place, and his or her name; then the witness is to introduce him or herself, stating his or her name, date of birth, and birthplace. After that, the witness is to begin telling us his or her story. What we are trying to do is figuratively and literally give ownership of the taping session to the subject.

As we listen, we often feel as though we are sitting across from someone who is viewing a movie in his or her head and describing it to us. Memories invoke other memories. The testimonies are often episodic rather than chronological. Our only questions try to help the survivor place his or her story in time and place. The questions are phrased so that if the witness does not know the answer, we can either assist him or her or just move on. We have found that if too many questions are posed, the witness becomes passive and simply waits for the next question. The free association stops; the mental movie ceases to run. The result is far less information from the survivor and few, if any, reflections.

Programs for Classroom Use

At Yale, we have created edited programs of these recorded testimonies specifically for classroom use. The edited programs are significantly shorter than the full testimonies so that they can be used in a class period. Fifteen programs can be streamed from our website.[5] These programs provide an opportunity for teachers to introduce students to the concept of a *primary resource* and then to actually use the primary resource in the classroom. Keeping Yehuda Bauer's words in mind, however, we encourage teachers to use these testimonies within a unit dealing with the Holocaust. History must be taught so students have a context and can then make connections. Map work provides another crucial context.

Programs are either single-witness accounts or thematic compilations. There are eight single-witness accounts, seven of which include survivors who were age sixteen or under when the Nazi occupation began for them. Of these seven survivors, four were eight or younger. The focus on young people allows students to identify with someone who is their age or younger. The images are of nicely dressed, well-groomed people who look like the students' parents or grandparents, not like the skeletal atrocity photographs in which the subjects hardly look human at all. The "history" becomes a "story" of one person with a mother, father, sister, brother, like all of us. Teachers and students are no longer dealing with an abstraction, like the number six million.

Testimonies deal with a reality that we seldom see portrayed in other moving images dealing with the Holocaust. In the August 16, 2012, issue of *The New York Review of Books*, Christopher Browning discussed a conceptual term, "choiceless choice," developed many years ago by Holocaust scholar Lawrence Langer. A "choiceless choice," wrote Browning, succinctly "capture[s] another infernal aspect of Nazi rule, in which the absolute asymmetry of power meant that the Germans could insidiously and consciously design situations in which Jewish leaders never had the choice between good and bad or even lesser and greater evil, but only between catastrophically disastrous alternatives." I would add that it was not only Jewish leaders, but *every* Jew who on a regular basis faced myriad situations of "choiceless choice." We hear examples of "choiceless choices" in the survival strategies survivors talk about in their testimonies: "I always volunteered"; "I never volunteered"; "I stayed with my siblings"; "I separated from my siblings." Regardless of the circumstances or the so-called "choice" of action, there is a consistent "but" – "***but***, I was lucky." Marion L., who was eleven when she was liberated from Bergen-Belsen, notes, "It was so serendipitous why we survived and others did not. It was truly the luck of the draw."[6]

Fred O. was a physician in Hrubieszów, Poland. He was clandestinely treating a German official for impotence. This man did not want to be treated by a German physician for obvious reasons, thus giving Fred O. some small bargaining power. When all the Jews in his town were rounded up to be shot in nearby pits, he tried to use his connections to save himself and his family:

> **Fred O.:** At that time they already had kept out of that group, I think ten people, so they could bury those that they were going to shoot. So he says, "*Ach, schon, gut.*" That means, "I am accepted to be spared from the rest." […] Then I had the courage to say, "*Sturmbannführer*, I have here my parents" – no, my brothers, first I said my brothers. So he must have promised Wagner to make an exception. So Felix came out, "Good." Accepted. Then Sam came out. Sam looked like hell. He was thin. He was gray. He was unshaved. He looked forty years older than his age. He says, "He's *schwach*. He's weak; he won't be able to work." I said, "*Sturmbannführer*, leave it to me. In three days, with good food he will look as good as I do." "Agreed." Then I had the guts to say, "*Und meine Eltern.*" That means, "My parents."

Interviewer: And Henry?

Fred O.: Oh, Henry, too, of course. Henry was accepted. He heard the word "*Eltern.*" He says, "*Was?* What? Old Jews?" To him, *meine Eltern* had to be old Jews. I said, "They are not old." And all of a sudden, I could see a fury in his eyes and he says, "*Nichts mehr, zurück zum Haufen.*" In other words, "The whole deal is off, back to the group." We should go back to the whole thing and be treated like the rest. And that's it. We stand there. And while he was selecting the five, the five of my family, he also selected three or four, I don't even know […] young people from the group to join us. But he got mad when I asked about my parents; he says, "*Zurück zum Haufen,* back to the bunch. No more." The deal is off, kind of. So we stand there, waiting what to do. Then the chief of Gestapo, a little man who was the chief, the nominal chief, but Ebner was the executioner. He came down and he wanted, because they were making the last preparations, to take all the people out into the trucks and take them away to be shot. And he saw this group, our group still standing separate, the way Ebner selected us. "*Was machen diese hier?* What are, what are these doing here?" So a Polish policeman, who couldn't understand a word of German, he says, "Ebner." That means, "Ebner selected us." And the little guy probably was scared from him as we all were because he was, he was a pathological killer. "*Ach Ebner, schön, oh, ja gut.* Up." We should go up the stairs to the building because he was going to take care of the rest. I try not to be emotional. Then my mother, she turned to me and she says, "*Rette die Kinder.* Save the children." And I saw my father helping her by the elbow to go out through the gate to be put into the truck. They were killed that night.[7]

This episode illustrates that it was not Fred O.'s connections, cleverness, medical skills, or ability to speak both German and Polish that saved him, his siblings, and a few others and that led the Nazi officer to order his group to rejoin all the others. It was not Fred O.'s actions, skills, or privilege, but simply dumb luck that the Polish policeman did not speak German that led to their survival that time. Fred O.'s luck did not continue indefinitely: his sister and one brother were killed, but through a series of "lucky" circumstances, he and two of his brothers did survive.

In another example that I think illustrates Langer's concept of "choiceless choice," Abe P. tells about his arrival at Auschwitz/Birkenau:

And I told my little brother, I said to him, "*Solly, geh tsu tate un mame.* Go with my [mother and father]." And like a little kid he followed. He did!

Little did I know that, that I sent him to the crematorium. I am, I feel like I killed him. My brother, who lives now in New York, he used to live in South America, every time we see each other he talks about that. He says, "No, I am responsible, because I said the same thing to you." And it had been bothering me, too. I've been thinking whether he has reached my mother and father. And when he did reach my mother and father, he probably told them, "*Avramham hot gezogt ish zol geyn mit aykh* [Abraham said I should go with you]." I wonder what my mother and father were thinking, especially when they were all, they all went into the crematorium. I can't get it out of my head. It hurts me, it bothers me, and I don't know what to do.[8]

Abe P.'s "choice" upon arrival at Auschwitz/Birkenau to send his younger brother with his parents, thinking they could care for him better than Abe P. himself could, not knowing what a selection was, resulted in both his brother's murder in the gas chamber and in Abe's life-long feeling of guilt that he "killed" his brother. It is the ultimate cruelty that not only did the Nazis kill Abe P.'s brother and parents, but that this good, kind man now lives with such guilt.

Survivor Testimonies about Starvation

We and our students also must begin to understand the impact of starvation suffered by survivors month after month, year after year. One Holocaust survivor, Martin S., described what it was like:

I remember the hunger, that wrenching, twisting pain that lived with you on a daily basis. All you could ever think of is to get something to eat. You could never fill your belly. It used to be uppermost in your mind. You used to dream of a feast. Just one day you kept hoping you could go through the day without this twisting pain that you constantly felt. That is an indescribable feeling.[9]

Survivor Testimonies about Corpses

Other survivors described what it was like to live with corpses all around them:

Steven H., a survivor of Bergen-Belsen at age nine: I remember always walking and learning how to count on bodies, but it was perfectly unremarkable. The bodies, in the morning, people were dead, either the person you slept with or someone else. They just collapsed. This was a constant kind of thing. People were literally dropping like flies, and it was totally unremarkable because it was part of the existence there.[10]

Hanna F., a survivor of Birkenau: I was very sick. I got diarrhea. I was already recuperating a little bit from the malaria. And I walked out with two pails of human waste, and I was going towards the dump. I walked out, and between the barracks was a mountain of people as high as myself. Of course I was in those, you know, those wooden shoes, the Hollander shoes. And whatever, the people that died at night were just taken and on the dump, a big pile of people. And I said to myself, "Oh, God. Must I walk by?" But meanwhile I couldn't hold back, and I just put down the two pails and sat down because I had a sick stomach. [long pause] And the rats were standing and eating the people's faces, eating, you know. […] Anyway, I had to do my job. I was just looking, what's happening to a human being. That could have been my mother. That could have been my father. That could have been my sister or my brother.[11]

Hanna F.'s testimony goes on to belie the pervasive myth of liberation as a joyous or celebratory event. Asked what she felt at liberation, she said,

What I felt when the liberation came? That I am alone in the whole world. I escaped from the transports. I run away two weeks before, two and half weeks before the liberation, I run away in Czechoslovakia. I had no desire to live. I had no place to go. I had nobody to talk to. I was just simply lost, without words.[12]

In other testimonies, former GIs with no previous knowledge or preparation for what they would encounter relate stumbling upon concentration camps or prisoners on death marches. These combat-hardened veterans found themselves shocked beyond anything they had previously experienced, often unable to communicate with these prisoners, wanting to assist them and not knowing how. Thousands of concentration camp prisoners survived to encounter these allied soldiers, only to die when these well-intentioned soldiers shared their rations, which the malnourished prisoners could not digest, with them.

After Liberation

What was next for the survivors after liberation from the camps? Where could they go? For most survivors of the ghettos and camps, there was no home to which they could return. Some who returned to Poland were murdered. Jan Gross's book, *Fear: Antisemitism in Poland after Auschwitz: An Essay in Historical Interpretation*, documents the 1946 Kielce pogrom on an almost minute-by-minute basis and relies upon survivor testimonies as an important source. When that murder of over forty Jews by a Polish mob became known, most survivors traveled to Ally-occupied territory to be safe, but then survivors found themselves once more in camps, this time Displaced Person camps. Although they were not concentration camps, the survivors were once again behind barbed wire with no place to go due to immigration quotas and political circumstances.

Most survivors, their educations ended or interrupted, eventually did emigrate to new countries, but in their new countries, they had to learn new languages, acquire vocational and professional skills, and support themselves and their new families. Life went on, but their memories and losses never left them.

In an October 9, 2012, obituary in *The New York Times* for Shlomo Venezia, an Italian Jew who arrived in Auschwitz-Birkenau at age twenty on April 11, 1944 – he was immediately selected for the *sonnderkommando* – it was noted that for fifty years he remained silent about his experiences, "Not because I didn't want to talk, but because people didn't want to listen, didn't want to believe it." His book, *Sonderkommando Auschwitz*, published in 2007 as an oral history, "offers page after page of harrowing detail […] The last question that Mr. Venezia answered in his book was: 'What was destroyed in you by that extreme experience?' His response: 'Life. Since then, I've never had a normal life. Everything takes me back to the camp. Whatever I do, whatever I see, my mind keeps harking back to the same place. It's as if the 'work' I was forced to do there had never really left my head. Nobody ever really gets out of the crematorium."

Another survivor of the Holocaust, Jacob K., in his video testimony illustrates the same point:

> The scars, the German behavior toward us, the tortuous days and nights, it is something what we have. It is in our minds. You can't forget about that. Six million people is just women and children? I can't tell you everything in an interview. I couldn't even tell you, describe one day in the ghetto. I don't want to live with that pain, but it's there. It's there. It forms its own entity and it surfaces whenever it wants to. I go on a train, and I will cry. I will read something, and I'll be right back there where I came from. And I can't erase it. I'm not asking for it. It comes by itself. It has formulated something in me. I'm a scarred human being among human beings.[13]

Educational Resource

The edited programs from Yale University's Fortunoff Video Archive for Holocaust Testimonies provide a valuable educational resource. Students immediately recognize the contrast with fictional film accounts and also with many documentaries. These testimonies are of real people conveying their real-life stories, not actors and actresses on an artificial set. The authenticity of these programs is reinforced by the absence of a soundtrack. After many years of showing these programs to students, I have found it does not take them long to realize the often manipulative function of a soundtrack. They quickly notice that there is no narrator, that the only faces they see are those of witnesses to the Holocaust.

Students and other viewers note the importance of body language, facial expression, tone of voice, and silence often more eloquent than words. These added dimensions should be carefully parsed. A skilled teacher using these programs can help students learn visual literacy skills that apply to watching these programs, but also to other programs.

By now, there is general agreement in the scholarly community concerning the value of eyewitness accounts. The possibilities are almost limitless for using these testimonies for research purposes. Books, articles, conference papers, musical compositions, works of art, documentaries, museum exhibits, poems, plays, and dissertations (not to mention countless student papers) have been based on materials in the Fortunoff collection,.

Although it is more than sixty-five years since the end of World War II, there is still much that is yet unexamined or missing, and much that still needs to be scrutinized. With the opening of the archives in the former Soviet Union, scholars have available a new source of information. Timothy Snyder's 2010 book, *Bloodlands: Europe between Hitler and Stalin*, makes extensive use of previously unavailable archival materials and provides a vital new perspective on Holocaust historiography. There are still myriad documents, diaries, letters, photographs, and other records that are coming to light all over the world, and some that will never surface.

At the Yale Fortunoff Library and Archive, we are trying to put together a jigsaw puzzle without an image of the finished picture on the outside of the box. Furthermore, we know in advance that many pieces are missing and may never be found. While it is a daunting challenge, we would be remiss if we did not try to solve the puzzle, knowing full well there is not one definitive solution and that we may find many partial solutions, or not find solutions in our lifetimes, aware that future generations of puzzle-solvers will continue our work and reveal more and more of the finished picture. Finally, they will have enough so that the missing pieces can be roughly sketched, with many variants but all based on informed, intelligent analysis. We have many pieces of this complex puzzle, and it would behoove us not to ignore any of them.

Yehuda Bauer in his book, *Rethinking the Holocaust* states, "Above all, we need the witness. There is no Holocaust history without witnesses. Direct testimony of the survivors and the authentic surviving descriptions (diaries, letters) by Jews who did not survive themselves"[14] add to our understanding. All evidence must be the subject of critical analysis, regardless of its form. Bauer cautions that some of the contemporary Jewish documents are suspect since it was feared at the time that they might be read by Germans, just as we know many German documents were written with the intent to communicate, but at the same time, obfuscate the information contained therein.

Christopher Browning notes that "it is no act of disrespect to subject survivor testimony to the same critical analysis that we would the conflicting and fallible testimony of other historical witnesses, even as we recognize that the survivors have lived through events that we cannot even remotely imagine on the basis of our own personal experiences." He found in his research that "[s]urvivor memories proved to be more stable and less malleable than I have anticipated."[15]

Challenges

I have heard Yehuda Bauer say that the Holocaust can be a precedent or a lesson, and an examination of the events that have occurred since the end of World War II supports the argument that it has been a precedent. Knowing about the Holocaust has not prevented other genocides. The Holocaust occurred, and other genocides occur, based on power and the abuse of power. Hitler lost World War II, but he won the war against the Jews. European Jewish culture and one-third of the world's Jewish population at that time were destroyed. If in your teaching you are looking for positive lessons, happy endings, or redemptive messages, do not teach about the Holocaust. We can teach about rescue and resistance, but with the understanding that these are the exceptions, or "footnotes," as Bauer calls them. All Jews were intended to be murdered, and those that survived did so because the war was lost, not because they were rescued. Browning notes:

> [I]t is not a particularly edifying story. One of the saddest "lessons" of the Holocaust is confirmation that terrible persecution does not enable victims. A few magnificent exceptions notwithstanding, persecution, enslavement, starvation, and mass murder do not make ordinary people into saints and heroic martyrs. The suffering of the victims, both those who survived and those who did not, is the overwhelming reality. We must be grateful for the testimonies of those who survived and are willing to speak. But we have no right to expect from them tales of edification and redemption.[16]

David Boder's book title, *I Did Not Interview the Dead*, is a profound recognition of a major limitation of witness testimony. Primo Levi reminds us, "All of us survivors are, by definition, exceptions because in the *Lager* you were destined to die. If you did not die it was through some miraculous stroke of luck. You were an exception, a singularity, not generic, totally specific."[17] The Holocaust is about being killed, not about surviving. Levi also observed that "the story has been almost exclusively written by those who have not fathomed the depths of human degradation. Those who did have not come back to tell the tale."[18] It is incumbent upon us to try to reconstruct those stories, using all the resources we have to do so.

Lawrence Langer reminds us of the importance of the survivor perspective in conjunction with other documents.

> Historians have granted a kind of immortality to certain key documents: the minutes of the Wannsee conference; the Jaeger report (enumerating executions by Einsatzkommando 3 after invasion of the Soviet Union); the Korherr report (a survey of victim deaths by Himmler's statistician); the Broad report (written by former SS guard Perry Broad in British captivity after the war about gassings in Auschwitz); even the self-serving autobiography of former Auschwitz commandant Rudolf Hoess, written in prison before his execution. All have been authored by men who enjoyed power under the Nazi regime. Used judiciously, they enhance our understanding of the German program of mass murder. But exactly the same can be said about the testimonies of those who were lucky enough to have escaped that doom. Granting their voices an equivalent immortality should not be seen as a sentimental homage to a kind of mystical suffering, but as a necessary gesture to history. Their spoken record, [also] used judiciously, extends and sometimes qualifies the written one, in ways that no other sources can supply.[19]

We must acknowledge that not everything will ever be told. Some incidents will never be told because the survivors refuse to tell them, in spite of remembering them very well. Some will not be told because survivors think no one could possibly believe them.[20] In Fred O.'s words:

> No matter what I said here, these episodes and things like that, these are only words that try to describe emotions, feelings, situations, and whatnot. But these are only words that are too-feeble expressions of what really they should mean. You can't, you can't, you can't exteriorate from your deep well, deep hidden emotions. You can't exteriorate them and show them in words. It's impossible. There are things that will never be told because they cannot be told.[21]

The testimonies provide a few pieces of the puzzle we are trying to construct. Our challenge in teaching this history is to try to make it meaningful to our students through the use of many genres and primary documents, including survivor testimonies; to develop the skills to use this genre for research; and to honor the memory of the murdered, Jews and non-Jews alike.

The jigsaw puzzle will continue to intrigue us, our children, and our children's children, and we will all keep working on it. Testimonies, as Yehuda Bauer writes in *Rethinking the Holocaust*, are one of the most important sources of our knowledge of the Holocaust. Survivors are "documents' walking among us on two legs."[22] Our continuing challenge is to record Holocaust survivors' testimonies with care and integrity, preserving them for future generations, carefully cataloging them so as to facilitate their use, then using them wisely and well.

Questions

1. *What is the difference between a memoir, an autobiography, a biography, a videotaped testimony, an interview, a documentary, a fiction film, a novel, and a speech related to Holocaust survivors and witnesses? How are they read and interpreted differently?*

2. *What is a primary source "document?" How do primary source documents differ from secondary sources?*

3. *What skills and tools are needed to understand and analyze primary source documents related to the Holocaust?*

4. *What are some of the issues one must be aware of when a primary source is translated from one language to another? Does translation make any difference?*

Bibliography

Bauer, Yehuda. *Rethinking the Holocaust*. New Haven, CT: Yale University Press, 2001.

Browning, Christopher R. *Nazi Policy, Jewish Workers, German Killers*. Cambridge, MA: Cambridge University Press, 2000.

Browning, Christopher R. *Collected Memories: Holocaust History and Postwar Testimony*. Madison, WI: University of Wisconsin Press, 2003.

Fred O. Holocaust Testimony (HVT-8075). New Haven, CT: Fortunoff Video Archive for Holocaust Testimonies, Yale University Library, 1998.

Langer, Lawrence L. *Holocaust Testimonies: The Ruins of Memory*. New Haven, CT: Yale University Press, 1991.

Parallel Paths (HVT-8064). New Haven, CT: Fortunoff Video Archive for Holocaust
   Testimonies, Yale University Library, 1989.

Witness: Voices from the Holocaust (HVT-8076). Old Westbury, NY: Stories to
   Remember, 1999. Archived at Fortunoff Video Archive for Holocaust
   Testimonies, Yale University Library. (A Teacher's Guide is available at
   http://www.library.yale.edu/testimonies/education/index.html.)

Notes

1. Omer Bartov, *Murder in our Midst: the Holocaust, Industrial Killing, and Representation* (New York: Oxford University Press, 1996), p. 8.
2. Ibid, p. 168.
3. Ibid, p. 170.
4. See further, http://legacy.www.nypl.org/research/chss/jws/ yizkorbooks_intro.cfm.
5. See further, http://www.library.yale.edu/ testimonies/education/ index.html.
6. Joanne Weiner Rudof, ed., *Parallel Paths* [HVT-8064] (New Haven, CT: Fortunoff Video Archive for Holocaust Testimonies, Yale University, 1990).
7. Rudof, ed., *Fred O. Holocaust Testimony* [HVT-8075], 1998.
8. Joshua Green, Shiva Kumar, and Joanne Weiner Rudof, *Witness: Voices from the Holocaust* [HVT-8076], Old Westbury, NY: Stories to Remember, 1999. Archived at Fortunoff Video Archive for Holocaust Testimonies, Yale University Library.
9. Ibid.
10. Rudof, *Parallel Paths*.
11. Green, Kumar, and Rudof.
12. Ibid.
13. Ibid.
14. Yehuda Bauer, *Rethinking the Holocaust* (New Haven, CT: Yale University Press, 2001), p. 23.
15. Christopher R. Browning, *Nazi Policy, Jewish Workers, German Killers* (New York: Cambridge University Press, 2000), p. 92.
16. Christopher R. Browning, *Collected Memories: Holocaust History and Postwar Testimony* (Madison, WI: University of Wisconsin Press, 2003), p. 86.
17. Primo Levi, *The Drowned and the Saved* (New York: Vintage International, 1989), p. 122.
18. Ibid., p. 30.
19. Lawrence L. Langer, "Reflections," *Fortunoff Video Archive for Holocaust Testimonies Newsletter* (Spring 2000): 5.
20. Lawrence Langer and Dana Kline, interviewers, *Leo G. Holocaust Testimony* [HVT-977] (New Haven, CT: Fortunoff Video Archive for Holocaust Testimonies, Yale University, 1988).
21. Rudof, ed., *Fred O. Holocaust Testimony* (HVT 8075).
22. Bauer, p. 24.

Rescuers of Jews during the Holocaust: Implications for Today

Eva Fogelman

Psychotherapist, Independent Scholar, and Filmmaker, New York, NY

The notion of rescue is well-established in the realm of Jewish law. But when Jews think of "rescue," it generally refers to the redeeming of captives and hostages, a trope that has played out numerous times in the course of Jewish history. However, Jews have another construct of "rescue," that of *Hasidei Umot Ha-Olam* (literally, "the righteous ones of the nations of the world"). "The righteous among the nations of the world shall have a share in the world to come" became an accepted doctrine in traditional Judaism. Non-Jews who rescued Jews during the Second World War are modern exemplars of the *Hasidei Umot Ha-Olam*.

In 1953, the courageous acts of these non-Jews played prominently in the creation of Yad Vashem in Israel, the National Museum and Archive that Prime Minister Ben-Gurion established not only to remember the victims of the Holocaust, but also to honor those non-Jews who risked their lives to save Jews. The museum established criteria that the rescuers needed to meet in order to qualify as belonging to the "righteous among the nations." Primarily, they could not have acted because of financial gain or other rewards, and they had to have risked their lives to help Jews during World War II and the Holocaust.

What Motivated the Righteous?

Motivations are a tricky subject, especially when decided by committee. For example, what if a non-Jew hid a Jewish family in his attic for money, but when the money ran out he kept them hidden for another few years? Or, conversely, what if a Christian saved a Jewish child, but when the parents came back, she did not want to give the child back without being forced by the courts? Did he or she still qualify as righteous?

As of 2012, the State of Israel has honored 24,000 rescuers. Surely there were more. One-hundred thousand? Two-hundred thousand? When you think of the fact that 700 million people lived under German occupation, we are talking about a very small percentage of the population. The rescuers did not change the course of history, but their behavior shows us that even under the worst conditions of terror, there are people who disobey malevolent authority and risk their own lives and the lives of their family members to save a human being.

In 1981, while I was a graduate student in social and personality psychology, I embarked on a journey that took me to Yad Vashem and around the world to find out who these *Hasidei Umot Ha-Olam*, these righteous among the world, were. I interviewed more than 300 rescuers from Poland, Holland, Italy, France, Belgium, Denmark, and the countries of the former Soviet Union. I found them in Europe, Israel, the US, and Canada. What motivated these rare individuals to act differently from the majority of those who were passive bystanders, and indeed, from those who became the killers?

During my years of research, I met Anne Frank's rescuer, Miep Geis; Oskar Schindler's wife, Emily; children and relatives of diplomats including Sempo Sugihara, who rescued Jews in Lithuania by giving them passports to go to Curacao. I met the children of Aristedes DeSouses Mendes, a Portugese Ambassador in Bordeaux who gave visas to about 30,000 Jews to escape to Portugal, and I met the daughter of Feng Shun Ho, who was the Chinese Ambassador to Austria who provided thousands of Jews with visas to go to Shanghai. I also met some very ordinary people: seamstresses, farmers, teachers, social workers, nannies. The kind of people you could see on the street and never imagine they could be capable of taking action that put at risk themselves, their families, and, in the case of rescuers who worked through rescue networks, their comrades. I tried to learn answers to my questions, and my book, *Conscience and Courage: Rescuers of Jews during the Holocaust*, is the result of this quest.

My interest in the motivation of rescuers was sparked because I grew up knowing that my father was rescued when a Russian baker protected him, while the rest of Illya's Jews, 1,000 men, women, and children, were intercepted on their way to work on Purim morning in 1942, stripped of their clothes, and shot in the town square. The whole exercise took less than half a day.

Each rescue story is unique, but I found commonalities among the rescuers that transcend their social class, education, religion, politics, and gender. The internal struggle to "do the right thing" transcended all the external hardships faced in rescuing relationships.

The Story of Jean Kowalyk
One of my interviewees was Jean Kowalyk, a Polish rescuer. When the Russians took

over the eastern part of Poland, Jean was a single Ukrainian Catholic in her early twenties, living with her recently widowed mother in a tiny two-room house with an attic and a backyard in a small village. Several other siblings lived nearby. One of her brothers was snatched into the Russian army, never to be seen again. Jean gave private sewing classes and helped with farming their small patch of land.

As it happens, Jean was friendly with one of the only Jewish girls in her village. In 1941, after the Germans invaded her part of Poland, they built a labor camp next door to Jean's house. Jean started to bring food to her friend and other inmates. She was caught by the Germans and shot in the leg; luckily, the bullet exited her leg. Conditions for the local inhabitants began restricting their lives. Local farmers had to give all their cattle to the occupiers. Jean's aunt was incarcerated for disobeying the Germans; she left nine children behind.

When Jean's mother took ill, her brother asked the German guard if one of the Jewish inmates could examine her. The Jewish doctor came daily to check on her. In the meantime, he asked if he could be hidden if the labor camp was ever liquidated. Jean's brother had four small children and could not risk their lives, so it was up to Jean and her mother, who agreed to help. One night, a knock on the window was followed by 14 Jews showing up outside their house. Jean and her mother took five Jews and other relatives took the rest.

For the next two years, they lived in constant danger. Neighbors were suspicious of the unceasing smoke from the chimney. Clothes had to be washed and dried inside, lest the neighbors suspect that men were living there. When the doctor had diarrhea, Jean's mother told her sewing student that the cats in the attic made love all year long. One day, a suspicious neighbor came to check up on the house while Jean was shopping for food. The neighbor discovered cigarette ashes and cards in the attic. Jean's 9-year-old nephew told the neighbor, "Shhh, please don't tell my aunt, but my friend who just left and I were smoking and playing cards." But the diarrhea and the cigarettes were nothing compared to trying to keep five people under control when a love triangle broke out.

A few days after liberation, Jean got an anonymous letter that said, "Because you saved Jews, if you do not leave the country, you could expect the same thing to happen to you." She fled the village and came to the United States. From the above story, one can begin to appreciate the conditions that made it almost impossible to save a life.

Who Might Be a Rescuer?

Who was most likely to be a rescuer? Was someone more likely to rescue if he was poor or she was rich? Might we expect religious people to be at the forefront of rescue efforts? Would left-wingers be more inclined to help than nationalists or apolitical people? And what about someone's education level? So many of the perpetrators were highly educated, which makes one wonder what happened to the notion that people with higher education would be too sophisticated to accept Nazi propaganda. Were the rescuers also among the educated elites in their society? How did their education differ from the education of the perpetrators? Does our stereotype that women tend to be more nurturing than men hold up in a situation of extreme terror?

The rescuers were not a monolithic group of people. They were very different from one another and came from all strata of society. The classic socio-economic variables of political affiliation, social class, gender, education, and religion were not reliable indicators whether a bystander would be moved to rescue. Rescuers came from all socio-economic classes, from peasants to aristocrats. They were apolitical, as well as very active in various political parties. They included both very religious people and the anti-religious Communists. Some, of course, were the kind of people whose philosophy and training were to help people – doctors, social workers, nurses, nuns. On the whole, however, age, gender, politics, religion, and class did not determine who became a rescuer.

I had to look more deeply into the rescuers' character and personality. Were they alienated types who were used to being ostracized? Were they oddballs, loners, or mavericks? Oskar Schindler was a member of the Nazi Party, a cynical entrepreneur whose original motive was to profit from the war. He maneuvered to acquire an enamel factory where Jewish slave laborers made pots and pans for the German Army. Schindler was a war profiteer, bon vivant, and womanizer who also was a Good Samaritan that saved more than 1,000 Jews. Obviously, all that cynicism did not reflect his real character. When he faced the challenge, his true values rose to the occasion.

Digging Deeper

Being a psychotherapist in addition to a social psychologist, I also asked rescuers about their childhood: What kind of upbringing did they have that made them take responsibility for saving another person's life, even if it meant putting themselves and often their family members at risk? Were the values that they learned as children any different from those of others around them? What values were more important than their education, religious commitment, and social class? Four values stand out: respect for other people's differences, altruism, competence, and independence of mind.

In talking with rescuers from all kinds of homes, I found that one quality above all others was emphasized time and again: familial acceptance of people who were different. This value had been the centerpiece of many of the rescuers' childhoods. From their infancy, rescuers were taught that people are inextricably linked to one another by a common bond of humanity; no one person or group was better than any other. They held the conviction that all people, no matter how downtrodden, were of equal value. People are people, whatever their religion, national origin, or ethnic group. This value was conveyed to children in both religious and non-religious households. If a child came home and said something negative about an individual who was different, the parent explained that that individual was a human being like him or her.

The second value, parental altruistic behavior in daily life, became a model for shaping rescuers. Furthermore, involving the children in helping others in their family or community enhanced "virtue as a habit."

The third value, parents teaching children to be independent, and the fourth value, parents instilling competence in their children, ultimately provided rescuers with ego strength to stand up for their beliefs and withstand pressure from critics.

As for personality characteristics, the unusual empathy exemplified by the rescuers toward the victims of Nazi persecution came from several sources: loving, warm, nurturing, and cohesive family environments; discipline by inductive reasoning rather than corporal punishment for misbehavior; a personal separation, loss, or illness experienced in childhood, together with the response from others that facilitated coping with the emotional and physical pain; and personal experiences with Nazi mistreatment. Other factors such as being resourceful, having a strong equilibrium, role-playing, and being able to withstand extreme anxiety and terror made it possible to continue to engage in rescuing relationships that extended into months and years.

From Bystander to Rescuer

The transformation from bystander to rescuer was at times planned and other times decided in the moment. But in both cases, there were three stages in the process of becoming a rescuer: first, awareness; then, interpreting the situation as one in which help was needed; and, finally, assuming the responsibility for another person.

Awareness: Becoming a rescuer meant becoming conscious of the imminent danger and probable death of Jews. It took a determined effort to attain such consciousness and discover the truth. Those who became rescuers made that effort. Their heightened sense of empathy overrode both Nazi propaganda and their own instincts for self-preservation. They saw the victims of Nazi persecution as individuals who were perhaps different, but still part of the same human community as they were. The Jewish plight touched a deeply personal chord. They felt empathy for the Jews.

The ability to see clearly beyond Nazi propaganda, strip away the gauze of Nazi euphemisms, and recognize that innocent people were being murdered was at the heart of what distinguished rescuers from bystanders. It was the necessary first step that made the subsequent rescue activity possible and, in some cases, inevitable. Where possible, the Germans camouflaged their persecution by deporting Jews before dawn. Jews were told they were being relocated for work purposes. Some packed their finest clothes and silverware. At times, non-Jews had to convince Jews that unless they hid, they were going to their deaths.

Interpreting a situation as one in which help was needed: While many local non-Jews were aware that Jews were losing their civil liberties, most interpreted this change as temporary, not fatal, and not necessarily warranting intervention. Oskar Schindler moved from awareness to interpreting the situation as one requiring his help during the liquidation of the Cracow Ghetto. It was after that murderous scene that he developed the scheme to establish a phony munitions factory to save his Jewish workers.

Assuming responsibility: Assuming responsibility was the third most crucial state in becoming a rescuer. It was because potential rescuers had reached this stage that they were able to make spontaneous responses to immediate life-and-death situations.

Moral Dilemmas

Rescuers framed their moral dilemma this way: "Can I live with myself if I say no?" Aware that turning down a request for help meant that Jews would die, rescuers weighed the consequences of saying no against their own safety: "What if I decide to give a Jew refuge and he or she jeopardizes the well-being of my family?" This was a real moral dilemma. Why?

Let's say a jeopardized Jewish person has an infectious disease and everyone could catch it. What do you do? Since a Jew cannot be taken to a quarantine room in a hospital, his or her presence could jeopardize everyone else's health. What if a person you are trying to help becomes mentally disturbed and disrupts the lives of the other Jews and your own family, but if you send this person out to survive on his or her own, everyone's life could be in jeopardy? To whom does one have the greater obligation?

What if your spouse objects strenuously to harboring Jews and you feel you could not live with yourself if you didn't help? What then? What if your spouse actually makes your life miserable because he has to live with your decision?

What if you have taken on the responsibility to help but feel that after a year, two years, three years, you can't take the extreme stress, but neither can you throw the rescued Jew or Jews out to be killed? What then?

What if a very Jewish-looking person is at your door and asks for a place to sleep for the night? He claims he was sent by the underground. You are already hiding several Jews and if you take this person in and he is an informer, it may jeopardize your whole operation. If you send him away and he is a legitimate Jew seeking refuge, he may be caught.

As you can tell, none of these questions have an easy answer, but all reveal actual, ongoing moral dilemmas faced by non-Jews who tried to help Jews in German-occupied Europe during World War II and the Holocaust.

Marion Pritchard

On a September day in 1942, Marion Pritchard left her apartment in Amsterdam and went across town. She picked up two Jewish youngsters from members of a rescue network of which she was a part. She took those children to her parent's summer cottage outside Amsterdam. One day Marion was preparing to take them out for a walk when there was a knock at the door. She quickly hid the children before four German Gestapo officers and a collaborationist Dutch police officer entered and demanded to know where the Jews were. Obviously, someone had tipped them off – a danger with which rescuers and their charges were constantly threatened. When the men didn't find the children, they left. But Marion and the children were not yet out of the woods. Just as they were getting ready to leave, the Dutch collaborator returned. The baby began to cry. Marion had a small revolver in her purse, and as she told me in an interview several decades later, "I had no choice except to kill him. There should have been another way, but there wasn't."

Now Marion had two problems: getting the children into hiding and getting rid of the body. What did she do? She picked up the phone and called another member of the rescue network who happened to work in a mortuary. "No problem," he told her. "I have a coffin here with a body in it; I'll just put the man in with him." So that's what he did. The family never found out that a Dutch collaborator was buried with their own loved one. Marion Pritchard was honored by Yad Vashem as a "Righteous among the Nations of the World" in March 1981.

Rescue Networks

Being one of many, belonging to a group, strengthened rescuers' resolve and gave them psychological support. With a group behind them, network rescuers felt what Freud described as the influence of a group: "An unlimited power and an insurmountable peril." Such psychological support allowed some rescuers to step outside the old parameters of their lives to lie, steal, and do whatever else had to be done to save lives. Networks also provided extra food-ration cards, money, and the necessities to buy food, information, and safe hideouts when necessary.

In Belgium, the networks to rescue children formed a sophisticated system, with Jews and non-Jews working cooperatively. Jews fetched children from their parents and non-Jews escorted the children to their hideouts without the parents' knowledge of the hiding place – in a private home, boarding school, convent, or orphanage. If one was in a rescue network, much more was at risk than the lives of one's own family members. One wrong move could jeopardize a whole group of people, as well as the entire operation. This meant an added nightmare facing a network rescuer – the fear of what one might reveal under torture in an interrogation.

Religiously motivated networks were exemplified by the Huguenots of Le Chambon Sur Lignon in France. These villagers were French Protestants with a history of persecution and of helping dissenters and refugees. Confronted with a Jewish refugee woman knocking at her door, Magda Trocme, the wife of the Protestant pastor of the village, did not think twice. She responded to the knock on the door with, "Come in! Come in!" She obviously took to heart the biblical mandate to "show kindness to the stranger, for by this some have entertained angels unawares" (Hebrews 13:2).

Rescuers' belief in their own competence and resourcefulness was crucial. They were neither foolish nor suicidal. They were not about to offer help unless they felt there was a good chance they could pull it off. They had faith in their capacity to evaluate situations and find solutions. There was seldom time for measured thought, only quick assessments. This was especially true in the case of the people in the helping professions, who were supremely confident about their ability to help. It was what they were trained to do. Whatever their particular jobs – social worker, nurse, firefighter – these rescuing professionals held to the highest ideals of their professions and applied them to the situation.

In summary, the making of a rescuer is complex, and sustaining such courageous behavior is often beyond our imagination as we think about whether we would be able to undertake such life-and-death risks for so many years. But my research shows that if we imbue our children with love; inculcate them with values that promote tolerance rather than constantly creating "us" and "them" categories; and provide them with independence, competence, and opportunities to help others, we will increase the probability of having more caring and giving citizens.

What about Today?

In every situation in which there is genocide, there will be rescuers – from Pharaoh's daughter saving Moses, to the abolitionists' efforts during the Civil War, to the Hutus' rescue of the Tutsis in Rwanda. The late Rabbi Marshall Meyer understood the power of a group to affect change. When he was a rabbi in Argentina under the brutal regime of the military juntas, he went beyond the risky work of counseling individual prisoners to actually trying to help individual prisoners. He and the late Israeli Consul Ram Nirgad organized an "underground railroad" to smuggle Jewish and non-Jewish Argentines to safety out of the country at risk of being "disappeared" – that is, murdered in secret Argentine concentration camps.

After relocating to New York City in 1985, Rabbi Meyer realized that giving a few cents or even a dollar to every homeless beggar he encountered daily on the streets of New York was not going to solve the problem of the homeless. It required a communal effort. His congregation, B'Nai Jeshurun, became the community through which Rabbi Meyer could channel the moral responsibility he and his congregants felt for those whom society had written off as pariahs. He organized a community shelter for the homeless and conducted special Passover Seders for people with AIDS.

Educators cannot ask students to contemplate how they could have stopped genocide in Rwanda in 1994 or in Sudan today. These places do not exist in the cognitive map of American youngsters. What can be discussed with students, however, is how to stop bullying of students who are different in the classroom, neighborhood, or even one's own family. Tolerance and acceptance of those who are different begins at home. Helping those in need begins at home, even in doing such a simple thing as helping a sibling with his or her homework. These everyday acts of kindness ultimately can have a ripple effect on the community, society at large, and the work world we inhabit.

The annihilation of European Jewry has no redemptive meaning. But that terrible event in history can teach us about the evil – and the good – of which human beings are capable. Whether 70 or 80 years ago, or today, in our cities and towns, schools, and work places, those who are able to transcend their narrow self-interest and see others as human beings like themselves, those who can reach beyond their own religions, ethnicities, and nationalities to embrace "others," those who can act on behalf of "others" who are at risk – they should be our models and our children's and grandchildren's models. Like the *Hasedei Umot Ha-Olam*, the "Righteous among the Nations of the World," such good people light the world for "humanity." If we want to honor them, we should follow their lead.

Questions

1. *What were some of the motivations of people who tried to help Jews during the Holocaust? How did a rescuer's education, family upbringing, and/or religious outlook influence his or her actions to help Jews during the Holocaust?*

2. *What were some of the moral dilemmas rescuers faced during the Holocaust? How do you evaluate and decide what you are going to do when faced with moral dilemmas like those faced by rescuers?*

3. *Who was Rabbi Marshall Meyer? What did he do that made Dr. Fogelman draw attention to him? Can you think of others today who are taking risks and standing with people who are marginalized because they are different? Give some examples of people, their actions on behalf of others, and the moral dilemmas they face or have faced.*

4. *Some people say that "one person can make a difference in our world." Do you or do you not believe this? Explain your answer.*

Bibliography

Fogelman, Eva. *Conscience & Courage: Rescuers of Jews during the Holocaust*. New York: Anchor Books, 1994.

Gushee, David P. *Righteous Gentiles of the Holocaust: Genocide and Moral Obligation*. 2nd ed. St. Paul, MN: Paragon Press, 2003.

Haillie, Philip. *Lest Innocent Blood Be Shed: The Story of Le Chambon and How Goodness Happened There*. New York: Harper & Row, 1979.

Isay, Jane, ed. *You Are My Witnesses: The Living Words of Rabbi Marshall T. Meyer*. New York: St. Martin's Press, 2004.

Kidder, Annemarie S., ed. *Ultimate Price: Testimonies of Christians Who Resisted the Third Reich*. Maryknoll, NY: Orbis Books, 2012.

Oliner, Samuel P. *Do Unto Others: Extraordinary Acts of Ordinary People*. Boulder, CO: Westview Press, 2003.

Rittner, Carol and Sondra Myers, eds. *The Courage to Care: Rescuers of Jews during the Holocaust*. New York: New York University Press, 1986.

Zuccotti, Susan. *Père Marie-Benoît and Jewish Rescue: How a French Priest Together with Jewish Friends Saved Thousands during the Holocaust*. Bloomington & Indianapolis, IN: Indiana University Press, 2013.

Jewish Women's Experiences and Artistic Expression of the Holocaust

. . . .

Myrna Goldenberg

Independent Scholar; Professor Emerita, Montgomery College, Rockville, MD

"We expected the worst, not the unthinkable." Charlotte Delbo

Ever since Carol Rittner and John Roth posed the question, "Where are the women?" the field of women and the Holocaust has attracted emerging and established scholars who have delved into archives and other repositories of testimony to examine women's experiences during the Third Reich.[1] A backlash[2] followed, claiming that a focus on women was a distraction that would draw attention away from antisemitism and towards gender. At the outset, it must be remembered that the Holocaust was not about gender; it was about Jews, both male and female. However, to ignore one-half of the targeted population is to know less, not more, about the Holocaust. Indeed, to ignore the issue of gender suggests that women's lives and suffering were less important than those of men.[3] The furor raised, primarily by Gabriel Schoenfeld, editor of *Commentary*,[4] was eclipsed by the wealth of research on women and the Holocaust. Our work has changed the field of Holocaust studies and, equally important, has influenced the study of genocide.[5] No longer do researchers ignore the issue of women's victimhood or agency in genocide.

Twenty-five years ago, I began a presentation on women and the Holocaust with a catalog of horrors: beatings, nakedness, starvation, humiliation, and other abuses – all of which were part of every female survivor's memoir or testimony;[6] the list did not include rape or sexual torture. Decades ago, we did not know that we

105

should ask about rape. Nor did I think about women's expressions of their Holocaust experiences through needlework and other non-traditional art forms. I have become sensitive to the missing passages and have learned to interpret them and to ask questions I had not previously known to ask. I now recognize more fully than I had before that memoirs, whether written, spoken, painted, or embroidered, are "filtered by protective memory."[7]

In the intervening years, however, I met women survivors who introduced me to two very divergent aspects of the Holocaust that neither I nor many other Holocaust scholars had previously explored or anticipated. A number of women whom I interviewed at some length reluctantly told me that they had been raped by German soldiers. They whispered this information out of earshot of their husbands and asked me not to include rape in anything I would write about them.

At the other extreme, I met Bernice Steinhardt, the daughter of a Polish survivor whose mother, Esther Nisenthal Krinitz, created thirty-six large wall-hangings to depict her experiences from the pre-Nazi occupation of her village to her emigration to America in 1949. While my further research revealed the prevalence of rape and other sexual tortures, primarily in Poland, the Baltics, Ukraine, and western portions of the former Soviet Union, I have found no other Holocaust survivor story told through needle and thread.[8] Clearly, the subjects of this chapter – sexual violence and one woman's fabric art – seem to have no common theme. In fact, their only connections are that they focus on Jewish women who had lived under Nazi control and that I learned about them in the past fifteen years or so. While I have not discovered any other common elements, both have taught me to listen and look for absences, for what is not in the text, on the tape, or on the canvas.

Post-Holocaust mass murders and genocides have shone a light on rape as a weapon of war (e.g., Bosnia-Herzegovina, Rwanda) and on women's transmission of genocidal experiences through textile art (Hmong story cloths).[9] Perhaps those events influenced Holocaust and other genocide scholars to explore these two quite disparate issues (i.e., rape and sexual abuse, as well as narratives told through story cloths). Consciously or not, after the ethnic cleansing of the former Yugoslavia became public, Holocaust scholars began to question and survivors spoke about rape more freely than they had previously. Ironically, at a genocide conference in Sarajevo in 2007, I delivered a paper on sexual violence and the Holocaust and was interrupted by a participant who, insisting that Nazi law prohibited rape, bellowed, "There was no rape because it was against the Nuremberg laws!" Notwithstanding his objections, scholars have begun to pay attention to sexual abuse of Jewish women[10] as well as to the expression of memory through art. In this chapter, I will explore these two disparate issues: women's sexual vulnerability during the Holocaust and the transmission of Holocaust experience through textile art, normally identified as women's work. Other than the fact that sexual violence and representation of memory are both subsets of the Holocaust as it was lived and remembered, these topics appear to have no connection to each other, as I stated above. Although books on rape and sexual violence have been published recently, there is much more to learn. Much less is known about fabric art as a medium of Holocaust narrative. I hope to begin to remedy that gap.

Part I: Sexual Violence during the Holocaust

Although *all* Jews were targeted for death during the Shoah, Jewish women faced what Joan Ringelheim called "double jeopardy."[11] That is, they were marked for death just as men were, but their biology also played a substantial role in the Nazi treatment of women. Women's physiology made them vulnerable to rape and other forms of sexual violence, in spite of the fact that any contact between an Aryan male and a Jewish female or between an Aryan female and a Jewish male was forbidden by the Nuremberg Law for the Protection of German Blood and Honor, which forbade race-mixing, or *Rassenschande*.[12] From 1935 and the implementation of the Nuremburg Laws to the end of the war, rape against Jewish women was not a crime in and of itself. *Rassenschande*, or race defilement, on the other hand, was a serious crime. Speculation about the motivation of rapists and sexual torturers and the sporadic effectiveness of *Rassenschande* leads us into issues of unchecked male violence,[13] which is beyond the scope of this paper.

Almost every woman survivor I have read about or spoken with has described the sexual humiliation they faced when they entered the camps: prolonged nakedness,[14] examination of their genitals, jeering by the SS men, body shaves, and rough physical treatment. One anecdote of sexualized violence represents many other similar incidents: When Judith was eight and imprisoned in a labor camp, she was bored, wandered from her post, and was noticed by a guard who questioned her. Because she had forgotten to wear her "patch" identifying her as a Jew, he swung a stick into her face, breaking her nose and knocking out some teeth. He ordered his dog to attack her: "The dog bit me and ripped my clothes off. Then the guard came over to me and burned his cigarette into my face. [...] Then he put his penis inside my mouth and peed. I started choking and vomiting. So he shot me in my leg, and left me there alone."[15] Others have testified that opened mass graves revealed that women's breasts were cut off. Olga Lengyel said that another prisoner told her when both were imprisoned in Birkenau that "she was forced to undress her daughter and to look on while the girl was violated by dogs, whom the Nazis had specially trained for this sport. That happened to other young girls."[16]

The "Black Book" about Jews in the Soviet Union describes another episode of sexualized violence. In Riga, a regiment "celebrated their successes. They herded several dozens of Jewish girls to their orgy, forced them to strip naked, dance, and sing songs. Many of these unfortunate girls were raped right there and then taken out in the yard to be shot." One of the officers replaced the seats of two chairs with tin sheets and then tied two young Riga University students to the chairs. He lit Primus stoves under the seats. He and other officers danced around the gagged girls who writhed in pain: "The room filled with the nauseating smell of burning human flesh. The German officers just laughed, merrily doing their circle dance."[17]

Seldom had survivors mentioned rape. After many hours of successive interviews, two survivors in two different interviews blurted out their experiences in a whisper. They asked me not to include the rapes in anything I would write about them. They trusted me with the information and with respecting their request to keep their secret. I have done so because they did not want their husbands, children, and grandchildren to know they had been raped. For decades, they carried what they believed to be their shame. I have not written about them because I feel just as conflicted about omitting this violation of their personhood as I do about including it.

Rape during the Holocaust is a complex issue. During that period, it was not a weapon of war as it was during the Bosnia-Herzegovina ethnic cleansing. Rape "reduces the civilian population [...], [instills] fear, submission, compliance, and flight from areas of contested territory."[18] It was not a tool to cleanse a culture, nor was it a political tactic to implement a goal of the war. It was a violent act of sexual aggression, often accompanied by torture and followed by death. Wartime rape, in contrast to genocidal rape, has been called a "ritual" of war: a physical manifestation of the domination of vulnerable victims. It was seen as a "recreational act" of a conqueror to prove that his victims, both male and female, were powerless.[19] As Susan Brownmiller stated, "Rape [...] destroys remaining illusions of power and property for the men of the defeated side. The body of a raped woman becomes a ceremonial battleground, a parade ground for the victor's trooping of the colors [...] vivid proof of the victory for one and loss and defeat for the other."[20] Just consider the rape of Nanking in 1937-38, the rape of thousands of women by the Russians in 1945, and even the wholesale rape of northern European women by the Allies after D-Day.[21]

Rape during the Holocaust had a profoundly demeaning and useless dimension. During the Holocaust, the Nazis dominated the Jews of Europe; the implementation of the Final Solution was evidence of their physical and political superiority. Though rape is sometimes explained as an assault on the community, the European Jewish community did not need any proof of their diminished status. Therefore, rape and other acts of sexual violence against Jewish women were redundant tools of terror and dominance. Jewish men had already been rendered impotent and unable to protect their families, and Jewish women in labor and concentration camps were anything but attractive. But we know that rape has little or nothing to do with sex appeal. Yet, sexual imagery coupled with sexual violence is ubiquitous in popular depictions of the Holocaust, namely, movies and works of fiction. What is it about the denigration and dehumanization of women – Jewish women in this context – that so captivated the Nazi imagination and continues to influence contemporary creative work on the Holocaust? The gratuitous episodes of nudity and intercourse in *Schindler's List* and *In Darkness*, for example, do not illuminate the mechanics or motives of the genocide against the Jews. Rather, these types of scenes make sexual victimhood a commodity, as it was in the pages of *Der Sturmer*, where "hostility to the Jews was sexualized in Nazi hate propaganda."[22]

Reticence about rape during the Holocaust is to be expected. We are talking about a different era, over half a century ago in a tradition-bound area of the globe, an era in which women who were raped were labeled "damaged goods." Whether or not most or some women internalized this label, almost all were uncomfortable talking about it. The "persistent silence" on the topic reflected not only the survivors' reluctance to talk about it, but as Joan Ringelheim has suggested, the reluctance of researchers to raise it.[23] It is reasonable to assume that headlines about rape camps in the former Yugoslavia and wide condemnation of the perpetrators coupled with sympathy for the victims loosened the lid on the topic. Unwarranted shame and reticence had obscured the depths of the Holocaust – a world devoid of morality as defined by the pre-1933 western world. It was a world characterized by anti-morality.

Diaries, such as Mary Berg's, report rapes in Warsaw right after the Germans occupied Poland.[24] Helene Sinnreich writes of multiple instances or rape in ghettos, labor camps, and concentration camps almost as a routine distraction for the invaders.[25] The irony is that while rape of Jewish women was made illegal in 1935, murdering them was not; SS and Wehrmacht soldiers raped, tortured, maimed, and often murdered their victims. No victims, no crime of *Rassenschande*.

Indeed, rape occurred in the ghettos and the camps but most conspicuously in the eastern provinces. As the four *Einsatzgruppen* squads proceeded to murder Jews in eastern Poland and the former Soviet Union, they virtually ritualized the death process of Jewish women. Jewish women were stripped publicly, often raped in the presence of their families, and murdered. The various "Black Books," which are compendia of contemporaneous eye witness reports of atrocities, describe a plethora of violent acts against women. In 1940, in Warsaw, Jewish women and young girls were snatched from the streets and raped or raped in homes and shops:

> A mass rape took place in a mirror shop: "orgies" on the part of German officers took place in the house of M. Szereszewski, a well-known Warsaw Jew in Pius Street. Another mass rape occurred during a raid in Franciszkanska Street. "40 Jewish girls were dragged into the house which was occupied by the German officers. There, after being forced to drink, the girls were ordered to undress and to dance for the amusement of their tormentors. Beaten, abused and raped, the girls were not released till 3 A.M."[26]

The Black Book: The Nazi Crime against the Jewish People explains that in the Tulchin camp, "from which no one returned alive," the commandant "asked each night for two Jewish virgins."[27] An underground newspaper in L'vov, October 1941, tells of rapes that occurred during pogroms: "Women were raped in the middle of the streets. The murderers dragged Jewish women out of their apartments and cut off their breasts […] It is estimated that the number of victims reached a few thousand."[28] The "Molotov Note," so named for V. M. Molotov, the Russian foreign minister who prepared it in January 1942, was entered into evidence at Nuremberg. It listed attacks on women in the occupied areas, including one that took place in L'vov: "Thirty-two women working in a garment factory were first violated and then murdered by German storm troopers. Drunken German soldiers dragged the girls and women into Kesciuszko Park, where they savagely raped them."[29]

Occasionally, women survivors reported witnessing sexual violence committed against someone else, not to themselves. In these memoirs and testimonies, women talk about a friend who had been raped or "used," and it is quite likely that the introduction of another woman as the victim spares them from revealing a humiliating personal experience or facing a terrible incident in their own lives. Besides, most Jewish women who were raped did not live to talk about it, and those who did live were likely to protect themselves from painful memories and suspicion of collusion. In fact, we find instances of rape in Holocaust fiction or on the movie screen much more than we do in memoirs.

Some victims of rape and torture did survive and have told about abuse by both German soldiers and Jewish foremen. Thirteen-year-old Tova, for example, was raped by the husband of the woman who hid her and by the Jewish foreman of a clothing factory who promised her "an easier job and some food." He, she said, "did the same like the Germans. I got better food from a German guy."[30] About the so-called protector, she mused, "[T]he truth is that for a bit of warmth and bread, I would have done it anyway. How should I relate to that as rape, since he actually saved me?" In despair to this day, she reflected:

> There were others who had used us for sex, including the Jewish foreman, who had not provided for us. It doesn't matter if men are Germans or Jews, all men are rapists. All of them knew that these children and young women were going to die, so when they had a chance, that's their nature . . . to take advantage.
>
> The rapes took place in the face of the loss of my family, our abiding hunger, and the wide-ranging tortures we and others endured. I was in such a shock that I didn't care much where I was, what people said to me, and whether I was raped or not. I was finished.
>
> I never spoke about being raped during the Holocaust. We inmates

spent our time thinking about food because we were starving. I think the Germans did what they did to us because when a person is hungry, you can do whatever you want with him. When you are hungry, have no bread, whether you die or are raped, it is all the same. Death is not just being shot at. Being raped is death . . . . The world is dead, I thought, and no one cares.[31]

Tova's history raises a sensitive issue – non-consensual sex or sex for survival – by fellow Jews and non-Jewish male prisoners. Many women survivors describe bartered sex, often as witnesses but occasionally as near-victims. Olga Lengyel self-righteously prides herself on refusing potatoes in payment for quick sex.[32] Women who bartered sex for survival internalized the shame others unjustly imposed on them: "What [a woman] experienced as a survival strategy during the Holocaust became a source of shame."[33] Yet, we have survivors who tell us that their parents ordered them to do anything to stay alive. Felicia Berland Hyatt did not understand her mother's order to "[D]o anything anybody asks you to do, just so you stay alive," until her mother told her explicitly, "[I]f a man wants to hide you and he asks you for anything, you just go ahead and give it to him if it means you can save yourself." Hyatt traded sex for "temporary rescue from the German authorities."[34]

Soon after Anna and her family arrived in Birkenau, her father told her that she "was no longer a child but a woman and that if anything were to help save my life I shouldn't hesitate a minute."[35] Transferred to another camp, she was "protected" by a German Jewish prisoner whose interest in her "was not fatherly. I didn't put up much of a resistance; I didn't have the strength nor even the will. It seemed to me that whoever behaved decently towards me would sooner or later want to sleep with me, that I wouldn't succeed in staving it off anyway."[36] Saving oneself by trading sexual favors for food or shoes or a sweater is not to be judged outside the context of Holocaust. While it is not the same as being raped, it is also not consensual sex. Withholding food or other sustenance in return for sex exploits the victim. The shame belongs to the perpetrator, particularly those who were Jewish and shared the same "life unworthy of living" category, not to the victim.

Primary sources of rape include episodes of torture and barely credible examples of sadism, especially to infants and children. These sources are profoundly troubling because they expose humankind at its worst; they should lead us to examine our culture, which tolerates and, in the worst cases, encourages sexual violence.

Part II: Narrative through Fabric Art
Not every woman survivor uses language to tell her story. Survivors of any genocide live with the text of their experiences imprinted on the insides of their eyelids. They close their eyes and re-live experiences of their own terror and of the terrors they

witnessed, not just once, but over and over and over again. Some survivors need a different medium to tell their story; they use art, whether literary, musical, or visual. Art about the Holocaust counteracts the anonymity of death, particularly mass murder. And viewing that art makes us secondary witnesses. In the process, we acquire two types of memories, those of the survivors and those that are our responses to the art.

To paraphrase Adam Zych, a poet and compiler of *The Auschwitz Poems*, art enabled one to survive – not in the biological sense, but in the psychological – because it helped preserve self-esteem.[37] Art of the Holocaust "ought to be treated not only as exceptional documents of the bygone years but also in the psychological dimension. […] Literature and the arts in the world of collapsing values aroused faith in [fellow humans] and in the salvation of human ideals."[38] Art was a defense mechanism both in the camps and later in the post-Holocaust world. Zych goes on to state that art enabled people to "preserve internal freedom, and it even gave an opportunity to develop one's personality and allowed self-realization."[39] Esther Nisenthal Krinitz, for one, did not create her art during the Holocaust. Her wall hangings – their clarity and detail – are remembered episodes of her life before and during the Holocaust. She relived these episodes as she felt the need to share that time with her family. Words may have failed her, but needle and thread did not.

Esther Nisenthal Krinitz was a survivor who spent the years under occupation as a Polish worker for an old farmer who needed an extra hand. However, having no means to do so, she did not produce art during this period. Born in 1927 in a tiny rural village in central Poland, Esther started learning how to sew when she was about nine. After the war, she filled notebooks in Yiddish and English with stories of her family and her experiences during the war. Her stories recorded her memories, but she felt that she lacked the verbal skills necessary to communicate what happened. She worked on reproducing her memories through story cloths throughout the 1970s and 1980s, and by the mid-1990s, she had completed thirty-six magnificent story cloths, all of which are made of fabric and yarn, embroidery and collage. She created them to tell her story to her children and grandchildren. Her daughters have used them to tell their mother's story to the world; they constitute a traveling exhibit, often as part of a program on the Holocaust or on genocide. The wall hangings are gripping scenes that engage us by their content and by their artistic merit.

Figure 1: "Cover of the Book – Jews leaving Mniszek"[40]

Esther was one of five children and lived an entirely rural existence in a house of split logs with a thatched roof and walls and floors of packed earth. Her father was a horse trader; her mother raised chickens and geese and sold eggs at the market. Her life was marked by celebrations of the Jewish holidays; services were led by her grandfather and his neighbor – the elders of the village conducted services in the largest and nicest

Figure 1

home in the village. One wall hanging depicting her childhood home is an early work that, though primitive in its perspective, is three-dimensional and extraordinarily detailed. Each embroidered flower, split log, thatch on the roofs, curtain, hasp, and latch is distinct. The flower gardens and bushes in bloom are different species. Although no more than twelve homes comprised this tiny village, each is distinct from the others.

Figure 2: "Childhood Home in the Village of Mniszek"

Several wall hangings depict children's activities before World War II: for example, swimming in one of the tributaries of the Vistula River, walking on stilts to her grandparents' house, and holiday preparations, including baking matzo.

In September 1939, when the Germans invaded Poland, the Jews of Esther's region began to fear for their lives. The Germans

Figure 2

made the village women do their laundry and cook. Because she had eggs, her mother was ordered to bake for a major. The young Jewish men were ordered to dig trenches. For her region, an area just southwest of Lublin, the first year of occupation was relatively free of the brutality that followed, but the war affected their livelihood and everyone was forced to find work. Esther and her ten-year-old sister Mania each worked for nearby farmers, for which they were given a small amount of money and some food.

In April 1941, two German soldiers walked into their house and, seeing the table set for Passover, they tore off the tablecloth, sending all the food and dishes flying. They began to tear her father's prayer shawl from him. The major's aide, quartered in a nearby house, heard the commotion and stopped the attack on Esther's father. However, the soldiers came back and found the goose under the table, now no longer hidden by the tablecloth. They grabbed the goose and killed it, thereby killing the family's source of eggs. After Esther's brother was ordered to report to the slave labor camp the Germans had established, her father took her brother and hid him in the pine forest where they had spent summers collecting pine tar, which they sold to local farmers for turpentine. In October 1942, the Germans began the Final Solution in the region, stepping up the killing process by deporting Jews to the death camps.

It is obvious that Esther's ability to show perspective began to develop around that time. In Figure 3, the flowers are either oversized or diminished, but each large plant is differentiated from the others by shading, just as each leaf on the trees is unique. The bleeding heart bush between the house and the barn stands out against the monochromes of buildings and the sky. The girls' dresses are appliqued as are her grandfather's sleeves. Notice the horses' eyes, averting from the Nazi soldier's abuse of her grandfather.

Figure 3

Figure 3: "Nazis Arrive in Mniszek" "September 1939. My friends and I run to see the first Nazis entering our village, Mniszek. They stopped in front of my grandparents' house, where one got off his horse to rough up my grandfather and cut his beard as my grandmother screamed."

Figure 4: "Dawn Raid" "September 1942. Before dawn one morning, the soldiers returned and marched the family, still in their nightclothes, across the road. They were ordered from their house twice that day. At one point, they scattered and returned home much later."

Figure 4

Figure 5

Figure 5: "Fleeing across the Fields." "September 1942. After the morning raid, the Gestapo were returning. We fled across the fields to the woods, my mother directing me to separate."

On October 15, 1942, the family was ordered to leave and join all other Jews on the road to the Krasnik railroad station. Figure 5 is busy, almost frantic with color and content. The grain is taller than the girls, covering part of the skirts. Their braids and their mother's hair and shawl fringes add another dimension to the otherwise flat canvas. The woods that border the fields are interspersed with flowering bushes, all in exquisite detail and distinctiveness. The night before the family was ordered to leave the village, Esther begged her parents to send her to a farmer where she could work. She left with her sister, Mania; they were the only members of the family to survive the Holocaust.

Figure 6

Figure 6: "Leaving for Good"

On October 15, 1942, two wagons carried the villagers to the railroad station, while Esther and Mania followed a woman to the house of her father's friend. Note that the sky is ominous, the garden is nearly bare, the birch leaves are turning yellow, but the apples are ready for harvest. The two sisters were later abandoned by the woman who was paid to take them to the home of her father's friend, where they were turned away. They went to the homes of other family friends, only to be turned away again.

Figure 7: "They are turned away from their friend's house" (October 1942)

This story cloth (Figure 7) depicts a narrative – asking for help, being turned away while friends watch, and hiding in a pile of debris for the night. Note the black clouds and generally dark "canvas."

Esther created a Catholic persona for each of them: she was Josephine or Juszia, and Mania became Maria or Marisha. She instructed Mania never to speak Yiddish again. They made their way from village to village, fleeing each time they were asked for identity papers. They ran to the woods and realized that if they were found

Figure 7

there, they would certainly be taken for Jews. So they went to a further village called Grabowka, where they got jobs as farm hands with two different farmers. They endured more close calls until July 1944, when Russian infantrymen marched into the village. Several wall hangings track Esther's episodes of near-disaster, dreams and after liberation her trip to the concentration/death camp Maidenak to look for her family. Esther labeled the shoe pile, the crematorium, and the gas chambers. She is taller here, stepping through the barbed-wire gate. The cheerful flowers outside the barbed-wire fences are grim in contrast to the huge cabbages on the mound of ashes at the rear of the camp.

Figure 8: "Maidenak" "August 1944. I went through piles of worn shoes but they all looked the same. After seeing the gas chambers, the crematorium, and the giant cabbages growing on human ashes, I joined the Polish and Russian armies stationed there."

In March 1945, the 5th Division of the Russian Army, of which she was now a part, crossed the Oder River into Germany to reach Berlin. Another wall hanging depicts the trucks driving between a row of German soldiers that had been hanged by the Russians and a field of dead Germans.

Figure 8

Figure 9:

"Victorious Polish and Russian Armies Shot or Hanged German Soldiers" (March 1945)

Once the War was over, Esther and Mania reunited and went to a Displaced Persons (DP) camp, where each married. Esther and her husband Max went to America, while Mania and her husband went to Israel. Esther told her daughter Bernice that coming to America meant that she'd never again be persecuted for being Jewish. Her wall hanging (Figure 9) depicting the Statue of Liberty as seen from the ship reflects a cloudless blue sky and welcoming birds.

Figure 9

Figure 10: "Coming to America" (June 1949)

Esther's textile pictures are as strong as was her determination to survive. They reflect a variety of simple and complicated techniques, each stitch as distinct as each episode in her life during those harrowing years. Some critics see the wall hangings as too cheerful, thereby distorting the horror of the Holocaust. Others claim that the bright colors and beautiful scenes belie the horror of the Holocaust. They fail to see the nuances of texture and composition, the details that fill a

Figure 10

canvas or leave it stark. These art works are compositions that reveal not just specific losses, but also triumphs of will and humanity. They are also evidence of her struggle to survive and of the life the Nazis had destroyed. The women who were tortured, raped, and murdered left us no evidence of their existence except mutilated bodies in mass graves.

It is clear that there are millions of stories, six million of which ended tragically and will always be missing. Indeed, in all the testimonies – written, painted, or sewn – the recurring themes are violence, absence, and loss. Esther Nisenthal Krinitz begins her textile narrative with a picture of a large family of three generations and ends with a family of three, including the infant Bernice. It is up to us as secondary witnesses to remember and honor the survivors and victims by teaching their stories and celebrating their lives. It is up to us to analyze those cultural and political values that foster sexual violence and valorize male dominance, particularly in times of war and mass murder. Finally, it is up to us to respect and treasure survivor stories though whichever media they are told.

I wish to thank Megan Lewis, reference librarian at the United States Holocaust Memorial Museum, for her prompt help in verifying sources. I also want to thank Bernice Steinhardt, president of Art & Remembrance Foundation, Washington, DC, for permission to use photographs of all the artwork in Part II of my essay.

Questions

1. *Defend the proposition that (wartime) rape is/is not the "aggressive manifestation of sexuality but rather a sexual manifestation of aggression."*

2. *What do you think are the reasons for the Nazis' preoccupation with sexuality?*

3. *In what ways can art be an expression of resistance? Of anonymity?*

Bibliography

Apenszlak, Jacob, ed. *The Black Book of Polish Jewry: An Account of the Martyrdom of Polish Jewry under the Nazi Occupation.* American Federation for Polish Jews, 1943. Westport, CT: Brohan Press, 1999.

Baer, Elizabeth R. and Myrna Goldenberg, eds. *Experience & Expression: Women, the Nazis, and the Holocaust.* Detroit, MI: Wayne State University Press, 2003.

Berg, Mary. *The Diary of Mary Berg: Growing Up in the Warsaw Ghetto, 1945* (Edited by Susan Pentlin). Oxford, UK: One World Publications, 2007.

Brownmiller, Susan. *Against Our Will: Men, Women, and Rape*. New York: Bantam, 1967.

Ehrenburg, Ilya and Vasily Grossman, eds. *The Black Book: The Ruthless Murder of Jews by German-Fascist Invaders throughout the Temporarily-Occupied Regions of the Soviet Union and in the Death Camps of Poland during the War 1941-1945*. New York: Holocaust Library, 1980.

Goldenberg, Myrna and Amy H. Shapiro, eds. *Different Horrors, Same Hell*. Seattle, WA: University of Washington Press, 2013.

Hedgepeth, Sonia and Rochelle Saidel, eds. *Sexual Violence against Jewish Women during the Holocaust*. Waltham, MA: Brandeis University Press, 2010.

Hmong Textile Art. www.//en.wikipedia.org/wiki/Hmong_textile_art.

Lev-Weisel, Rachel and Susan Weinger. *Hell within Hell: Sexually Abused Child Holocaust Survivors*. Lanham, MD: University Press of America, 2011.

MacKinnon, Catharine. *Are Women Human? and Other International Dialogues*. Cambridge, MA: The Belknap Press of Harvard University Press, 2006.

Rittner, Carol and John K. Roth, eds. *Different Voices: Women and the Holocaust*. St. Paul, MN: Paragon House, 1993.

Rittner, Carol and John K. Roth, eds. *Rape: Weapon of War and Genocide*. St. Paul, MN: Paragon House, 2012.

Stiglmayer, Alexandra, ed. *Mass Rape: The War against Women in Bosnia-Herzogovina*. Lincoln, NE: University of Nebraska Press, 1994.

Notes

1. See Carol Rittner and John K. Roth, eds., *Different Voices: Women and the Holocaust* (New York: Paragon House, 1993).
2. See Elizabeth R. Baer and Myrna Goldenberg, eds., Introduction, *Experience & Experience: Women, the Nazis, and the Holocaust* (Detroit, MI: Wayne State University Press, 2003), pp. xvii-xxviii.
3. Myrna Goldenberg, "Sex-Based Violence and the Politics and Ethics of Survival," *Different Horrors, Same Hell: Gender and the Holocaust*, eds. Myrna Goldenberg and Amy H. Shapiro (Seattle, WA: University of Washington Press, 2013), p. 100.
4. Gabriel Schoenfeld, "Auschwitz and the Professors," *Commentary*, June 1998: 42-46.
5. See, for example, Cynthia Enloe, "Have the Bosnian Rapes Opened a New Era of Feminist Consciousness?," *Mass Rape: The War Against Women in Bosnia-Herzegovina*, ed. Alexandra Stiglmayer (Lincoln, NE: University of Nebraska Press, 1994), pp. 219-230; Choman Hardi, *Gendered Experiences of Genocide: Anfal Survivors in Kurdistan-Iraq* (Burlington, VT: Ashgate Publishing Company, 2011); Carol Rittner and John K. Roth, eds., *Rape: Weapon of War and Genocide* (St. Paul, MN: Paragon House, 2012); Samuel Totten, ed., *Plight and Fate of Women During and Following Genocide*, Genocide: A Critical Bibliographic Review, Vol. 7 (New Brunswick, NJ: Transaction Publishers, 2012).
6. Myrna Goldenberg, "Different Horrors, Same Hell: Women Remembering the Holocaust," *Thinking the Unthinkable: Meanings of the Holocaust*, ed. Roger S. Gottlieb (New York: Paulist Press, 1990), pp.150-166.
7. Ibid, p. 151.

8. Esther Nisenthal Krinitz and Bernice Steinhardt, *Memories of Survival* (Washington, DC: Art and Remembrance, 2005). All details of Krinitz's life and work come from this book and Bernice's explanations.

9. See Hmong Textile Art at http://en.Wikipedia.org/wiki/Hmong_textile_art. See also Judy Chicago, *Holocaust Project: From Darkness into Light* (New York: Penguin Books, 1993).

10. Goldenberg, "Sex-Based Violence."

11. Joan Ringelheim, "Women and the Holocaust: A Reconsideration of Research," *Different Voices: Women and the Holocaust* (New York: Paragon House, 1993), pp. 373-405.

12. This law preserved racial purity (i.e., contamination of Aryan blood could pollute the Aryan race for generations, and Jews were the chief pollutants according to Nazi ideology). The law was stern and often led to the death of the perpetrator; by 1945, it was one of forty-three crimes that called for the death penalty. Certainly in the case of contact between an Aryan woman and Jewish man, the man was tried and almost always found guilty and executed. See one famous case, portrayed in the 1961 film *Judgment at Nuremberg* and examined in Christine Kohl, *The Maiden and the Jew: The Story of a Fatal Friendship in Nazi Germany* (Hanover, NH: Steerforth Press, 1997).

13. Jonathan Gottschall, "Explaining Wartime Rape," *Journal of Sex Research*, May 2004, 41 (2): 129-136.

14. Anna Hyndrakova-Konanica, "Letter to my Children," *The World without Human Dimensions: Four Women's Memories*, trans. Olga Kuthanova, The Menorah Series. (Prague, Poland: State Jewish Museum, in cooperation with the Federation of Jewish Communities, 1991), p. 163.

15. Rachel Lev-Weisel and Susan Weinger, *Hell within Hell: Sexually Abused Child Holocaust Survivors* (Lanham, MD: University Press of America, 2011), p. 50.

16. Olga Lengyel, *Five Chimneys: A Woman Survivor's True Story of Auschwitz, 1947* (Chicago: Academy Chicago Publishers, 1995), p. 199.

17. Ilya Ehrenburg and Vasily Grossman, eds., *The Black Book: The Ruthless Murder by German-Fascist Invaders throughout the Temporarily-Occupied Regions of the Soviet Union and in the Death Camps of Poland during the War 1941-1945* (New York: Holocaust Library, 1980), p. 302.

18. Allison Ruby Reid-Cunningham, "Rape as a Weapon of Genocide," *Genocide Studies and Prevention*, December 2008, 3 (3): 279-296. (See p. 281)

19. Goldenberg, "Different Horrors," pp. 101-103, 121-122, note 2.

20. Susan Brownmiller, *Against Our Will: Men, Women, and Rape* (New York: Bantam, 1967), p. 31.

21. Iris Chang, *The Rape of Nanking* (New York: Penguin Books, 1997); William Hitchcock, *The Bitter Road to Freedom* (New York: The Free Press, 2008).

22. Catharine A. MacKinnon, "Genocide's Sexuality," *Are Women Human? and Other International Dialogues* (Cambridge, MA: The Belknap Press of Harvard University Press, 2006), pp. 212-220.

23. Lev-Wiesel and Weinger, pp. 22-25.

24. Mary Berg, *The Diary of Mary Berg: Growing up in the Warsaw Ghetto, 1945* (Oxford, UK: One World Publications, 2007), p. 60. See also Lyn Smith, *Remembering: Voices of the Holocaust* (New York: Carroll and Graf, 2005), p. 161. Men, too, testified that Jewish women were raped: Roman Halter, a Polish Jewish youth, described the intake process into Auschwitz-Birkenau, recalling that the women in his transport were not taken to the "women's block, but rather in the big block next to us." The men in his block heard "the Kapos and their deputies [...] rape the women at night and there were terrible screams and groans coming from that block, and the husbands in our block wept because they could understand the shouts" and presumably recognize their wives' cries.

25. Helene J. Sinnreich, "The Rape of Jewish Women during the Holocaust," and Zoe Waxman, "Rape and Sexual Abuse in Hiding," *Sexual Violence against Jewish Women during the Holocaust*, eds. Sonja M. Hedgepeth and Rochelle G. Saidel (Waltham, MA: Brandeis University Press, and Hanover, NH: The University of New England Press, 2010), pp. 108-123 and 124-135, respectively.

26. Jacob Apenszlak, ed., *The Black Book of Polish Jewry: An Account of the Martyrdom of Polish Jewry under the Nazi Occupation*. American Federation for Polish Jews, 1943 (Westport, CT: Brohan Press, 1999), p. 29; Brownmiller, p. 48.

27. Jewish Black Book Committee, *The Black Book: The Nazi Crime against the Jewish People* (New York: Duell, Sloan, and Pearch, 1946), p. 164.

28. Nomi Levenkron, "Death and the Maidens," *Sexual Violence against Jewish Women during the Holocaust*, eds. Sonja M. Hedgepeth and Rochelle G. Saidel (Waltham, MA: Brandeis University Press, and Hanover, NH: The University of New England Press, 2010), pp. 17-18.

29. Brownmiller, pp. 51-52.

30. Lev-Wiesel and Weinger, p. 70.

31. Lev-Wiesel and Weinger, p. 71.

32. Lengyel, pp. 60-63. Lengyel also describes the "lovemaking" that took place in the latrines of Birkenau.

33. Esther Dror and Ruth Linn, "The Same Is Always There," Sexual Violence against Jewish Women during the Holocaust, eds. Sonja M. Hedgepeth and Rochelle G. Saidel (Waltham, MA: Brandeis University Press, and Hanover, NH: The University of New England Press, 2010), pp. 275-289.

34. Felicia Berland Hyatt, *Close Calls: The Autobiography of a Survivor* (New York: Holocaust Library, 1991), pp. 76-77.

35. Anna Hyndrakova-Konanica, *The World without Human Dimensions: Four Women's Memories*, trans. Olga Kuthanova (Prague, Poland: State Jewish Museum, in cooperation with the Federation of Jewish Communities, 1991), p. 163.

36. Hyndrakova-Konanica, p. 181.

37. Adam Zych, ed., *The Auschwitz Poems: An Anthology* (Oswiecim: Auschwitz-Birkenau State Museum, 1999), p. 5.

38. Ibid, p. 6.

39. Ibid, p. 8.

40. Permission to use the photographs of all the artwork (Figures 1-10) in Part II of this essay was granted by Bernice Steinhardt, president of Art & Remembrance Foundation, Washington, DC.

Recovered, *2005 by Samuel Bak*
Image Courtesy of Pucker Gallery

PART III:
GENOCIDE IN RWANDA
(1994)

Becoming Evil:
How Ordinary People Commit Genocide and Mass Killing

■ ■ ■ ■ ■ ■ ■ ■ ■ ■ ■

James E. Waller

Cohen Professor of Holocaust and Genocide Studies,
Keene State College, Keene, NH

Aptly dubbed the "Age of Genocide," the past century saw a massive scale of systematic and intentional mass murder coupled with an unprecedented efficiency of the mechanisms and techniques of mass destruction. On the historical heels of the physical and cultural genocide of American Indians during the nineteenth century, the twentieth century writhed from the near-complete annihilation of the Hereros by the Germans in Southwest Africa in 1904, the brutal assault of the Armenian population by the Turks between 1915 and 1923, the implementation of a Soviet man-made famine against the Ukrainian kulaks in 1932-33 that left several million peasants starving to death, the extermination of two-thirds of Europe's Jews during the Holocaust of 1939-45, the massacre of approximately half a million people in Indonesia during 1965-66, and mass killings and genocide in Bangladesh (1971), Burundi (1972), Cambodia (1975-79), East Timor (1975-79), Rwanda (1994), and the former Yugoslavia (1992-95). All told, it is estimated that at least 60 million men, women, and children were victims of genocide and mass killing in the last century alone.[1]

The dawn of the twenty-first century brought little light to the darkness. In Darfur, the western region of Sudan, at least 300,000 people have died as a result of a Sudanese government-sponsored campaign of violence and forced starvation that began in early 2003. The impact of that violence is still felt in the Nuba Mountain and Blue Nile regions of Sudan. A recent risk assessment analysis by Barbara Harff lists 20 countries currently considered high-risk for genocide and mass atrocity.[2]

There is one unassailable fact behind this ignoble litany of human conflict and suffering: Political, social, or religious groups wanting to commit mass murder do. Though there may be other obstacles, they can always recruit individual human beings who will kill other human beings in large numbers and over an extended period of time. That is the one constant upon which they can count. In short, people are the weapons by which genocide occurs. How are people enlisted to perpetrate such extraordinary evil?

Ironically, we know more about the broad mechanics of mass murder than we do about the mindset of people who have carried it out. So, unlike much of the research in perpetrator behavior, I am not interested in the higher echelons of leadership who structured the ideology, policy, and initiatives behind a particular genocide or mass killing. Nor am I interested in the middle-echelon perpetrators, the faceless bureaucrats who made implementation of those initiatives possible. Rather, I am interested in the rank-and-file killers, the soldiers, police, militia (paramilitary), and civilians at the bottom of the hierarchy who personally carried out millions of executions. These people were so ordinary that, with few exceptions, they were readily absorbed into civil society after the killings and peacefully lived out their unremarkable lives – attesting to the unsettling reality that genocide overwhelms justice. One point stands clear: to understand the fundamental reality of mass murder, we need to shift our focus from impersonal institutions and abstract structures to the actors, the men and women who actually carried out the atrocities.

The goal of this chapter is to offer a psychological explanation of how ordinary people commit genocide and mass killing. It is an attempt to go beyond the minutiae of thick description (who, what, when, and where) and look at the bigger questions of explanation and understanding: to *know* a little less and *understand* a little more.

Ordinary Origins of Extraordinary Human Evil

The origins of extraordinary evil cannot be isolated in the extraordinary nature of the collective; the influence of an extraordinary ideology; psychopathology; or a common, homogeneous, extraordinary personality type.[3] A myopic focus on the extraordinary origins of extraordinary evil tells us more about our own personal dreams of how we wish the world to work than it does about the reality of perpetrator behavior. In that role, such explanations satisfy an important emotional demand of distancing us from them.

The truth seems to be, though, that the most outstanding common characteristic of perpetrators is their normality, not their abnormality; they are extraordinary only by what they have done, not by who they are. Perpetrators of genocide and mass killing cannot be identified, *a priori*, as having the personalities of killers. Most are not mentally impaired, nor are they identified as sadists at home or in their social environment, nor are they victims of an abusive background. They defy easy demographic categorization. Among them, we find educated and well-to-do people, as well as simple and impoverished people. We find church-affiliated people, as well as agnostics and atheists. We find people who are loving parents, as well as those who have difficulty initiating and sustaining satisfying personal relationships. We find young people and old people. We find people who are not actively involved in the political, religious, or social groups responsible for institutionalizing the process of destruction, as well as those who are. We find ordinary people who went to school, fought with siblings, celebrated birthdays, listened to music, and played with friends. In short, the majority of perpetrators of genocide and mass killing are not distinguished by background, personality, or previous political affiliation or behavior as being men or women unusually likely or fit to be genocidal executioners.

We are then left with the most discomforting of all realities – ordinary, "normal" people committing acts of extraordinary evil. This reality is difficult to admit, to understand, to absorb. We would rather know extraordinary evil as an extra-human capitalization. This reality is unsettling because it counters our general mental tendency to relate extraordinary acts to correspondingly extraordinary people. But we cannot evade this discomforting reality. We are forced to confront the ordinariness of most perpetrators of mass killing and genocide. Recognizing their ordinariness does not diminish the horror of their actions; it increases it. As we look at perpetrators of genocide and mass killing, we need no longer ask who these people are. We know who they are. They are you and I.

There is now a more urgent question to ask: *How* are ordinary people like you and me made into perpetrators of genocide and mass killing? The importance of this question is only matched by the complexity of its answer. The precise "how" of the transformation process remains veiled from us, as it may have remained veiled from the men and women who experienced it. The multiplicity of variables that lead an ordinary person to commit genocide and mass killing is difficult to pin down. It is impossible to establish general "laws" that apply to all individuals in all contexts and at all times.

Regardless, we are now in a position to advance some hypotheses that may offer a solution more right than wrong. The remainder of this chapter outlines a general explanatory model (see Figure 1) of the making of perpetrators.[4] The model – drawing on existing literature; eyewitness accounts by killers, bystanders, and victims from a wide range of genocides and mass killings; and classic and contemporary research in social and evolutionary psychology – is not an invocation of a single broad-brush psychological state or *event* to explain the making of perpetrators. Rather, focusing less on the outcome, it is a detailed analysis of a *process* through which the perpetrators themselves – either in committing atrocities or in order to commit atrocities – are changed.

Figure 1
A Model of How Ordinary People Commit Genocide and Mass Killing

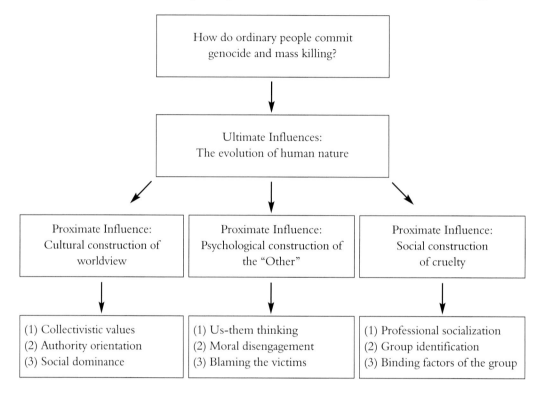

The model recognizes that human behavior is multiply influenced and that any answer to the question, "Why did that person act as he or she did?" can be examined at two levels of analysis – the proximate and the ultimate. As Pinker describes, "A *proximate* cause of behavior is the mechanism that pushes behavior buttons in real time, such as the hunger and lust that impel people to eat and have sex. An *ultimate* cause is the adaptive rationale that led the proximate cause to evolve, such as the need for nutrition and reproduction that gave us the drives of hunger and lust."[5] In other words, proximate influences refer to those immediate influences closest to the present moment, "how" a behavior occurs in the here and now. Ultimate influences, conversely, refer to those deeper influences from our evolutionary past, "why" a behavior evolved by natural selection. It is these ultimate influences that reveal the nature of human nature and, in so doing, help us understand the "why" behind "how" ordinary people commit genocide and mass killing.

While evolutionary psychology describes the ultimate evolutionary capacities common to all of us, this understanding must be couched in the context of the more proximate and immediate cultural, psychological, and social constructions that converge interactively to activate these capacities. Building on these ultimate influences, the model emphasizes three proximate here-and-now constructions that impact individual behavior in situations of collective violence. The Cultural Construction of Worldview examines the influence of cultural models that are widely shared by the members of a perpetrator group. The Psychological Construction of the "Other" analyzes how victims of genocide and mass killing simply become the "objects" of perpetrators' actions. Finally, the Social Construction of Cruelty explores the mechanisms used in creating an immediate social context in which perpetrators initiate, sustain, and cope with their cruelty.

Cultural Construction of Worldview

All cultures leave their fingerprints on the members within them, most often through the transmission of a worldview. A worldview includes the presuppositions, intentions, meanings, rules, norms, values, principles, practices, and activities through which people live their lives. Cognitive anthropology understands worldview in the rich theoretical context of cultural models. As Hinton describes, "[C]ultural models are largely tacit knowledge structures that are both widely shared by and mediate the understanding of the members of a social group."[6] In other words, cultural models are the constituent elements of a worldview that give us the background, or lens, through which we interpret our social world and make judgments about appropriate responses. There are three specific cultural models – related to *collectivistic values*, *authority orientation*, and *social dominance* – that are particularly relevant to understanding the making of perpetrators.

Collectivistic values of obedience, conformity, tradition, safety, and order form a worldview in which group membership shapes and completes individuals. Group-based identity – whether centered on race, ethnicity, tribe, kin, religion, or nationality – becomes a central and defining characteristic of one's personal identity and overshadows the self. Group goals become indistinguishable from individual goals. Conflict in a collectivistic culture is intergroup since group membership (often based on mythic blood ties or shared history) is enduring, stable, and permanent, and has an existence beyond the individual. When group membership is seen as impermeable and fixed, the potential to view other groups as perpetual threats is heightened.

Historically, genocidal regimes have emphasized collectivistic values that make group membership central to personal identity. Such regimes have been particularly adept at using such collectivistic values to highlight boundaries between in-groups and out-groups by making extreme categorical judgments based on the polar opposites of "good us" versus "bad them." Our cause is sacred; theirs is evil. We are righteous; they are wicked. We are innocent; they are guilty. We are the victims; they are the victimizers. It is rarely *our* enemy or *an* enemy, but *the* enemy – a usage of the definite article that hints at something fixed and immutable, abstract and evil.

A cultural model of collectivistic values often is cultivated in concert with a highly salient cultural model of *authority orientation*, a way of ordering the social world and relating to people according to their position and power in hierarchies. This is a cultural model exemplified by a preference for hierarchical, vertical relationships with a clear delineation of spheres of power. Such a cultural model cultivates individuals who enjoy obeying authority and exercising power over those below them, who prefer order and predictability. While a certain degree of authority orientation is required in all social systems, a culture that inculcates an excessively strong authority orientation nurtures individuals who are less likely to oppose leaders who scapegoat, or advocate violence against, a particular target group.

Finally, aside from the sexual drive, evolutionary psychology suggests that one of the most universal and powerful motivating forces in animals is the desire for *social dominance*. This desire, leading to differences in rank and status, can be defined as the set of sustained aggressive-submissive relations among individual animals. In a group, these relations form a hierarchical structure, commonly called a social dominance hierarchy. In a social dominance hierarchy, some individuals within a group reliably gain greater access than other individuals to key resources, particularly resources that contribute to survival and reproductive success.

In addition to recognizing the ultimate adaptive value of social dominance hierarchies, it is important to understand the real-time behavioral consequences of a psychological adaptation for social dominance and the ways in which cultural models of social dominance are often perpetuated and legitimated by ideologies, myths, and symbols. Occasionally, our desire for social dominance has prosocial consequences as we realize that helping others creates friendships and coalitions that are useful in our struggle for power. At other times, however, our evolved desire for social dominance means that we have a predisposition to respond to certain kinds of situations aggressively (sometimes even violently) to get our way. Violence works as a means of getting some contested resource by increasing the cost of that resource to another individual. Moreover, once we get past initial inhibitions against aggressive and violent behavior, such behavior rapidly escalates and increases over time and seems, in part, to become self-reinforcing. In short, aggression and violence often function to increase our status and power within a social dominance hierarchy.

Psychological Construction of the "Other"

Implied in these cultural models, and certainly inherent in a genocidal worldview, is the obliteration of a common ground between perpetrators and victims. How do victims simply become objects of the perpetrators' actions? How do perpetrators define the target of their atrocities in such a way as to "excommunicate" them from a common moral community? There are three mechanisms central to understanding the psychological construction of the "other" – *us-them thinking*, *moral disengagement*, and *blaming the victims*.

Human minds are compelled to define the limits of the tribe. Kinship, however defined, remains an important organizing principle for most societies in the world. Knowing who is kin and who is in our social group has a deep importance to species like ours. We construct this knowledge by categorizing others as "us" or "them." We have an evolved, universal capacity for *us-them thinking* in which we see our group as superior to all others and may even be reluctant to recognize members of other groups as deserving of equal respect.

Us-them thinking does not lead us to hate all out-groups. Social exclusion, let alone genocide and mass killing, is not an inevitable consequence of us-them thinking. We are reminded, however, that once identified with a group, we find it easy to exaggerate differences between our group and others, enhancing in-group cooperation and effectiveness and frequently intensifying antagonism with other groups. This process helps us understand how the suggestive message of us against them can be ratcheted up to the categorically compelling "kill or be killed."

The *moral disengagement* that often results from us-them thinking is not simply a matter of moral indifference or invisibility. Rather, it is an active, but gradual, process of detachment by which some individuals or groups are placed outside the boundary where moral values, rules, and considerations of fairness apply. How do perpetrators regulate their thinking so as to disengage, or not feel, their moral scruples about harming others?

There is a variety of disengagement practices used by perpetrators to make their reprehensible conduct acceptable and to distance them from the moral implications of their actions. For instance, there is a moral justification in which mass murder is made personally and socially acceptable by portraying it as serving socially worthy or moral purposes. Perpetrators may believe this rationalization to such an extent that their evil is not only morally justifiable (right to do), but becomes an outright moral imperative (wrong not to do it). Perpetrators can then justify their evil as essential to their own self-defense – to protect the cherished values of their community, fight ruthless oppressors, preserve peace and stability, save humanity from subjugation, or honor their national commitments.

Moral disengagement also is facilitated by the dehumanization of the victims – categorizing a group as inhuman either by using categories of subhuman creatures (that is, animals) or by using categories of negatively evaluated superhuman creatures (such as demons and monsters). Dehumanization is most likely when the target group can be readily identified as a separate category of people belonging to a distinct racial, ethnic, religious, or political group that the perpetrators regard as inferior or threatening. These isolated subgroups are stigmatized as alien and memories of their past misdeeds, real or imaginary, are activated by the dominant group.

The dehumanization of victims helps perpetrators to justify their hurtful behavior. A common form of dehumanization is the use of language to redefine the victims so they will be seen as warranting the aggression. The surreal gentility of the euphemistic labeling of evil actions central to the moral disengagement of the perpetrators is complemented by a barbarity of language that dehumanizes the victims. Perpetrators so consistently dehumanize their victims that the words themselves become substitutes for perceiving human beings. Before the Japanese performed medical experiments on human prisoners in World War II, they named them *maruta* – logs of wood. The Greek torturers studied by Gibson and Haritos-Fatouros referred to their victims as "worms."[7] The Hutu extremists called the Tutsi *inyenzi*, meaning cockroaches or insects. Haing S. Ngor, the late Cambodian doctor and actor who found fame for his role in "The Killing Fields," notes of the plight of those persecuted by the Khmer Rouge: "We weren't quite people. We were lower forms of life, because we were enemies. Killing us was like swatting flies, a way to get rid of undesirables." There is even a quantitative process of dehumanization in which victims become mere statistics – bodies to be counted and numbers to be entered into reports. Reduced to data, dehumanized victims lose their moral standing and become objects requiring disposal.

Such dehumanization often leads to an escalation of the brutality of the killing. Dehumanizing victims removes normal moral constraints against aggression. The body of a dehumanized victim possesses no meaning. It is waste, and its removal is a matter of sanitation. There is no moral or empathic context through which the perpetrator can relate to the victim.

Perpetrators further facilitate moral disengagement by using euphemistic language to make their atrocities respectable and, in part, to reduce their personal responsibility for it. By masking their evil in innocuous or sanitizing jargon, their actions lose much of their moral repugnancy. Mass murder becomes "ethnic cleansing," "bush clearing," or "liquidation." The camouflage vocabulary used by the Nazis to cover their extraordinary evil was especially striking – "final solution," "special treatment," "evacuation," "spontaneous actions," "resettlement," and "special installations," among many others.

Finally, the psychological construction of the "other" feeds on itself and is driven by our brain's remarkable capacity to seek, and find, explanation in the events surrounding us, our actions, and the behaviors of people with whom we interact. We recognize that victims can be grouped into two broad categories – those who deserve their suffering and those who do not deserve their suffering. We know that bad things do happen to good people. To a large degree, we recognize the reality that it is not a just world.

But we do not so easily relinquish our hopeful illusion of a world that is fair and just. We hold on to that notion, however misguided, to give us the courage to go out into the world and to send our children out into the world. Our need to believe in a just world overwhelms our recognition that bad things can happen to good people. As a result, we often assume that victims deserve, and can be blamed for, their fates. Indeed, we show a hardy cognitive tendency to search for ways to blame individuals for their own victimization. On the whole, the general tendency of *blaming the victims* for their own suffering is a central truth about human experience. For perpetrators, this tendency is invaluable in its striking propensity to devalue victims and their suffering. We will rearrange our perception of people and events so that it seems everyone is getting what they deserve. Victims must be suffering because they have done "something," must somehow be inferior or dangerous or evil, or because a higher cause is being served. The belief that the world is a just place leads us to accept the suffering of others more easily, even of people we ourselves have harmed.

Social Construction of Cruelty

In addition to the cultural construction of worldview and the psychological construction of the "other," a thorough understanding of how perpetrators are made requires an analysis of the real-time power of situational influences on individual behavior. A social construction of cruelty makes each perpetrator believe that all people are capable of doing what they do. It is an inverted moral universe, shaped by a process of brutalization, in which right has become wrong; healing has become killing; life has become death. A social construction of cruelty envelops perpetrators in a social context that encourages and rewards evil. We must borrow the perspective of the perpetrators and view their actions, not as the work of "madmen," but as actions with a clear and justified purpose – as defined by a social construction of cruelty. There are three momentum-inducing features of a social construction of cruelty that enable perpetrators to initiate, sustain, and cope with their cruelty – *professional socialization*, *group identification*, and *binding factors of the group*.

Newcomers to a social context of cruelty are typically in the position of someone who does not know his or her way around and knows it. It is natural for them to seek information from others to learn which behaviors are acceptable or not acceptable in the organization. *Professional socialization*, usually institutionalized in military or paramilitary organizations, often takes the form of a sequence of seemingly small, innocuous incremental steps – a series of escalating commitments. From 1967 through 1974, the process of escalating commitments was used by the military regime then in power in Greece to train torturers.[9] In a systematic process of escalating commitments, recruits underwent physically brutal initiation rites. At the same time as they were cursed, punched, kicked, and flogged, they were told how fortunate they were to be invited into such an elite organization. They were then subjected to torture themselves (as if it were a normal act), then assigned to guard prisoners, then made to participate in arresting squads, then ordered to hit prisoners, then made to observe torture; finally, they were ordered to practice torture in group beatings and a variety of other brutal methods. Once the training was complete, a carrot-and-stick strategy of special benefits coupled with threats and punishment for disobedience kept the perpetrators committed to their tasks.

Perhaps most relevant to professional socialization, however, is a merger of role and person through which evil-doing organizations can change the people in them over time. When one performs the behaviors appropriate for a given role, one often acquires the attitudes, beliefs, values, and morals consistent with that role and its behaviors. Seen in this light, the egregious brutality of perpetrators does not automatically indicate an *inherent*, pre-existing brutality; not everyone playing a brutal role has to have sadistic traits of character. Rather, brutality can be a consequence, not only a cause, of being in a duly certified and legitimized social hierarchy committed to evil. In other words, the nature of the tasks of atrocity may have been sufficient to produce that brutality even if the perpetrators were not initially sadists. It may be a vicious social arrangement, and not the preexisting viciousness of the participants, that lead to the cruel behaviors exhibited by perpetrators.

As we saw in our discussion of collectivistic values, *group identification* – an emotional attachment to a group – is a potent influence on an individual's thoughts, emotions, and behaviors. Group identification, whether centered on race, ethnicity, tribe, kin, religion, or nationality, can become a central and defining characteristic of one's personal identity and may even overshadow the self. These group identities can even become such an important source of self-definition and esteem that other groups are perceived as threats – thus sowing the seeds for intergroup conflict by evoking suspicion of, hostility toward, and competition with an out-group. At the extreme, group identification may be mobilized into collective violence or a genocidal imperative as it is used to forge in-group solidarity and undermine the normal inhibitions against killing out-group strangers. We can identify with a group, and against other groups, to such a degree that group identification comes to dominate our individual thoughts, emotions, and behaviors, often against the interests and welfare of other groups.

Group identification carries with it a repression of conscience where "outside" values are excluded and locally generated values dominate. Such a repression of conscience serves a self-protective function, as well as having a progressively desensitizing effect on the perpetrators, and is facilitated in social contexts that promote diffusion of responsibility and deindividuation.

Diffusion of responsibility is accomplished by bureaucratic organization into cells and columns, as well as by a routinization of bureaucratic subroutines – a segmentation and fragmentation of the killing tasks – in which responsibility for evil is divided among members of a group. Such division of labor, in addition to making the killing process more efficient and effective, allows perpetrators to reduce their identification with the consequences of their evil. Once activities are routinized into detached subfunctions, perpetrators shift their attention away from the morality of what they are doing to the operational details and efficiency of their specific job. They are then able to see themselves totally as performers of a role – as participants *in*, not originators *of*, evil. It is easier for perpetrators to avoid the implications of their evil since they are focusing on the *details* of their job rather than on its *meaning*.

The segmented activities of bureaucratic organizations also provide a cloak of deindividuation that facilitates the commission of evil. Deindividuation refers to a state of relative anonymity in which a person cannot be identified as a particular individual, but only as a group member. The concept usually includes a decreased focus on personal identity, loss of contact with general social norms, and the submergence of the individual in situation-specific group norms. These are conditions that confer anonymity and increase the likelihood of evil as people partially lose awareness of themselves as individuals and cease to evaluate their own actions thoughtfully.

In addition, it is important for us to examine the ways in which group identification fulfills and shapes perpetrators' rational self-interests, both professionally and personally. Generally speaking, most perpetrators of genocide work within the context of a military or paramilitary organization. In that context, there is a logic of incentives enmeshed with professional self-interest – ambitions, advancement, and careerism – that certainly plays a role in understanding their behavior. Moreover, there often is a mutually reinforcing and deadly compatibility of one's professional self-interests with a larger political, religious, or social interest in annihilation of a specific target group.

Genocide and mass killing is replete with examples of perpetrators who used the situations of extremity to advance their personal self-interest by claiming power, property, and goods. The following account of a Hutu perpetrator from the Rwandan genocide is illustrative of this reality:

> A failed student turned killer, Shalom [Ntahobari] became a big man in Butare once the slaughter began. He swaggered around town with grenades hanging from his belt, often armed with a gun which he once aimed in insolent jest at a local burgomaster. One witness asserted that even military officers saluted Shalom. He controlled his own barrier in front of the family house near the university campus where he bullied his militia subordinates as well as passersby. One witness who had known Shalom as a fellow student witnessed him killing a man in order to rob him of his cattle.[10]

Finally, a social construction of cruelty relies on *binding factors of the group*, or cementing mechanisms that endow a social context with at least minimal stability.

Such binding factors are the pressures that work to keep people within an evil-doing organization or hierarchy. They constitute the social authority of a group and hold the individual tightly to a rigid definition of the situation, closing off the freedom of movement to focus on features of the situation other than its authority structure.

One significant binding factor is the explicit, or implicit, dynamic of conformity to peer pressure. Military science is replete with assertions that the cohesive bonds soldiers form with one another in military and paramilitary organizations are often stronger than the bonds they will form with anyone else at any other point in their lifetimes. Among people who are bonded together so intensely, there is a powerful dynamic of conformity to peer pressure – or "mutual surveillance" – in which the individual cares so deeply about his comrades and what they think of him that he would rather die than let them down. Conformity to peer pressure certainly helps sustain perpetrators' involvement in evil. It is difficult for anyone who is bonded by links of mutual affection and interdependence to break away and openly refuse to participate in what the group is doing, even if it is perpetrating atrocities.

Another significant binding factor is kin-recognition cues that allow us to move from a biological definition of kinship to a social definition of kinship (that is "fictive kin"). Such cues are important because kin recognition is so strongly related to altruistic behavior in many species. Johnson has suggested that altruism for the benefit of non-kin can be fostered by cues of *association*.[11] In other words, we are evolutionarily primed to define kin as those with whom we are familiar due to living and rearing arrangements. So genetically unrelated individuals can come to be understood as kin – and subsequently treated as such – if introduced into our network of frequent and intimate associations (for example, family) in an appropriate way. In addition, Johnson suggests *phenotypic matching* as another indirect kin-recognition cue. By assuming a correlation between genotype (internally coded inheritable information) and phenotype (outward physical and behavioral characteristics), we can recognize likely kin by comparing our own phenotype with theirs. Though somewhat less reliable than the primary kin-recognition cue of association, perceived phenotypic matching is still capable of eliciting altruistic behavior on behalf of non-kin.

Because the kin-recognition cues of association and phenotypic matching are indirect, they are subject to errors, as well as manipulation. It is the manipulation of kin-recognition cues that gives us a new lens through which to view the mechanisms that military and paramilitary organizations use to bind individual members to the group and, subsequently, evoke the type of loyalty and emotional bonding that promotes the altruistic and self-sacrificing behaviors that are normally reserved for genetically related kin. The kin-recognition cue of association is manipulated by military and paramilitary organizations through the training of recruits in extremely close and intense physical proximity that replicates natural kin contexts. In addition, the use of identifying and rhetorical language characterized by such kin terms as "motherland," "fatherland," the "homeland," "brothers-in-arms," and "sisters-in-arms" encourages a social redefinition of kin through association. The supplemental kin-recognition cue of phenotypic matching is manipulated by having individual members of a military or paramilitary organization resemble each other as much as possible by means of uniforms, emblems, accoutrements, identical haircuts, weaponry, habits and mannerisms, tattoos, and so on. In such ways, military and paramilitary organizations manipulate kin-recognition cues to bind individual members to a larger group and, in so doing, to maintain and reinforce altruistic behavior (such as volunteerism, risking one's life in combat, and altruistic suicide) in a non-kin setting.

Conclusion

To resist the compelling cultural, psychological, and social constructions that influence our behaviors requires a rare degree of individual strength – psychological, moral, and physical. Regardless, we know that some people do resist, and it is in that knowledge that we both take hope and reserve the right of condemnation for those who perpetrate mass atrocities of any type. To offer a psychological explanation of how ordinary people commit genocide and mass killing is not to forgive, justify, or condone their behaviors. We must not confuse explanation with exculpation; to explain behavior is not to exonerate the perpetrator. There are no "perpetrator-less" acts of terror. Perpetrators of genocide and mass killing are not just the hapless victims of human nature, culture, psychology, or their social context. On the road to committing atrocities, there are many choice points for each perpetrator. Sometimes the choosing may take place without awareness or conscious deliberation. At other times, it is a matter of very focused and deliberate decision-making. Regardless, what perpetrators decide to do makes a great difference in what they eventually do. The perpetrators, in willfully failing to exercise their moral judgment, retain full moral and legal accountability for the atrocities they committed. No explanatory model or "psychological insight" will ever take that away.

My argument – that it is ordinary individuals like you and me who commit genocide and mass killing – is not an easy sell. None of us likes to be told that we are capable of such brutality. It is a pessimistic point of view that flies directly in the face of our sincere, but misguided, optimism that human evil can be obliterated by reforming society. We must not, however, avoid the hard task of trying to extract the comprehensible from the unthinkable. We must not let "evil" be a throwaway category for the things we are afraid to understand. We must not let it be the impenetrable term we use when we come to the limit of human comprehension. We must not consider perpetrators so irrational, so atavistic, as to be beyond human understanding. We must not place human evil beyond human scrutiny. To do so is to give it the benefit of our ignorance. In this sense, our refusal to attempt to understand human evil is a willful failure to know our own hearts and, if anything, only facilitates the continuation of evil in human affairs.

The lesson that ordinary people commit genocide and mass killing need not be compartmentalized only as "bad news" – a disturbing, unsettling, disquieting truth about the human condition. The lesson does contain potentially "good news," as well – the making of perpetrators need no longer be a mystery. We are beginning to understand the conditions under which we can be transformed into killing machines. The more we know and the more open we are to seeing ourselves as we are, the better we can control ourselves. It is only in accepting the limits of who we are that we have a legitimate chance to structure a society in which the exercise of human evil is lessened. Civility, after all, is a chosen state, not a natural condition. Ultimately, being aware of our own capacity for evil – and how to cultivate the moral sensibilities that curb that capacity – is the best safeguard we can have against future genocide and mass killing.

Questions

1. *Why is it so difficult for us to embrace the notion of the "ordinariness" of people who commit genocide and mass killing? Why do we want them to be so different from ourselves?*

2. *From the factors described in the explanatory model, which do you consider most potent in the making of perpetrators? What factors seem to you to be most influential?*

3. *How could you use this explanatory model to inoculate a society against the making of perpetrators? In other words, how can the model be "reversed" to develop cultural, psychological, and social influences to encourage help rather than harm?*

Bibliography

Chung, Lee Isaac, dir. *Munyurangabo*. Film Movement, 2009.

Gibson, Janice T. and Mika Haritos-Fatouros. "The Education of a Torturer." *Psychology Today* 20 (1986): 50-58.

Egoyan, Atom, dir. *Ararat*. Miramax, 2003.

Hatzfeld, Jean. Machete Season: The Killers in Rwanda Speak. New York: Farrar, Straus and Giroux, 2003.

Hinton, Alexander L. "Why Did You Kill? The Cambodian Genocide and the Dark Side of Face and Honor." *The Journal of Asian Studies* 57 (1998): 93-122.

Johnson, Gary R. "Kin Selection, Socialization, and Patriotism: An Integrating Theory." *Politics and the Life Sciences* 4 (1986): 127-140.

Johnson, Gary R. "The Role of Kin Recognition Mechanisms in Patriotic Socialization: Further Reflections." *Politics and the Life Sciences* 8 (1989): 62-69.

Jones, Adam. "Gender and Genocide in Rwanda." *Journal of Genocide Research* 4 (2002): 65-94.

Ngor, Haing S. *A Cambodian Odyssey*. New York: Grand Central Publishing, 1987.

Pinker, Steven. *The Blank Slate: The Modern Denial of Human Nature*. New York: Penguin, 2002.

Smith, Roger W. "Human Destructiveness and Politics." *Genocide and the Modern Age: Etiology and Case Studies of Mass Death*. Eds. Isidor Wallimann and Michael N. Dobkowski. Syracuse, NY: Syracuse University Press, 2000.

Tanovic, Danis, dir. *No Man's Land*. MGM, 2001.

Wajda, Andrezej, dir. *Katyn*. Akson, 2007.

Waller, James E. *Becoming Evil: How Ordinary People Commit Genocide and Mass Killing*, 2nd ed. New York: Oxford University Press, 2007.

Notes

1. Roger W. Smith, "Human Destructiveness and Politics: The Twentieth Century as an Age of Genocide," *Genocide and the Modern Age: Etiology and Case Studies of Mass Death*, eds. Isidor Wallimann and Michael N. Dobkowski (Syracuse, NY: Syracuse University Press, 2000), p. 21.
2. See http://gpanet.org/webfm_send/120, accessed December 12, 2012.
3. For a complete critique of the work of those who argue that the origins of extraordinary human evil lie not in ordinary individuals but in extraordinary groups, ideologies, psychopathologies, or personalities, see James Waller, *Becoming Evil: How Ordinary People Commit Genocide and Mass Killing*, 2nd ed. (New York: Oxford University Press, 2007).
4. Ibid.
5. Steven Pinker, *The Blank Slate: The Modern Denial of Human Nature* (New York: Penguin, 2002), p. 54.
6. Alexander L. Hinton, "Why Did You Kill? The Cambodian Genocide and the Dark Side of Face and Honor," *The Journal of Asian Studies*, 1998, 57: 96.
7. Janice T. Gibson and Mika Haritos-Fatouros, "The Education of a Torturer," *Psychology Today*, 1986, 20: 50-58.
8. Haing S. Ngor, *A Cambodian Odyssey* (New York: Grand Central Publishing, 1987), p. 230.
9. Gibson and Haritos-Fatouros.
10. Quoted in Adam Jones, "Gender and Genocide in Rwanda," *Journal of Genocide Research*, 2002, 4: 76.
11. Gary R. Johnson, "Kin Selection, Socialization, and Patriotism: An Integrating Theory," *Politics and the Life Sciences*, 1986, 4: 127-140. Commentaries and an author's response follow on pp. 141-154 of the same issue. See also Johnson's "The Role of Kin Recognition Mechanisms in Patriotic Socialization: Further Reflections," *Politics and the Life Sciences*, 1989, 8: 62-69.

Genocide in Rwanda, 1994

▪ ▪ ▪ ▪ ▪ ▪ ▪ ▪ ▪ ▪ ▪

Carl Wilkens

Former Head of the Adventist Development and Relief Agency International, Rwanda;
Director, World Outside My Shoes, *Spokane, WA*

Carol Rittner, R.S.M.

Distinguished Professor of Holocaust & Genocide Studies and
Dr. Marsha Radicoff Grossman Professor of Holocaust Studies,
The Richard Stockton College of New Jersey, Galloway, NJ

"Much of what the world remembers about the Rwandan genocide are grim tales of betrayal among neighbors and of the slaughter of innocent civilians. [But there] are other stories of people who resisted the urge to kill and who risked their lives to save the lives of others." Carl Wilkens is one of those people. The following is an interview with him, edited by Carol Rittner and based on his presentations at the 2012 Ethel LeFrak Holocaust Education Conference held at Seton Hill University's National Catholic Center for Holocaust Education.

Carol Rittner: Please share with us a little bit about yourself, your extraordinary wife, Teresa, and the work the two of you have been doing for many years.

Carl Wilkens: Unfortunately, as you know, Teresa could not join me here at Seton Hill University. She's in Zimbabwe at the moment helping her aunt who started an orphanage there more than 20 years ago. Her aunt, who is 78 and hasn't been in such good health for awhile, sent a desperate plea in an email a few weeks ago, and Teresa said, "I have to go to help her." I said, "Yes, you do have to go and help her." So that's where she is and why she can't be here this week.

Teresa and I met in high school. When we went on to college, we started doing accounting homework together. Obviously, that added up real well! A week after graduating from college – she with a business degree and me with an industrial education degree – we got married. Six weeks later, we moved to Zimbabwe to do work with the Seventh Day Adventist Church in Africa. Our daughters were born in Zimbabwe. We spent six years there and in Zambia, then moved back to the USA, where I got an MBA – and we got a son, Shaun, who was born in the States. We have a great family. After our kids graduated from college, they all did some teaching in China for awhile, but now they are back in the USA.

Not long after Shaun was born, Teresa, the kids, and I moved to Rwanda. We went there with the Adventist Development and Relief Agency, the humanitarian arm of the Seventh Day Adventist Church. One of the things we did in Rwanda, a gorgeous land of a thousand hills, was build schools, which was very rewarding work. We loved working and living in Rwanda. We had a comfortable home, many friends, and great work to do. It was a wonderful place to raise our kids.

Rittner: Sounds very idyllic, and yet we know awful things happened in Rwanda in 1994. What can you tell us about what you remember about April 1994?

Wilkens: Well, I am sure most of you know about how the plane carrying Rwanda President Juvenal Habyarimana and Burundi President Cyprien Ntaryamira was shot down the night of April 6, 1994, as it was making its approach to land at Kigali's international airport. We heard the explosions from our house but didn't know what it was, much less that this double assassination would be used to launch a well-planned genocide. In less than an hour, shooting broke out around the city.

Several weeks earlier, we had sent a fax to the Adventist Church world headquarters in the US saying that we felt like we were sitting on a "keg of dynamite." In coordination with the US embassy, we had evacuation plans in place for all the missionaries. Contributing to the mounting tensions were RTLM hate radio's songs, speeches, and comedy, along with newspaper cartoons like the one that had a patient saying to his doctor, "I'm sick" and the doctor replies, "What is your sickness?," to which the patient responds, "The Tutsi, the Tutsi, the Tutsi." Later, as we reflected back on that time, we realized this was part of a very intentional process in which people were constructing an enemy. First you have words and images, then you have actions.

One of the first people killed in our neighborhood was a banker. Every morning, he would leave in his beautiful three-piece suit heading off to work. He had a large home with a big satellite dish in his yard. Remember those? They were before the internet. Anyway, he had one of those dishes, and no doubt he knew about all sorts of international affairs, like world stock markets and other sorts of things.

The Thursday morning after the President's plane was shot down, he did not head off to work. I imagine it was because he was thinking about his wife and children. They had to make some extremely difficult decisions. What they ended up doing was boosting their children up over the wall into the orphanage next door with its 30 children. The couple responsible for the orphanage would flee in several days, but the night watchman, whose name was Heri, would courageously care for those children throughout the genocide.

The banker neighbor – they were Tutsis – after doing what they could for their children went back inside their home and tried to hide in a small closet under their stairway. We could hear the pounding and smashing and screams as gangs of thugs tried to find them, which they did eventually. I'll spare you the details, except to say that they draped the mother's lifeless body over their fence. Maybe it was a warning, as if to say, "This is what happens if you are sympathetic to the enemy." I don't really know, but we watched these killers walk down the street in front of our house carrying a couch from our neighbor's home, and a television, and microwave.

That Thursday night – the night after the plane was shot down – a band of militia came to the gate of our home. They assembled there, but they never came in because the moms, grandmas, and the aunts who lived in our neighborhood and with whose children our children played, when they heard that these Hutu militia were threatening us, they came and stood in front of our gate. They said to these menacing men and boys, "No, you can't go in there!"

Now if the situation were reversed and I was in their place, I am sure that I could think of a thousand reasons not to go out and stand in front of a gang of adrenaline-driven guys with bloody machetes in their hands, or who were holding clubs they were swinging with spikes they had driven through the wood to make them more torturous. It is likely these guys had barely pulled up their pants after what they probably had done to women in the neighborhood before they killed them. Yes, I could give you a thousand reasons why someone would not want to come and stand between them and us. And yet, these ladies, these moms and grandmas, these aunts, courageously came and stood there and told those guys, "No! You are not going in there."

Many of us know that one of the most powerful weapons anyone has is not a traditional weapon – a club, a knife, a gun – but a story. The power of stories is just incredible. And that day, those ladies told stories. Grandmas are masters at telling stories. They told those thugs stories about how in the middle of the night a neighbor would be having a difficult delivery, and their friends would come and ring our bell and ask Teresa or me to take them to the hospital. Simple acts of kindness. Those are the stories they told. They said, "You can't go in that home. Their kids play with our kids."

Somehow, these ladies, these wonderful women, changed the thinking, feeling, and actions of that Hutu mob outside our gate that night. We didn't know until the next morning, Friday morning, that there had been a mob at our gate the night before. When I think back about it, they could have robbed or even killed us, but no, those moms and grandmas saved us. They stood up for us.

Rittner: Do you think the genocide that happened in Rwanda was spontaneous?

Wilkens: There's nothing spontaneous about genocide. You can't just say, "Oh, the Hutus hate the Tutsis," and then boom! Genocide just breaks out. No. It's hard to pull off a genocide. It requires planning. You have to break the bonds between people, and that's not always easy to do. There are obstacles to genocide that have to be overcome. For example, in Rwanda, we had 2,500 United Nations peacekeepers in town. They were highly visible. And they were there not just for the Rwandans, but for us foreigners, too, so we felt a sense of security. These guys used to patrol the streets in groups of eight, and you often saw these big, white, armored personnel carriers with the bold black UN letters marked on them. As you can imagine, their presence was potentially a huge obstacle to widespread and massive violence. What's the strategy to overcome this obstacle? As we saw in the documentary, *Ghosts of Rwanda*, the Hutu-power people decided to kill ten Belgian peacekeepers. They knew this would get the attention of the world, and they gambled that the UN – or the Belgians – would pull the rest of their men out of Rwanda. And that's exactly what happened. But all of this was planned. None of this was spontaneous.

Rittner: Would you say that foreigners, particularly if they were white, were just as vulnerable as Rwandans who were Tutsi, or "moderate Hutu"?

Wilkens: Well, those Belgian soldiers weren't very safe, and they were white. But I would say that, generally speaking, if you were white, you were somewhat safer. In fact, if Tutsis were injured by these Hutu mobs and could manage to get to a hospital staffed by white foreigners – like missionary hospitals, or the Red Cross hospital set up by Phillipe Gaillard and his colleagues, places like that – they usually had a chance to survive, because those *Interahamwe* (Hutu-power militia) did not want to tangle with foreigners, at least, not normally.

Rittner: How important would you say was the presence of foreigners – white foreigners particularly – during those terrible weeks of genocide in 1994?

Wilkens: Important? Oh, they were so important. The power of presence! There was nothing more important. I am sure you are familiar with the story about the Rape of

Nanking and just how important the presence of those 18 or so foreigners in Nanking were to the survival of 200,000 people of Nanking? Well, Teresa and I were faced with a decision about whether to stay or to leave. It wasn't easy.

We had a friend, a young woman who had worked for us for three years. Her ID card said "Tutsi," and we knew that if she left our house, she would be in danger. And our kids also knew there was danger, even though we tried to shelter them as much as possible from everything that was going on around us. We tried to play games to distract them and so on. But they knew this young Tutsi woman – her name was Anita – was in danger. They loved her. We all did. There also was a young man who worked for us as a night watchman – he also was in danger. These two people put a very human face on the Tutsi people of Rwanda for us. Having them with us in our home kept our hearts engaged in our decision for me to stay, preventing logic or fear from dominating our thoughts.

It's amazing how the physical presence of a person can change the outcome of a situation. Sometimes simply "being there" is often the most powerful factor in making the right decision, a decision we will not regret the rest of our lives. The presence of Anita and that young man impacted our thinking and kept me in Rwanda. The power of presence. It is something I am learning about more and more every day.

Rittner: OK, so you stayed, but what about Teresa and your kids?

Wilkens: After much prayer and talking with each other, Teresa and I made the decision that I would stay and she would evacuate with the kids and with my mom and dad. They were visiting us in Rwanda and got caught in the violence. Great timing, huh? My dad was helping us to rebuild health centers that had been destroyed in the three-year war before the genocide. We also were getting ready to move about a million displaced people back into their homes around the same time as when the violence broke out. When we decided that everyone but me would go in the evacuation organized by the American embassy, my dad drove the camper we had. The trip was difficult and frightening at times, but they got out okay to Burundi, then flew to Nairobi where Teresa and the kids stayed until we were reunited when the genocide ended three long months later.

Rittner: Did you have any contact with your family after they left? They must have been worried out of their minds about you, particularly if they were watching the news on BBC Television, or some other international station. I remember seeing horrible images coming out of Rwanda during April, May, and June 1994.

Wilkens: Every day Teresa would get someone to watch the kids, and she would walk or catch a ride to either the American embassy in downtown Nairobi or to one of the humanitarian aid organizations we knew. There she would get access to a short-wave radio – I had one in our house in Kigali – and every single day I would hear her sweet voice. My call number was 76 and hers was *Tango Whiskey* – her initials, *TW*, in radio talk. Sometimes we would talk for hours. She would talk as if she had nothing else to worry about. Her? In her situation? Literally, a single mom in a strange country with three kids, helping them to do their homework, doing laundry in the bathtub – nothing to worry about? But there she was, giving me this incredible sense of support and love. What an amazing gift it is when you have someone to stand with you. Teresa did just that.

When we said goodbye in Kigali, I told her, "Two weeks, Love, this thing can't last more than two weeks." But I was so wrong. As it dragged on, Teresa was with me, supporting me all the way. She was rock solid. Can't imagine having done this without her. I have found that on those days when we seem to weaken physically, our beliefs help to reinforce our actions.

After three weeks of being stuck in my home under 24/7 curfew, we heard via the local radio that the colonel who was now in charge of the city was announcing that the curfew restrictions were being loosened and if someone had a legitimate reason to leave their home, they could come to his office for a travel permit. So I thought, "OK, I am going to try to get to his office and get one of those passes and see how I could help those who must be in need around the city."

So I arrived at his office – I won't go into details, except to say that he was shocked I was still in Kigali. After exchanging greetings, I said, "You announced on the radio that all the aid organizations except the Red Cross had left Kigali." I went on to say that as the director of the Adventist Development and Relief Agency, I was still here and I wanted to help those in need. Long story short, he gave me travel papers and directed me to two orphanages that were in desperate, desperate need of help.

As I started moving around the city, I soon learned I was the only American, along with nine Europeans who had stayed in the portion of the city controlled by the Hutu extremists. But not long ago, I discovered I *wasn't* the only American who stayed in Rwanda. Three guesses who else stayed. Two American Sisters stayed in the southwest of the country to help. I found this out a few weeks ago. Those Sisters are now living in Texas. Boy, would I love to meet them! In Rwanda, those Sisters were Jesus with skin on to the people around them.

Last evening when Rabbi Greenberg spoke, he said that any religion – he didn't care which one – that has a way of labeling people, of making some people second-class – watch out! When religion *minimizes* the other – that's big trouble, very big trouble. I couldn't agree more. As far as I'm concerned, religion needs to be about connecting us with our Maker and our neighbor. If these two things are not largely evident, there is a serious problem; something isn't right. Religion is about loving God and loving our neighbor, not about classifying or minimizing anyone. Let me also just say a word about people, particularly people we think may be despicable because of what they have done.

Some years after the genocide, the colonel who was in charge of Kigali was convicted of genocide, mass atrocities, and inciting mass rape. This is the very same person who directed me to help people at the orphanage I told you about a little earlier. He did terrible things while he was "in power," and he should be held accountable, but amazingly, he was the one who told me about the orphans and that they needed help. There were other people I also met who helped me in 1994. Some did terrible things, but I had to negotiate with them so that I could get fuel for my truck, powdered milk, which they probably had stolen from somewhere, for the kids, and other things. I guess what I was trying to do was build relationships with people, relationships just as important as the ones Teresa and I and our children formed with our neighbors before the genocide started.

I can't stress enough about building relationships with people – that's the key. In any crisis, that's what we have to do. We have to look for allies to help us to do what we have to do. If we write off certain people because we think they are blood-thirsty killers, heartless savages, monsters – if we write off such people, we may miss some of our best allies for a certain time. Why? Because I honestly believe that as long as somebody is breathing, they have the potential to make just one decent choice. And today could be that day for a decent choice. I have to believe that, particularly when I'm in a terrible situation and need someone's help, even help from someone who may be less than honorable.

Rittner: Can you tell us more about the orphanage, what was happening, what you had to do, how you did it?

Wilkens: Yes, it was something else, incredible. Damas, a Rwandan man, was operating Gisimba orphanage. It had been started by his grandfather. Damas and the 80 orphans never had much. Now they had even less, and add to this that when the genocide started, people were looking for a safe place for their kids. The churches were not safe places, the government offices were not safe places, but this man's orphanage somehow became a safe place, a refuge. But he had to make hard decisions – and he did. He often had to tell parents, "I'll take your kids, but I'm sorry, you can't stay here." He believed this was his best chance at saving the children. But he couldn't always say no, so by the time the whole thing was over, he ended up with more than 40 widows there. And his 80 orphans grew to more than 400 kids before the killing stopped. All of them were desperate for safety, for food, water, and medicine.

The PBS documentary *Ghosts of Rwanda* tells part of the story, but not everything. Each day I would arrive at the orphanage with a truckload of water – clean water, such a simple thing, but without it children were dying. People there were living under constant threat.

Finally the day came that Damas was sure would be their last day. The *Interahamwe* had come the day before and told everyone to evacuate. They said they were coming back the next day, and they would kill all who remained. They said it didn't matter if they were Hutu or Tutsi. Anyone still there would be killed. Damas had left, desperately searching to find help.

Hardly a minute or two after I arrived that day with water, about 50 young Hutu militia men with assault weapons, machetes, and clubs began to surround the orphanage, with some of them coming in the main entrance. Most of them were wearing either military fatigue jackets or military pants. They wore bandanas marked with the well-known colors of the CDR (Coalition for the Defense of the Republic, or, in French, *Coalition pour la Défense de la République*, a Hutu power group). When they saw me, they paused. I don't know if it was the hand-held radio I was holding up to my mouth, or if it was just the fact that I was a white foreigner, but they stopped trying to come in. Instead, they moved toward the perimeter and stood with others, some of them defiantly. Others made a feeble effort at hiding.

A few minutes later, a dark green Mercedes station wagon came ripping into the parking lot, and a guy gets out dressed in full military uniform. He was the local head of the Hutu militia, which he ran like his own private army, and I'm thinking, "This is the guy who stole one of our vehicles, and I had to hunt him down trying to get it back." I called Philippe [Gaillard] at the Red Cross on the radio to tell him that we were surrounded by militia and about to be killed. Could he send someone to help us?

Somehow Philippe managed to get seven policemen to come to us. Now some police in Rwanda saved people and others slaughtered people. You just didn't know who to trust. Anyhow, when these police arrived, there was an officer with them. As he sized up the situation, I took a chance and said to him, "Thank you for coming, Lieutenant. Please, can you and your men spend the night here with the orphans?" After looking around again, he says, "No, no, we are outnumbered. We need reinforcements. You go talk to my commander to see if we can get more men." And I'm thinking to myself, "Is he just wanting to get rid of me so they can do a massacre?" Honestly, I didn't know what to do. Then, a young man at the orphanage says, "No, no, please don't leave. As soon as you leave, they'll just slaughter us all." And he starts to cry. I was so torn up. If I left, was it just to save my own skin; would I hear shooting as soon as I drove out, or could I trust this lieutenant guy? If I stayed, will the power of my presence continue to keep the killers back?

As many of you know from the film, *Ghosts of Rwanda*, I did trust that guy. A massacre did not happen. Somehow I was actually able to get to the Prime Minister, one of three persons in charge of the genocide, and talk to him. Don't ask me how this happened, but I was able to get him to help me, to help us at the orphanage. Literally, the Prime Minister stopped a massacre from happening there. And two days later, these orphans were moved by bus from the section of the city where they were to another area where they were a bit safer.

Rittner: Let me shift our focus and ask you a question about Christianity in Rwanda. I realize, of course, that you can only give your impression, your opinion, but nevertheless, here's the question, the issue: Rwanda, tiny country though it is, in 1994 was one of the most Christian-churched countries in all of Africa. What happened? What went wrong? Where did Christianity fail?

Wilkens: Oh, great questions: What went wrong? Where did Christianity fail? Let me go back to what I said earlier: When religion is used to separate people, to drive a wedge between them, something is wrong. When you have a church community in which you have an "us" and a "them," something is wrong. When that happens, we are modeling some of the worst things we could ever model.

For me, the genocide stemmed from the kind of thinking that says, "My world would be better without you in it." Unfortunately, this kind of exclusive thinking based on false notions about ethnic identity was present in the Christian churches – all of them, not just the Catholic Church, not just in the Seventh Day Adventist Church, but in just about any church you could name in Rwanda before and during my time in that beautiful, sad country. That kind of thinking is wrong. It certainly is not thinking like a Christian should be thinking. A Christian should be trying to find ways to include people, not separate people into "us" and "them." Unfortunately, too many baptized people thought that way, and too many pastors and priests and teachers reinforced that kind of thinking. It's something we have to address and do something about.

Rittner: Many people who will read this interview with you are going to be teachers, most of whom will teach about the Holocaust, but increasingly they also are teaching about other genocides as well – Armenia, Cambodia, former Yugoslavia, Rwanda, not to mention also terrible events like the Rape of Nanking, *gendercide* in Guatemala, using rape as a weapon of war in places like Congo. Do you have any final thoughts you would like to share with them?

Wilkens: Wow! That's heavy, but, okay, here are three thoughts. First, keep studying about these places and these issues. There are people who know a lot more than I do, and it's important to learn from them. The book you and John did, *Rape: Weapon of War and Genocide* – I have an essay in it, as you know – is one book with incredible essays and information about things teachers need to know if they are going to teach about genocide.

The second thing is the power of stories. Listen to what people have to say. Remember what they have to say. Pay attention to your own experiences. Share these stories with others, with each other. Stories are incredibly powerful. They can bring people together. So listen to and share stories.

Finally, the third thing: questions. Help people to ask questions. Ask your own questions. When people think you have all the answers to really complicated situations, issues, they'll stop listening to you, and that includes students. They will stop listening, but if you ask questions that make people think, that get them involved in discussion with you and each other, I think that helps – helps to bring people together to talk, to think, to share. I think there is nothing quite like a good question to get someone's attention, to get students' attention, to get our own attention.

I wish I could say I know how to prevent genocide. I don't. All I know is that we have to do what we can where we are everyday. I don't know if it will prevent genocide, but I really, really believe it will help us to make a difference for a few people, maybe even for many people.

Rittner: Thank you.

Questions

1. *What is genocide? How does it happen? Why does it happen?*

2. *What role does religion play in society? In what ways can it be a force for good? In what ways can it be a force for destruction? What, if anything, can we do to ameliorate religion's potential for negative effects in society?*

3. *What does Carl Wilkens mean by "the power of stories?" Can you give any concrete examples from your own experience about how telling a story can be powerful, both negatively powerful and positively powerful?*

4. *What does Carl Wilkens mean by "the power of presence?" How can just "being there" be helpful in a crisis?*

5. *Why are questions sometimes more important than answers?*

Bibliography

Barnett, Michael. *Eyewitness to a Genocide: The United Nations and Rwanda*. Ithaca, NY: Cornell University Press, 2002.

Gourevitch, Philip. *We Wish to Inform You that Tomorrow We Will Be Killed with Our Families: Stories from Rwanda*. New York: Picador, 1998.

Hatzfeld, Jean. *Machete Season: The Killers in Rwanda Speak*. New York: Picador, 2005.

Power, Samantha. *"A Problem from Hell": America and the Age of Genocide*. New York: Basic Books, 2002.

Rittner, Carol, John K. Roth, and Wendy Whitworth, eds. *Genocide in Rwanda: Complicity of the Churches*. St. Paul, MN: Aegis, in association with Paragon House, 2004.

Rittner, Carol and John K. Roth, eds. *Rape: Weapon of War & Genocide*. St. Paul, MN: Paragon House, 2012.

Totten, Samuel and William S. Parsons, eds. *Centuries of Genocide: Essays and Eyewitness Accounts*. 4th ed. New York: Routledge, 2013.

Wilkens, Carl. *I'm Not Leaving*. Spokane, WA: World Outside My Shoes, 2011.

Genocide in Rwanda:
Introductory Comments for
Ghosts of Rwanda

■ ■ ■ ■ ■ ■ ■ ■ ■

Carol Rittner, R.S.M.

Distinguished Professor of Holocaust & Genocide Studies and
Dr. Marsha Radicoff Grossman Professor of Holocaust Studies,
The Richard Stockton College of New Jersey, Galloway, NJ

T. S. Eliot once wrote that "April is the cruelest month."[1] It certainly was true for Rwanda, where, on April 6, 1994, a genocide began that did not end until nearly a million people were dead. Many deaths, although not all, took place in that terrible month of April, "the month that would not end."

> Although the genocide in Rwanda of the Tutsis by the Hutu Power movement took place in a post-Holocaust world that had loudly declared: Never again, its progress can be looked at in stages of destruction similar to those defined by Raul Hilberg for the Holocaust: registration of victims, organized indoctrination of killing squads, systematic use of media, mobilization of armed groups, and escalation of violence. Moreover, the genocide of the Tutsis in Rwanda not only resembles that of the Jews in Nazi Germany but is thought by some to have been influenced directly by it.[2]

When the genocide ended and troops of the Rwandan Patriotic Front (RPF) searched President Juvénal Habyarimana's residence, they found a movie version of Hitler's *Mein Kampf*, plus other evidence that Habyarimana and his circle were likely admirers of Adolf Hitler. Philip Gourevitch, grandson of Holocaust survivors and author of *We Wish to Inform You That Tomorrow We Will Be Killed with Our Families* (Picador, 1999), put a human face on the genocide in Rwanda with that book. He also suggests the Hitler connection, as do others like the late Alison Des Forges in *Leave None to Tell the Story: Genocide in Rwanda* (Human Rights Watch, 1999).

Genocide

The 1948 United Nations Convention on the Prevention of Genocide states that genocide is "[a series of] acts committed with intent to destroy, in whole or in part, a national, ethnical, racial, or religious group." Genocide never happens by chance. It is always planned, deliberate, calculated. Nowhere was this more true than in Rwanda between April and July 1994, when thousands of hate-inspired Hutu extremists carried out a well-organized campaign of killing that left more than 800,000 of their countrymen and women dead. Most of those mutilated and killed during those 100 days of blood and mayhem were members of the minority Tutsi ethnic group. The rest were moderate Hutus who advocated peaceful co-existence with their Tutsi neighbors.

There are many books and reports one can read to fill in details about the 1994 genocide in Rwanda. The film *Ghosts of Rwanda* does not pretend to be a thorough history or analysis of that awful time not so very long ago, but it is filled with insights. Like all genocides, "the Rwandan whole is a prism with many sides, a study in which the forces of resistance, of international attitudes, of complicity of bystanders, and of the ultimate denials or rationales reflect coldly on one another, but do not let us penetrate deep inside."[3] Still, there are some things one should consider while viewing the film, keeping in mind that what lies at the heart of *Ghosts of Rwanda* is an effort by the filmmaker (Greg Barker) to penetrate the prism, to comprehend the evil thinking that led, and perhaps still leads, to the extermination of a people.

Context

Before World War I, Rwanda was a German colony. After World War I and Germany's defeat by the Allies, the League of Nations "awarded" Rwanda to the Belgians to administer. The Roman Catholic Church, powerfully involved in the life and culture of Belgium's people and government, sent missionaries – priests and nuns – to Rwanda to establish schools, clinics, hospitals, and other social services, and, of course, to establish churches and preach the Christian gospel to the native people. Suffice it to say that through its various institutions, the Roman Catholic Church became intimately involved in the life of the Rwandan people and in the colonial government, if not directly as appointed civil servants, then indirectly as advisers to many of the colonial government people and agencies. In short, the Catholic Church worked "hand-in-glove" with the colonial power, reinforcing many of its policies and practices.

While we usually think of Rwanda as largely composed of two distinct ethnic groups – Hutu and Tusi – until the 20th century, "Hutus" and "Tutsis" did not constitute separate "nations," to use Adam Jones' language.[4] In pre-colonial times, Hutus and Tutsis were viewed as "*social castes*, based on material wealth."[5] The Belgians were the first to rigidly codify Hutu and Tutsi designations, and in a tradition of divide and rule, Tutsis, because they were considered more "European-looking" by their Belgian colonial masters, became the favorites and protégés of the Belgian colonizers.[6] According to Adam Jones, "As was typical of imperial racial theorizing, the mark of civilization was grafted on to physiognomic differences, with the generally taller, supposedly more refined [thus, European-looking] Tutsi destined to rule, and the shorter, allegedly less refined Hutus [destined] to serve."[7] Consequently, in everything from educational opportunities to positions in the colonial civil governmental structures, as well as in the Roman Catholic Church's missionary structures, Tutsis were favored and Hutus were ignored. All of this occurred in a country where the "European"-looking Tutsis constituted about 12% of the population and the less "European"-looking Hutus constituted about 85% of the population, with the Twa [aka "pygmies"] constituting about 3% of the population.

One can only imagine the outright resentment and anger of the majority Hutu, who endured decades of discrimination at the hands of their Belgian colonizers, including Catholic Church leaders, and their fellow Tutsi countrymen and women. This widespread discrimination continued until Rwanda was given its independence as a sovereign country by Belgium in 1962, at which time the tables were reversed and the Tutsis became systematically discriminated against and periodically subjected to waves of killing and ethnic cleansing at the hands of the Hutu ethnic majority.

Tutsi refugees fled into neighboring countries. In 1987, Tutsi exiles in Uganda formed the Rwandan Patriotic Front (RPF). In 1990, the RPF launched an invasion of Rwanda, which ultimately contributed to increasing tension and conflict within the nation. The Hutu-dominated government adopted extreme measures to deal with the conflict, thus exacerbating the tension between the two groups. The RPF military invasion compounded an already fragile economic situation and living conditions worsened dramatically for ordinary people, Hutu and Tutsi alike. The RPF invasion, with its abuses and atrocities against Hutu civilians, contributed to a growing climate of fear among ordinary Hutus who were only too willing to be organized into armed militia groups, including the so-called *interahamwe*,[8] a flamboyant Hutu youth militia that gained enormous popularity in the wake of the invasion and subsequent fighting in the early 1990s.

The decisive event that marked the beginning of the genocide of the Tutsis occurred the night of April 6, 1994, when a plane carrying Rwandan President Juvénal Habyarimana, Burundian President Cyprien Ntariyamira, and other government officials returning from United Nations-brokered peace negotiations in Tanzania was shot out of the sky as it approached Kigali airport. To this day, it is not clear who exactly fired the missile that hit the airplane. Adam Jones writes that it was "either

Hutu Power[9] or RPF elements anxious to scuttle the Arusha[10] peace process."[11] Whoever it was, within moments of the crash, members of Habyarimana's Presidential Guard and militia groups began to set up roadblocks around the city of Kigali, the capital of Rwanda, and widespread massacres of Tutsis, political opposition leaders, and moderate Hutus began. This violence would not end until July 1994, when the RPF secured overall control of Rwanda, thus putting an end to the violence.

Of course, there is so much more that one could say about the 1994 genocide in Rwanda, but rather than go into more detail here, I would like to draw your attention to a few resources on the web that you can consult to inform your knowledge about the Rwandan genocide.

Web Resources

The website developed at the time *Ghosts of Rwanda* was originally shown on PBS (Public Broadcasting System) is a treasure trove of information.[12] Among other resources, there is a viewer's guide, a teacher's guide, and interviews with some of the principals who were in the American government and the United Nations at the time of the genocide. There are also interviews with, among others, Canadian General (now retired) Roméo Dallaire, who was the head of UNAMIR, the UN peacekeeping force in Rwanda in 1994; the head of the Red Cross Mission in Rwanda, Philippe Galliard; and Carl Wilkens, the only American as far as we know to remain in Rwanda throughout the genocide. The PBS website is an excellent source of information about both the film and the 1994 genocide.

Another good resource on the web is the United States Holocaust Memorial Museum's website, specifically the section of their site devoted to the "Committee on Conscience."[13] This is an excellent source of information about Rwanda, both during the genocide and after. There are podcasts about the genocide, videos, transcripts of lectures, and other helpful information. It is a particularly good site for teachers and students.

A third site you should explore is that of Aegis, a non-governmental genocide prevention organization in the United Kingdom. Aegis was started by the Smith brothers, Stephen and James, to complement the important work on the Holocaust they have done through the Holocaust Center they started in Nottinghamshire, UK. The Aegis website is http://www.aegistrust.org. There you can find all sorts of resources, including films, book titles, interviews with genocide survivors, photographs, suggestions for taking action when it comes to genocide prevention, and links to the Rwandan genocide memorial site in Kigali.

Controversies

It is only fair to mention that some controversies have arisen in the years since the 1994 genocide in Rwanda. While I do not want to suggest which side is right or wrong, I do want to draw your attention to a few of these controversies:

1. There are those who say that "Never Again!" as far as Rwandan President Paul Kagame[14] is concerned means that *never again* will Hutus achieve dominance in Rwanda politics. Thus, there is more than a little criticism of the current Rwandan government's human rights record.

2. Before her untimely death in 2009, Alison Des Forges, the well-respected genocide investigator who was a specialist on the Great Lakes Region of Africa and who wrote the monumental study about the Rwandan genocide for Human Rights Watch, *Leave None to Tell the Story*, was no longer welcome in post-genocide Rwanda. According to Des Forges' supporters, this was because she was extremely critical of the human rights record of the post-genocide government headed by former RPF General Paul Kagame.

3. There is criticism of the United Nations-established International Criminal Tribunal for Rwanda (ICTR) because it has only indicted alleged perpetrators of the genocide and has refused to launch any investigations into post-1994 Rwandan leaders who are alleged to have been involved in RPF-inflicted atrocities against Hutus in Rwanda and Eastern Congo.

Again, there is much more one could say about Rwanda and its sad recent history. The film *Ghosts of Rwanda* can serve as a starting point for teachers and students to delve more deeply into the 1994 genocide, even though it is now nearly ten years old. New research about perpetrators, victims, bystanders, and rescuers has since come to light and is available in books and journals. Still, *Ghosts of Rwanda* remains an important film resource to use with students when teaching about the 1994 genocide in Rwanda.

Questions

1. *What does "Never Again!" mean? Is it meant for some people but not for others? Explain your answer.*

2. *Can one hold Belgium "responsible" for the genocide in Rwanda in 1994? Explain your answer, providing evidence as well as rationale to support your position. What about the Roman Catholic Church? Should it be held "responsible" for the 1994 genocide? Explain. What about the United Nations? Does it share responsibility for what happened in Rwanda in 1994?*

> 3. Select two or three of the people interviewed for the film (e.g., General Dallaire, Laura Lane, Philippe Gaillard, UN Secretary General Kofi Annan, Carl Wilkens, or President Paul Kagame). What "role" did they play during the genocide? Do you admire them or not? Why?

Bibliography

Fujii, Lee Ann. *Killing Neighbors: Webs of Violence in Rwanda*. Ithaca, NY: Cornell University Press, 2009.

Longman, Timothy. *Christianity and Genocide in Rwanda*. New York: Cambridge University Press, 2010.

Melvern, Linda. *A People Betrayed: The Role of the West in Rwanda's Genocide*. London, UK: Zed, 2000.

Power, Samantha. *"A Problem from Hell": America and the Age of Genocide*. New York: Basic Books, 2002.

Rittner, Carol, John K. Roth, and Wendy Whitworth, eds. *Genocide in Rwanda: Complicity of the Churches?* St. Paul, MN: Paragon House, 2004.

Semelin, Jacques, Claire Andrieu, and Sarah Gensburger, eds. *Resisting Genocide: The Multiple Forms of Rescue*. New York: Columbia University Press, 2011.

Notes

1. See further, line 1 of T. S. Eliot's poem, "The Wasteland," written in 1922.
2. Helmut Walser Smith, ed. *The Holocaust and Other Genocides: History, Representation, Ethics* (Nashville, TN: Vanderbilt University Press, 2002), p. 201.
3. Ibid, pp. 201-202.
4. Adam Jones, *Genocide: A Comprehensive Introduction*, 2nd ed. (New York: Routledge, 2011), p. 348.
5. Ibid.
6. Ibid, p. 349.
7. Ibid.
8. Ibid, pp. 350-51.
9. Editor's note: Hutu Power was a violence-prone ideology advocated by Hutu extremists in Rwanda. This ideology contributed to the genocide against moderate Hutus and the Tutsi minority group in Rwanda in 1994.
10. Editor's note: In August 1993, the United Nations helped negotiate what became known as the Arusha Peace Accords (because they were negotiated in Arusha, a city in northern Tanzania), which put an end to hostilities and provided for a power-sharing agreement among the various major political and armed factions in Rwanda.
11. Jones, p. 352.
12. See further, http://www.pbs.org/wgbh/pages/frontline/shows/ghosts/.
13. See further, http://www.ushmm.org/genocide/.
14. Editor's note: Paul Kagame, an ethnic Tutsi, was born in southern Rwanda and as a two-year-old had to flee with his parents into Uganda after the Hutu revolution of the late 1950s and early 1960s overturned Tutsi dominance in Rwanda. He spent his childhood and early adulthood as a refugee in Uganda. He was the commanding general of the Rwandan Patriotic Front at the time of the 1994 genocide and is now president of Rwanda.
15. See further, Jones, pp. 360-362.

The Sheen, *1995 by Samuel Bak*
Image Courtesy of Pucker Gallery

PART IV:
THE ETHEL LEFRAK
OUTSTANDING
STUDENT SCHOLAR
ESSAYS

The Ethel LeFrak Outstanding Student Scholar of the Holocaust Award

National Catholic Center for Holocaust Education (NCCHE) benefactor Ethel LeFrak created *The Ethel LeFrak Outstanding Student Scholar of the Holocaust Award* to recognize the Seton Hill University student who writes a reflection paper that best demonstrates an advanced understanding of the lessons of the Holocaust.

The director(s) of the National Catholic Center for Holocaust Education and faculty teaching in Seton Hill University's Genocide and Holocaust Studies Program select the winning paper for this annual award, begun in 2009.

All students selected to receive the award have their papers included in the proceedings of The Ethel LeFrak Holocaust Education Conference, which are published on a triennial basis. Additional recognition includes a $1,000 award presented during a NCCHE-sponsored event and publication of an excerpt in the *Setonian*, Seton Hill's student newspaper.

Picturing a Better Future: Dehumanization in Advertising and the Role of Media Literacy in Holocaust Education

■ ■ ■ ■ ■ ■ ■ ■ ■ ■ ■

Josie L. Rush

Recipient of the 2011 Ethel LeFrak Outstanding Student Scholar of the Holocaust Award

Over the centuries, genocide has remained one of the most tragic and baffling problems of humanity. Despite advances in modern culture, we have had to make the promise of "Never Again" again and again. Scholars scramble for answers to what is perhaps humanity's deadliest question: Why can't we stop genocide? In an effort to deconstruct the progress of genocide, Gregory Stanton, president of Genocide Watch, suggests there are eight stages that encompass the process. Stanton acknowledges that "the process is not linear," but, despite the complexity of the crime, "at each stage, preventative measures can stop it."[1] The eight steps Stanton lists include classification, symbolization, dehumanization, organization, polarization, preparation, extermination, and denial.

While Americans often feel safe from the threat of genocide in their democratic country, the United States is not unfamiliar with several of the steps of genocide. In fact, dehumanization is prevalent throughout American society today, especially in advertisements. Because dehumanization is so common in advertising, Americans often become desensitized to one of the key steps of genocide; thus, they have difficulty both noticing and exerting concern when this step occurs in other cultures. In order to circumvent this problem, media literacy must become an integral part of genocide studies.

The Role of Dehumanization in Genocide and Propaganda

Along with the many other questions genocide provokes, one of the most common refrains remains, "How is this possible?" Indeed, the human mind shies away from numbers like six million killed or 800,000 murders in 100 days, even while we know that just because our minds cannot comprehend the reality of a number does not mean the number is false. Still, we circle back to questions like "Why?" and "How?" Sometimes our answers lead us somewhere: "How is it possible for people to kill other people on such a massive scale? The answer seems to be that it is not possible, at least not as long as the potential victims are perceived as people."[2] Chalk and Jonassohn's conclusion leads us back to Stanton's suggestion that dehumanization is a necessary step to committing genocide. After all, what harm is there in killing an *inyenzi*, or cockroach?[3] When anti-Tutsi propaganda flooded the Rwandan radios, the dehumanization of the Tutsis was no more accidental than when antisemitic propaganda had infiltrated German society. In order for genocide to be successful, an authority needs, at the very most, perpetrators, and at the very least, bystanders. If people are to take on either of these roles, they must view themselves as acting for the greater good, as cleansing their nation. Very often, such a conception requires the victims to be viewed as not only guilty, but also subhuman. So, while dehumanization is not the only step to committing genocide, it is a necessary and frightening part of the process.

In order for society to help stop this process in its tracks, we must reawaken our disgust for the practice of dehumanization, as well as our horror at genocide itself. It is neither novel nor controversial to say that advertisements, movies, video games, and television shows have helped desensitize people to death and violence. Yet, we must realize the compounded risk of "turning the Holocaust into a footnote of history" when considering both desensitization to violence and the passage of time. Vogel expresses explicit concern for Holocaust remembrance, stating, "Consider how sitcoms are now using references to Hitler to get a quick laugh or how often you have heard someone sarcastically called a 'Nazi' for following rules too stringently."[5] Clearly an emotional revitalization is necessary, and we must go through the uncomfortable process of not only allowing ourselves to be appalled by what we learn, but by showing ways in which genocide is relevant to the world today.

Connecting past genocides and the steps that lead to genocide to our lives today may prove difficult, as "it has become our firm belief that the tools of democracy remain our best hope in combating genocide and mass atrocity crimes."[6] Because America seems so safeguarded against genocide, instances of dehumanization do not seem like a matter of great concern, since in the minds of many citizens, these instances will likely not lead down the deadly path to genocide. Yet, any similarities that can be drawn between genocidal perpetrators and ourselves should be cause for alarm, not only because these parallels strengthen the possibility of inhumane action, but also because dehumanization in our own culture may blind us to dehumanization in other cultures. The Nazi regime was infamous for its usage of propaganda and the effectiveness of its "advertising" strategies. A concrete definition of "propaganda" has remained elusive throughout the centuries, but this essay shall function under the acceptance of Aristotle A. Kallis's definition, as quoted in *State of Deception: The Power of Nazi Propaganda*. According to Kallis, propaganda is "a systematic process of information management geared to promoting a particular goal and to guaranteeing a popular response as desired by the propagandist."[7]

Figure 1:
Poster, Der Ewige Jude
[The Eternal Jew], 1937; Hans
Stalüter, designer; Kunst im Druck,
Munich, printer; Offset color
lithograph; 33 1/8 x 23 5/8 inches
(84.1 x 60.0 centimeters).
Published with the permission of
The Wolfsonian—Florida
International University, Miami
Beach, Florida from The Mitchell
Wolfson, Jr. Collection, Accession
number XX1990.3107.
Photo by Silvia Ros.

Nazi Propaganda: The Eternal Jew

For the Nazis, propaganda remained a valuable tool in subconsciously preparing Germans for genocide and covering the tracks of the genocidal perpetrators with alleged good intentions. Prior to the implementation of overtly antisemitic legislation, "propaganda campaigns created an atmosphere tolerant of violence against Jews."[8] During the genocide, "[p]ropaganda also encouraged passivity and acceptance of the impending measures against Jews, as these appeared to depict the Nazi government as stepping in and 'restoring order.'"[9] Genocides cannot occur without a large group of people willing to comply through active participation or passivity, and propaganda's psychological priming helps prepare a nation for murder. Citizens become consumers, and the product is an ideology of hatred.

Propaganda such as *Der Ewige Jude*, or *The Eternal Jew*, a fictional film disguised as a documentary film (also reincarnated as a book and in exhibitions), drew countless German consumers. The film portrayed Jews as dirty, money-hungry people, and the book is comprised entirely of photographs that "generally make the Jews look as unpleasant as possible."[10] Figure 1, an image from *The German Propaganda Archive*, shows an example of an advertisement for the film and exhibition and is also used as a picture in the book. The Jew is shown cradling Russia under his arm, symbolizing the fear that Jews were supporters of Communism, while holding a whip and bloody coins, which portray a stereotypically cruel and greedy Jew. Furthermore, the grotesque appearance of the Jew, who is shaded darkly and has an unkempt beard, makes him frightening no matter what weapons he is brandishing. The menacing, unclean image of the Jew helped emphasize the idea that the Jews were subhuman. Clearly, the man in the picture is not someone a German citizen would want freely walking the streets, and "[a]fter years of being told that Jews were vermin, it became easier for Germans to accept what they would have rejected in 1933."[11] The Jews were portrayed as a threat not only to Germany's potential perfection, but also to the safety and well-being of the nation's citizens.

Dehumanization in American Advertising

The objectives of the Nazi propagandists were obviously different than the objectives of advertisers today. Whereas Nazis used propaganda to pave the way for genocide, advertisers' motives are not so malicious — they generally want to sell a product or support an ideology. However, the definition of propaganda as "a systematic process of information management geared to promoting a particular goal and to guaranteeing a popular response as desired by the propagandist" remains functional for both advertisements and propaganda. Today, the topic of women in advertising receives much attention from feminists and non-feminists alike, as people express concern over what sort of "information management" is being employed in an attempt to sell a product. Jean Kilbourne argues that consumers see so many instances of women being dehumanized, threatened, or objectified in advertising that "[m]ost of us become numb to these images, just as we become numb to the daily litany in the news of women being raped, battered, and killed."[13]

Figure 2: PETA ad featuring Pamela Anderson. Image courtesy of People for the Ethical Treatment of Animals: www.peta.org

Figure 2 is an ad from the website of People for the Ethical Treatment of Animals (PETA) intended to promote vegetarianism. Above a picture of a scantily clad Pamela Anderson is the phrase, "All animals have the same parts," words that clearly categorize Anderson as an animal. Anderson's body is labeled so that parts like "breasts," "ribs," and "rump" do not escape the viewers' notice. In this example of advertising, an organization attempts to sell an ideology to consumers. While PETA's goal may have been to draw in consumers with an alluring image of a beautiful woman and to remind consumers of the connections between animals and people, the phrase on top of the ad likening women to animals, along with the overly sexualized picture of Pamela Anderson, manages to devalue an entire gender. The unnecessary lack of clothing in figure 2 probably does not shock readers who are familiar with the advertising industry. However, while we may have grown accustomed to the onslaught of sexualized and objectified images of both men and women in the media, we must not grow complacent: "Sex in advertising is pornographic because it dehumanizes and objectifies people."[14] When a person is conveyed as a sexual entity, the person pictured becomes an object to be used for pleasure, not a person.

Problems Connected to Advertising

Advertising has been blamed for several tragic trends in the United States, from domestic violence to rape to eating disorders. In "Dehumanizing Women in Advertising," Kristen Tsetsi suggests the rise in female human trafficking victims in the US is partially due to the fact that "females have come to be considered a viable, and apparently an even somewhat palatable, commodity, particularly in the United States."[15] She states that while the cause of such disregard for human life is complex, advertising inarguably plays a major role in the issue of slavery in a nation known for freedom. Scott A. Lukas, chairman of anthropology at Lake Tahoe Community College, agrees, stating,

> [Objectification and dehumanization] say, "This person is different from us, this person is less than us, so we can do what we want to them." There's a movement toward something that leads to breaking down personal barriers that would normally prevent them from doing something wrong.[16]

The question then becomes, if we cannot care about dehumanization in our own culture, how can we care about dehumanization as it occurs in other cultures? Through our own culture's advertising, we often see strategies that should be horrific to us because they can lead down a dark and dangerous path, but instead of fear, we look at these advertisements with apathy.

The Role of Media Literacy in Holocaust Education

The role of technology in education has not escaped the notice of Holocaust and genocide educators. Irene Ann Resenly points out that "teachers and scholars have an unprecedented amount of resources available to them."[17] More technology means more exposure, and more exposure is a double-edged sword. While students are blessed with media like video testimonials of survivors and nearly ubiquitous access to websites for organizations like Genocide Watch and Amnesty International, students also have fewer moments away from the assault of dehumanization in advertising. The more often students are exposed to instances of dehumanization without being educated to combat both the stated and unstated ideologies being sold, the less likely they are to profess outrage. Luckily, Holocaust educators like Resenly are aware of the necessity to "teach students to think critically and *incorporate their life experiences in the classroom*" (emphasis mine).[18] What is more prevalent in the average American student's life than the media?

Implementing media literacy into genocide education will not be a difficult task, as Nazi propaganda is widely recognized for its effectiveness in helping to bring about the near-extermination of the Jews. Having students analyze propaganda like *The*

Protocols of the Elders of Zion, which was "a primary weapon used by the Nazi propaganda machine in winning over the German people's support for, or at least apathy towards, their answer to the 'Jewish question,'"[19] will allow students to see firsthand the strategies of Nazi propagandists. Adding examples of contemporary advertising will force students to look for parallels between the media. For example, the following question could be posed to a classroom: "The Nazis built on pre-existing prejudice towards the Jews. What pre-existing prejudice does this advertisement exacerbate?" If the students are analyzing Figure 2, for instance, they may suggest that the advertisers are playing on the belief that women are primarily sexual beings who function principally as sexual objects. Students should be aware of the unstated ideologies being sold by companies and ask themselves questions about the images they see instead of merely accepting dehumanization in any culture.

Conclusion

Genocide education should arm students against apathy and reawaken their concern for their fellow human beings. Warnings against objectification and dehumanization in the media have become so commonplace that students often regard them with annoyance, if they regard them at all. However, such disregard carries over to other areas of life as well, and students must allow themselves to be horrified and disgusted by what they see every day. The process of genocide is complex, and humankind's reasons for not stopping such atrocities are many-faceted. Political, psychological, and social explanations for our inability to put an end to genocide remain as tragically true as ever. Desensitization to dehumanization is one small factor in the question of why we cannot seem to stop genocide. But this answer presents a problem every person can begin correcting immediately. Returning to the idea of questions of genocide, one of the most important questions genocide provokes is, "What can I do?" While genocide will not be halted by the mere recognition of dehumanization, recognition awakens compassion, and compassion leads to positive action. In order to stop genocide in our time, we must reestablish the value of human life and not take such gifts for granted in any form.

Questions

1. *What is propaganda? How did the Nazis use it to support their "war against the Jews" during the Nazi era, World War II, and the Holocaust? Give some examples to support your position.*

2. *What is meant by "dehumanization"? Give some examples of how people – men, women, and children – were dehumanized during the Holocaust, the genocide in Rwanda, and another genocide or genocidal event about which you have studied.*

> 3. *Is all propaganda dehumanizing? Can propaganda ever be used to humanize or re-humanize people? How can one discern the difference between "dehumanizing" propaganda and "humanizing" propaganda? Give examples to support your position.*

Bibliography

Barnett, Victoria J. *Bystanders – Conscience and Complicity during the Holocaust*. New York: Greenwood Press, 1999.

Bartov, Omer. *The "Jew" in Cinema: From The Golem to Don't Touch My Holocaust*. Indianapolis: Bloomington University Press, 2005.

Haggith, Toby and Joanna Newman, eds. *Holocaust and the Moving Image: Representations in Film and Television since 1933*. New York: Wallflower Press, 2005.

Insdorf, Annette. *Indelible Shadows: Film and the Holocaust*. New York: Cambridge University Press, 2003.

Steinfeldt, Irena. *How Was It Humanly Possible? A Study of Perpetrators and Bystanders during the Holocaust*. Yad Vashem, 2002.

Switzer, Ellen. *How Democracy Failed*. New York: Atheneum, 1975.

Notes

1. Gregory Stanton, "The 8 Stages of Genocide," *Genocide Watch: The International Alliance to End Genocide* (1998).
2. Frank Chalk and Kurt Jonassohn, *The History and Sociology of Genocide: Analyses and Case Studies* (New Haven, CT: Yale University Press, 1990), pp. 27-28.
3. Fergal Keane, *Season of Blood* (London, UK: Penguin Books, 1995), p. 10.
4. Judith A. Vogel, "Children of the Holocaust," *Learn Teach Prevent: Holocaust Education in the 21st Century*, ed. Carol Rittner (Greensburg, PA: Seton Hill University, 2010), p. 171.
5. Ibid.
6. *The Last Survivor: A Genocide Happened Here* (Righteous Pictures, 2011), http://www.thelastsurvivor.com/.
7. Quoted in Susan Bachrach and Steven Luckert, *State of Deception: The Power of Nazi Propaganda* (Washington, DC: W.W. Norton & Company, 2009), p. 2.
8. United States Holocaust Memorial Museum, "Nazi Propaganda," *Holocaust Encyclopedia* (2011). Available at http://www.ushmm.org/wlc/en/article.php?ModuleId=10005202.
9. Ibid.
10. Calvin College, "The Eternal Jew," *German Propaganda Archive* (no date). Retrieved April 20, 2011 at http://www.calvin.edu/academic/cas/gpa/diebow.htm.
11. Ibid.
12. Ibid, http://www.bytwerk.com/gpa/images/diebow/cover.jpg.
13. Jean Kilbourne, "Two Ways a Woman Can Get Hurt," *Rereading America: Cultural Contexts for Critical Thinking and Writing* (New York: Bedford/St. Martin's, 2004), p. 462.
14. Ibid, p. 456.
15. Kristen J. Tsetsi, "Dehumanizing Women in Advertising," in Archived Articles (February 18, 2009). Available at http://tsetsiarchives.blogspot.com/2009/02/dehumanizing-women-in-advertising.html.

16. Quoted in Tetsi.
17. Irene Ann Resenly, "The Historian and the Holocaust: A New Holocaust Curriculum," *Learn Teach Prevent: Holocaust Education in the 21st Century*, ed. Carol Rittner (Greensburg: Seton Hill University, 2010), p. 144.
18. Ibid, p. 145.
19. Michelle Horvath, "Passivity of the 'Ordinary' German: Factors Leading to the Evolution and Implementation of the Final Solution," *Learn Teach Prevent: Holocaust Education in the 21st Century*, ed. Carol Rittner (Greensburg: Seton Hill University, 2010), p. 83.

Understanding the Holocaust through Personal Accounts

. . . .

Katherine Prange

Recipient of the 2012 Ethel LeFrak Outstanding Student Scholar of the Holocaust Award

The Holocaust was the planned extermination of the Jewish population. To understand how a group of people could conceive of the "Final Solution" is almost impossible. However, the Germans left much evidence behind, making it easier to understand how death factories worked and how two-thirds of a religious group perished during World War II. For years, research has focused on those who died; not much was asked of the survivors for many years after the war, and not many volunteered to tell their story.

Survivors' Memoirs

Slowly, though, the survivors of the Holocaust started talking. Abraham Foxman puts it best in his introduction to Jane Marks' book, *The Hidden Children*, when he says, "We came to realize the importance of other people hearing our stories so that they could understand the Holocaust in terms of the living as well as the six million Jews who died."[1] Learning about the Holocaust and the intolerance that led to the murder of six million Jewish people deserves much scrutiny because it could lead to the understanding that is needed in order to prevent further acts of genocide. Fred Spiegel writes about the Holocaust because he believes "[i]t is very important for survivors to bear witness in order to teach children what can happen when bigotry, racism, and antisemitism become the law of the land."[2] Through personal accounts of survivors, we have an insight into the inhumanity that was the Holocaust. Gone are the history books. What we have left are voices to bring the history of the Holocaust alive.

In his preface to the new translation of *Night*, Elie Wiesel says, "I don't know how I survived; I was weak, rather shy; I did nothing to save myself. A miracle? Certainly not. If heaven could or would perform a miracle for me, why not for others more deserving than myself?"[3] With his recounting of events that took place while he was in the concentration camps, Wiesel allows us inside his head and gives us such a personal glimpse into his thinking that, while we were not there with him, we begin to comprehend more fully his suffering.

There is really no way to fully understand or comprehend the events surrounding the Holocaust, however. If one did not witness firsthand the atrocities that took place in concentration camps, ghettos, and hiding places, one cannot truly understand the enormity and scope of the Holocaust: "After all, it deals with an event that sprang from the darkest zone of man. Only those who experienced Auschwitz know what it was. Others will never know."[4] Those who study the Holocaust get a clearer picture of the events, but *true* understanding is granted only to those who suffered at the hands of the Germans. Students of the Holocaust have a responsibility to try and understand enough to keep the stories alive and teach tolerance to younger generations. Most personal accounts of the Holocaust start with what life was like prior to the Germans' plan for the Jewish people; in other words, "[t]he story begins with Jewish children at home with their parents."[5] For most of the survivors, life was "normal." There was a family unit and an order to the day. For some Jewish children, life started to change with the election of Hitler in 1933; for others, a few years passed before they felt the hand of the Germans controlling their every move. Richard Rozen recalls, "We lived a very privileged life in the sense that our family had money, but I didn't get to see much of my father, a doctor who ran a big hospital and had little time to spend at home."[6] Life for him changed very quickly, though. He and his family were soon forced into hiding, where he went from living in a large house to living in a cabinet. From there, he went to live in the forest until the war was over. Leading a normal life was no longer an easy task for Rozen.

While events unfolded a little differently for Fred Spiegel, he writes that his early life included pleasant walks in the park with his grandfather. One of the first changes he noticed was how the park eventually became an unsafe place. What had once been a happy place for him and his grandfather became a place where kids would try to beat him up and friends started cursing his grandpa. He saw his world getting smaller: "Because we were no longer going to school with all the other children, I started to lose contact with many of my former classmates […] most non-Jewish students did not make an effort to stay in touch with us or play with us. We were being separated from the rest of the population."[7]

Who is a Jew?

Whatever circumstances befell the Holocaust's child survivors, their daily lives were greatly affected. Whether they were sent to concentration camps, ghettos, the Kindertransport, or hiding places, they were sent away from their families, their homes, and their lives. The events of the Holocaust began when the Germans first conceived a definition for a Jewish person: "The Nazis defined the Jews on the basis of a concept of race rather than religion."[8] While the mere definition of "a Jew" did not immediately affect the lives of average Jewish people, it served to set them apart from the rest of the population. They were the ones who could "never become part of the Aryan community."[9] New legislation based on this definition created significant changes in Jews' lives. At that point, children were affected by what was "filtered through their parents."[10] Charlotte Levy put it best when she said, "Then what constituted our life began to crumble away [...] The noose around our necks got tighter."[11]

Personal accounts illustrate how slowly and methodically the Nazis sought the extermination of the Jewish population. The new definition led to laws that purposefully isolated Jews from the rest of the population. Children were no longer allowed to go to school with their friends. Whereas before the new laws, some children had only been vaguely aware of their Judaism, the legislation forced many children to become aware of their religion; as Levy pointed out, "Until I was thrown out of high school I was subliminally aware of being Jewish."[12] Ursula Rosenfeld wrote that her family was not very religious, but when "Hitler came into power, we became conscious of our religion."[13] At that point, some Jewish families went into hiding; for them, holding the family unit together was of the utmost importance.

Decisions

It is interesting to learn how decisions were made about which path to take. Kim Fendrick recounts:

> I was so relieved when they agreed that we would take our chances together. [...] Of course the odds were against us. It was stupid for us to think we would survive. But my mother didn't want to be without my father, and I didn't want to be without my parents, so the slim, unlikely chance of surviving was more attractive than being separated.[14]

Levy, on the other hand, chose to send her son on the Kindertransport to England. Her rationale, different from Fendrick's, was to try to get out of Germany as quickly as possible. Levy's husband, recovering from surgery for cancer, had been arrested and they felt that their young son would be safer if he were out of the country. The Levys' decision demonstrates how much despair and turmoil were occurring at the time. As Harris and Oppenheimer point out, "The degree of despair to which you can be driven is best revealed by this reversal of one's normal feelings and principles. To feel happiness about what? About being able to send one's little boy of nine away to a foreign country."[15] Given a glimpse into the mindset of the affected families may lead to an understanding about the origins of their decisions and help create a clearer picture of survivors' lives during the Holocaust.

Life was not easy for those who went into hiding or were sent away on the Kindertransport, either. Many of them felt guilty: "We examined the guilt that continues to haunt us; the pain we felt at losing our loved ones; our anger; our inability to speak of these experiences with our family; our identity crisis; and our confused, frightening, lost childhoods."[16] Many of the hidden children did not believe anyone could fathom a comparison between their suffering and the experiences of those in the concentration camps. However, Leon Ginsburg's story is a testament to the suffering of the hidden children. After his mother was caught by the Germans and stabbed, Ginsburg had to figure out how to stay safe. He felt somewhat safer after finding a home and people who hid him and six other Jews, where he was able to stay for the duration of the war. In losing his family, though, Ginsburg's main goals in life became to remain safe and survive. It took him years to tell his story and open up about his experiences.

Hidden Children

It is clear from reading the hidden children's experiences that they lived with fear every day, just like every other child affected by the Holocaust. These children worried daily that they would be caught by Germans or evicted by the families that had taken them in and hidden them. For many people, Anne Frank's diary is the only first-person account of the Holocaust, but books like *The Hidden Children* also tell young survivors' stories, attempting to paint a bigger picture than Frank could in her diary. While Frank's story is compelling and moving, for many readers it has the air of romance and simplicity that only a child could see in such circumstances. Children's survivor accounts in books like *The Hidden Children* and *Children with a Star* give a more realistic picture of life in occupied Europe. These books teach readers that although hidden Jewish survivors' experiences had some similarities, they were actually quite unique.

The idea that the hidden children felt their ordeal was not as horrendous as that of other survivors is understandable – they did not suffer directly at the hands of the Nazis in the camps. Yet, they did suffer. Some children had to lead double lives by hiding their Jewishness every day. Other hidden children dealt with death on a daily basis: "Those who hid themselves among the partisans were eyewitnesses to the murder of their comrades by the Germans."[17] They, like the children in concentration camps, had to deal with thoughts of their own death every day, as well.

Children like Kristene Keren also faced terrible trials. Keren hid with her family in the sewers for fourteen months, scared every day that they would all be caught. They lived with sickness, rats, and little water or food. Keren never let her past hinder her future, however.[18]

Transports

Transported children also faced challenges. Some children felt abandoned by their parents, not understanding that what their parents were doing was best for them. Children who were transported dealt with leaving parents and family and with the guilt of surviving, especially when so many of their friends and family did not.

Hedy Epstein lives with the guilt of surviving. Epstein's parents decided that sending her to England was the best solution for their family. Since she was young, Epstein did not understand that her parents were doing what they thought was best. Because she was scared, Epstein accused her parents of wanting to send her away. Now, as an adult, she realizes that her parents did the best they could. While in England, Epstein lived with many families. She was lonely, and the families did not always treat her well. At one point, her parents asked her to attempt to get them out of Germany, but since she was so young, Epstein never really pushed the issue. Her parents later died in a concentration camp.[19] Like so many children, even though there was nothing else she could have done, Epstein has lived with the feeling that she could have or should have done more to help her family. Intellectually, she might know that she did not do anything wrong, but the guilt is always there in the back of her mind.

While Epstein and Keren had completely different experiences, both women suffered in their own way. Epstein was without her family, alone in a strange world trying to survive and figure out how to help her parents. Although with her family, Keren struggled to stay alive in the sewers of Germany against all odds. Epstein missed the loving care of her parents but had some semblance of safety. Keren had the love and companionship of her parents but lived in mortal fear of being caught every day.

Ghettos

Other Jewish children who did not go into hiding or on a transport often went to a ghetto. Most children in ghettos had some or all of their families with them, but they, like hidden and transported children, lost their innocence and childhood. While the ghettos were created within existing cities, these segregated areas were vastly different from the cities where most Jewish families had previously lived. According to Dwork in *Children with a Star*, the Warsaw ghetto was like a graveyard. Those who came to the ghetto were a mere shell of their former selves, and they were not allowed to bring money or anything else in with them. Coming to the ghettos after being forced out of their homes, the Jews thought there was some modicum of hope for a future; however, they were sadly mistaken. Whether it was a long- or short-term ghetto, Jewish people were sure of one thing—they did not know how long life in the ghetto would last. What was important for the inhabitants was "that families lived together and familial structure remained intact."[20] Wiesel does not recall his time in the ghetto negatively: "Little by little, life returned to 'normal.' […] We were entirely among ourselves […] People thought this was a good thing. The ghetto was neither ruled by German nor Jew; it was ruled by delusion."[21] While they had an opportunity to hide, the Wiesels chose family and stayed together.

Children in the ghetto were surrounded by family and allowed to play. However, hunger was a constant condition. Starvation was one of the cruelest forms of torture enacted by the Germans. Death was a slow process, and starving Jews had nothing but time to think about what the lack of food was doing to their bodies. Malnutrition meant some children were unable to walk or were impaired in other ways. With most of the food available allocated to other German citizens, Jews received a mere 184 calories a day. According to Dwork, "Hunger and famine were the basic elements of ghetto life. They dictated health."[22] The lack of food caused people to die every day and was dehumanizing to the Jews in the ghettos: "We were so dehumanized, we were so under-the-boot, so obsessed with satisfying this terrible hunger that nothing else mattered really."[23] For some, food was one of the only things to live for in the ghetto. Dwork writes:

> I don't think anything hurts as much as hunger. You become wild. You're not responsible for what you say and what you do. You become an animal in the full meaning of the word. You prey on others. You will steal. That is what hunger does to us. It dehumanizes you. You're not a human being any more.[24]

The lack of food forced elders in many ghettos to ration food. Their rationale for distributing the meager food supplies was based on who, if they lived, could keep the Jewish population alive. It was because of this thinking that the youngest members of the ghetto were given the largest rations.

Smuggling also became a part of daily ghetto life. Living with little or no food forced Jews into illegal activities to obtain something to eat. Large smuggling rings were very profitable for all involved. In order for smuggling rings to be successful, though, many people in the Aryan world had to be paid for their silence and/or cooperation. Martin Gray illustrates the large scale smuggling process in his book, *For Those I Loved*. Gray writes about how he, as a teenager, ran a large, rather profitable smuggling ring in the ghetto where he lived.[25] While his account seems somewhat exaggerated, Gray's narrative accurately portrays how large smuggling rings worked.

From the leader to the bribes, his description of the smuggling ring brings to life the story of how food and nourishment were brought to the ghettos. As Dwork points out, many young people snuck out of the ghetto to steal food for the family, but most of their operations were on a much smaller scale and "not especially lucrative."[26]

Although one commonality in the ghetto was starvation, another more important commonality was hope and faith: "Life wasn't difficult; it was unbearable. Many of us wished just to be finished with it. But there was always this glimmer of hope."[27] For some, hope was the one constant that kept people alive: "Living is hoping, and I kept hoping that somehow, something will happen and the war will end. One just had to be strong enough to wait and I took each day the way it came."[28] These sentiments illustrate the strength and courage that Jews had to possess in order to survive.

Even though Gray's writing describes many negative aspects of the ghetto, his tone is also hopeful. Whenever he was caught by the Germans, he always managed to get away. It was his confidence and positive thinking that allowed him to find the opportunities to escape so many times. But by the time he and his family were put on a cattle car and taken to a concentration camp, Gray used the word "hopeless." Wiesel illustrated what the loss of faith can do to a person:

> Poor Akiba Drumer, if only he could have kept his faith in God, if only he could have considered this suffering a divine test, he would not have been swept away by the selection. But as soon as he felt the first chinks in his faith, he lost all incentive to fight and opened the door to death.[29]

Nazi Concentration Camps

The last stop for most Jewish people who couldn't escape the Nazi death machine was the concentration camps. At the camps, prisoners suffered beatings, starvation, loss of family, and the defeat of any illusions they had about survival. Wiesel writes in *Night*, "The beloved objects that we had carried with us from place to place were now left behind in the wagon and, with them, finally, our illusions."[30] Wiesel's faith was sorely tested at Auschwitz. Upon his arrival at Birkenau, Wiesel writes, "For the first time, I felt anger rising with me. Why should I sanctify His name? The almighty, the eternal and terrible Master of the Universe chose to be silent. What was there to thank him for?"[31] As he recounts his time in the camps, Wiesel shares how much his faith is tested:

> In days gone by [...] I fully believed that the salvation of the world depended on every one of my deeds, on every one of my prayers. But now, I no longer pleaded for anything [...] I felt very strong. I was the accuser, God, the accused. My eyes had opened and I was alone, terribly alone in a world without God.[32]

Wiesel learned, though, that once faith is lost, hope for living is lost as well. Akiba Drumer lost faith and was selected, Meir Katz lost faith and died on the train to Buchenwald, and even though Wiesel tried to give his father hope, he died as well. Praying to stay true to his father, Wiesel never completely lost his faith. He has had to reconcile what happened to him in the war and how people in his life changed. Wiesel recounts the beginning of his journey to Auschwitz: "'Faster! Faster!' […] the Hungarian police were screaming. That was when I began to hate them, and my hatred remains our only link today. They were our first oppressors. They were the first faces of hell and death."[33] Wiesel still grapples with hatred for the Hungarian police today.

Twins in the Camps

Life was very different for "Mengele's twins" in Auschwitz. They were the only survivors, saved solely because they were twins. Excluded from the selections that were a part of every other prisoner's life and living next to the crematoriums, the twins underwent severe torture. They were tested, injected with diseases, and had horrendous operations performed on them in the name of science. They also watched people go to the crematoriums every day.

Being Mengele's children was both a privilege and a curse. Many twins have grappled with their image of the "Angel of Death." It is hard to believe that a doctor who brought about the deaths of thousands of people could "charm and beguile youngsters."[34] For this reason, Mengele is seen as both a "savior and demon."[35] If he hadn't picked these children, they would have gone to the gas chambers. Mengele's twins live with demons. Nightmares invade the sleep of some, the burden of their selection saving their lives weighs on others, while some deal with "the foundation of their childhood being filled with the smell of burning flesh and chimneys belching out the black smoke of our families."[36] The twins seem to have suffered emotionally more than physically. While other hidden children of the Holocaust went on to lead normal lives, making the best of their time during the war, many twins have been at a standstill since the war, not able to shake the images of their past. The Holocaust stays with all who endured it, but Mengele's twins carry in their minds a burden that is hard to move past. Sharing their pain and stories has been freeing for some twins. It has allowed them to move forward and to finally live.

Conclusion

As difficult as it is to understand how Mengele and his co-conspirators did what they did, examining the mindset of Nazis at the time is important. Some say that Mengele and all who performed these deeds were insane. Not true. At the time, propaganda allowed for the mistreatment of Jews, making it acceptable for the Germans to carry out their plans. Jews were seen as an alien race and slated for annihilation. Mistreating

Jewish children was not a crime. Creating death factories enabled the killing and experimentation of Jews a business, therefore legitimizing the acts.

Now we know. Learning how genocide occurs and how committing violent acts is not as difficult when the right conditions are present is key to putting an end to genocide. The Holocaust's children have come out and shared their stories, finding support where some thought there was none. We are now messengers, keeping history alive, so it doesn't happen again.

Questions

1. *What is a memoir?*

2. *What is the difference between a memoir and an autobiography?*

3. *Who is Elie Wiesel? Is* Night *a memoir or an autobiography? Explain.*

Bibliography

Dwork, Deborah. *Children with a Star*. New Haven, CT: Yale University Press, 1991.

Gray, Martin. *For Those I Loved*, 35th ed. Charlottesville, VA: Hampton Roads, 1971.

Harris, Mark Jonathan and Deborah Oppenheimer. *Into the Arms of Strangers: Stories of the Kinderstransport*. London, UK: Bloomsbury Publishing, 2000.

Lagnado, Lucette Matalon and Sheila Cohn Dekel. *Children of the Flames: Dr. Josef Mengele and the Untold Story of the Twins of Auschwitz*. London, UK: Penguin Books, 1992.

Marks, Jane. *The Hidden Children: The Secret Survivors of the Holocaust*. New York: Fawcett Columbine, 1993.

Nordheimer, Jon. "For Twins of Auschwitz, Time to Unlock Secrets." *The New York Times* 14 (April 1991).

Spiegel, Fred. *Once the Acacias Bloomed*, 2nd ed. Margate, NJ: ComteQ Publishing, 2011.

Wiesel, Elie. *Night*. New York: Hill & Wang, 2006.

Notes

1. Jane Marks, *The Hidden Children: The Secret Survivors of the Holocaust* (New York: Fawcett Columbine, 1993), p. viii.
2. Ibid, p. iii.
3. Elie Wiesel, *Night: A New Translation* (New York: Hill and Wang, 2006), p. viii.
4. Ibid, p. ix.
5. Deborah Dwork, *Children with a Star: Jewish Youth in Nazi Europe* (New Haven, CT: Yale University Press, 1991), p. 3.
6. Marks, p. 43.
7. Fred Spiegel, *Once the Acacias Bloomed* (Margate, NJ: ComteQ Publishing, 2011), p. 19.
8. Dwork, p. 8.
9. Ibid, p. 10.
10. Ibid, p. 13.
11. Mark Jonathan Harris and Deborah Oppenheimer, *Into the Arms of Strangers: Stories of the Kinderstransport* (London, UK: Bloomsbury Publishing, 2000), p. 31.
12. Dwork, p. 21.
13. Harris and Oppenheimer, p. 27.
14. Marks, pp. 57-8.
15. Harris and Oppenheimer, p. 84.
16. Marks, pp. vii-viii.
17. Ibid, p. 293.
18. Ibid, pp. 26-33.
19. Harris and Oppenheimer.
20. Dwork, p. 159.
21. Wiesel, p. 12.
22. Dwork, p. 197.
23. Ibid.
24. Ibid.
25. Martin Gray, *For Those I Loved* (Charlottesville, VA: Hampton Roads, 1971).
26. Dwork, p. 199.
27. Ibid, p. 196.
28. Dwork, p. 183.
29. Wiesel, p. 77.
30. Ibid, p. 29.
31. Ibid, p. 33.
32. Ibid, p. 68.
33. Ibid, p. 19.
34. Lucette Matalon Lagnado and Sheila Cohn Dekel, *Children of the Flames: Dr. Josef Mengele and the Untold Story of the Twins of Auschwitz* (London, UK: Penguin Books, 1992), p. 9.
35. Jon Nordheimer, "For Twins of Auschwitz, Time to Unlock Secrets," *New York Times* (April 14, 1991), Retrieved April 28, 2012 at http://www.nytimes.com/1991/04/14/us/for-twins-of-auschwitz-time-to-unlock-secrets.html.
36. Ibid.

Eva Fogelman:
Rescuer of the Hidden Truth

. . . .

Jennifer L. Sproull

Recipient of the 2013 Ethel LeFrak Outstanding Student Scholar of the Holocaust Award

When studying the Holocaust, it is nearly impossible to imagine the tragedy of Hitler's twelve-year reign in Germany. The death, destruction, and hopelessness witnessed by those who were targeted by Hitler's regime cannot even be summed up in words. However, there were many who disagreed with the wrath of the Nazis and did all they could to help save others. They risked their family's safety and the comforts of life to hide Jewish families and those sought out by the Nazi regime. Rescuing others placed a major burden on families, and because of the risks, they had to carry out their actions in secret. To this day, many will not discuss their experiences, but one individual has devoted her life's work to telling their stories.

Eva Fogelman

Eva Fogelman has brought to light victims' secrets hidden like the ruins of the Holocaust. Her birth to Holocaust survivors in a Displaced Persons (DP) camp led her to a career as a psychologist. From there, she began to focus in-depth on counseling and therapy. Her work at Harvard Medical School brought her into contact with other individuals interested in starting a Jewish mental health clinic. As a result, she and colleague Bella Savran began the first short-term therapy group for the children of Holocaust survivors.[1]

This first step in her work generated a number of groups for children of Holocaust survivors. Many of them embraced their Jewish identity, while others were only learning about their Jewish heritage as adults. These groups also gave them the support needed to be able to discuss the horrific events of their past. This open communication among second-generation Holocaust survivors encouraged them to make connections with others who had come from this unique situation. The tragedy that brought these individuals together became the driving force for the First International Conference on Children of Holocaust Survivors, which was held November 4-5, 1979, at the Hebrew Union College in New York City. Six-hundred second-generation survivors participated in the conference, and it inspired them to return to their communities to begin support groups for others like them. The first world gathering of Holocaust survivors occurred in 1981, where 10,000 survivors and descendants met in Jerusalem. Through these gatherings, The International Network of Children of Jewish Holocaust Survivors was founded, with Eva Fogelman as a founding member.[2]

Through all of Fogelman's encounters with Holocaust survivors and their children, she began to collect information on non-Jews who rescued Jews during World War II. This research eventually became her doctoral dissertation, *The Rescuers: A Socio-Psychological Study of Altruistic Behavior during the Nazi Era*. Fogelman's commitment to this study helped connect her in 1986 with Rabbi Harold Schulweis, with whom she would co-found the Foundation to Sustain Righteous Christians; a short year later, the organization would change its name to the Jewish Foundation for Christian Rescuers. Today, that organization is known as the Jewish Foundation for the Righteous.[3]

The Jewish Foundation for the Righteous

The Jewish Foundation for the Righteous (JFR) was originally established to fulfill the Jewish pledge of *hakarat hatov*, the searching out and recognition of goodness. The foundation has committed its resources to helping Righteous Gentiles in need. The rationale behind doing so is that during the Holocaust these people helped Jews, and they did so without expecting any recognition or reward. The founding members of the JFR felt that it was their duty to honor the Gentiles' efforts.[4]

Initially, the JFR assisted eight rescuers, but there was a time when the organization was helping as many as 1,750 rescuers. In recent years, the number of rescuers receiving support has declined due to the passing of these heroic individuals; however, rescuers are constantly recognized, and the foundation continues to receive new applications for support. Presently, the JFR extends its funding and support to over 750 rescuers in 22 countries.[5]

Through its Rescuer Support Program, the JFR gives financial assistance to needy rescuers at three different times during the year in U.S. dollars. The money can be used for any number of reasons, including for food, heating, medical care and medications, or for other emergency needs that may arise. Grants are also provided if requested to help defray the costs associated with funerals. To date, the foundation has awarded over \$31 million to these courageous individuals.[6]

While many may think that the only function of the JFR is to financially support individuals who were rescuers, it does serve the additional purpose of preserving the memory and legacy of the rescuers through the JFR's National Holocaust Education Program. The JFR's specific objectives include the following:

- To provide high quality Holocaust education that runs the gamut from an introduction of the subject to intense study at residential seminars and institutes;
- To improve Holocaust teacher education by working with established Holocaust centers across the country to complement the efforts of other organizations working in the field;
- To expose teachers to the best in current scholarship on the Holocaust, to develop their knowledge of the subject, and to treat teachers as serious learners and educators; and
- To develop a skilled network of teachers who teach history of the Holocaust and rescue.

Teachers from the United States and Eastern Europe, working with personnel at the JFR's Holocaust Center, learn about the Holocaust and about some of the rescuers of Jews during the Holocaust. As a result of this dedicated program, over 400 educators have been given the status of master teacher in Holocaust history and the subject of rescue. Teachers can achieve master teacher status through one of the four key elements included in the education program:

- JFR-published educational materials;
- The Alfred Lerner Fellowship program;
- A Holocaust Centers of Excellence program; and
- Educational seminars, institutes, and workshops for teachers and students.[7]

Various JFR Programs
The Holocaust Centers of Excellence Program was established to impact Holocaust education on a national level. In the spring of 2000, partnerships were made with sixteen centers, which have since invested their time and funds into these different communities. By agreeing to participate in the agreement with JFR, each center is allotted two scholarships to the Summer Institute for Teachers; they can then nominate two additional teachers every year. Each center also agrees to use JFR resources to teach the Holocaust and to specifically include the subject of rescue. Teachers completing the summer program are known as Alfred Lerner Fellows.[8]

The Alfred Lerner Fellowship Program was named in memory of Alfred Lerner, who was the founding chairman and chief executive officer of MBNA Corporation. Each summer, a program is held at Columbia University as a tribute to Lerner's commitment not only to the foundation, but especially to his interest in Holocaust education. To date, there are more than 400 Lerner Fellows.[9]

In June 2000, the National Holocaust Teacher Educator Program was launched through JFR. The program includes a residential summer program, an advanced seminar, an educators' study program to Germany and Poland, an academic newsletter, and partnerships with Holocaust centers throughout the country. The resource used in these programs is *Voices & Views: A History of the Holocaust* by Deborah Dwork, a leading Holocaust historian. A second book currently being written will include additional resources and ideas to integrate the topics and lessons learned in Voices & Views. To further assist educators in their classrooms, JFR offers a Speakers Bureau dedicated to Holocaust-related subjects. Speakers include Holocaust scholars, survivors, rescuers, and JFR staff members who are available to speak on a number of topics.[10]

Teachers are not the only recipients of the JFR's goodwill. In the New York/New Jersey area, schools that participate in the Holocaust Teacher Educator Program can send students and their teachers to the Annual Dinner. It provides the opportunity to meet the rescuer being honored at the dinner. Prior to the dinner, representatives from the JFR staff visit the students and teachers planning on attending the dinner in order to describe the work of the JFR and tell the story of the rescuer and of the rescue itself.[11]

One of the most intriguing programs offered by the JFR is the Bar/Bat Mitzvah Program. The program matches a Bar/Bat Mitzvah with a Righteous Gentile (or twin). The hope for this event is that it connects a special event in the family's life with their Jewish history and values, fulfilling the teaching of *tzedakah* (charity or justice), *tikkun olam* (repairing the world), and *hakarat hatov* (the seeking out and recognition of goodness). JFR also offers specially designed invitations to recognize this unique experience. The experience of involving Righteous Gentiles in the Bar/Bat Mitzvah can be extremely powerful not only for the family, but also for the young person as s/he becomes Bar/Bat Mitzvah. To participate in the Twinning Program or Invitation Program, a minimum donation to JFR is requested.[12]

Hidden Child Foundation

Eva Fogelman's footprints were not simply made in one organization. Her research led her to meet individuals like Myriam Abramowicz, who had a vision of bringing together surviving children of the Holocaust that had been hidden in convents, orphanages, non-Jewish homes, etc. The First International Gathering of Hidden Children, co-sponsored by the Anti-Defamation League, occurred in 1991, with over 1,600 hidden children and families attending from around the world. This gathering allowed the hidden children to speak of their own personal Holocaust experiences and relate to others their feelings of having their childhoods stolen. Participating in the Hidden Children gathering also opened doors for them to finally break down the walls of silence to their spouses, children, families, and the outside world. The Hidden Child Foundation was founded as a result of this gathering.

The mission of the Hidden Child Foundation is "to educate all people about the consequences of bigotry and hatred so that never again will anyone suffer the atrocity, the injustice, and the agony of the Holocaust." It was founded with help from Abraham H. Foxman, the National Director of the Anti-Defamation League and also a hidden child from Poland.[13]

The Hidden Child Foundation describes a very specific list of actions it considers important in reaching out to all former hidden children:

- Hold national and international conferences workshops, and gatherings;
- Sponsor Hidden Children speakers worldwide to share their stories of survival;
- Use our extensive database to help us act as a liaison of all Hidden Children, helping them find each other and learn about their pasts;
- Help Hidden Children and children of Holocaust survivors form support groups;
- Develop educational curricula and materials for schools;
- Publish *The Hidden Child*, the Foundation's newsletter, excerpts from which are online in "The Experiences of Hidden Children" section;
- Advocate for psychological and financial help for Hidden Children; and
- Honor rescuers through the Braun Holocaust Institute.[14]

The Hidden Children of the Holocaust witnessed unspeakable horrors that gave them their first taste of reality. Many have felt these children were too young to remember what they saw and reminded them of how lucky they were to have survived. Unfortunately, too often this is a false statement for the survivors, as it only worsened their suffering. Through the Hidden Child Foundation, many members have been able to find strength to overcome and turn their feelings about what they experienced into a way to live positive, productive lives.[15]

Scholarship

Many look at Eva Fogelman's achievements in founding various organizations and groups committed to the legacy of the rescuer as her greatest achievement, but I think her most important contribution to Holocaust history and research is the book she wrote, *Conscience and Courage: Rescuers of Jews during the Holocaust*.

For this project, Fogelman interviewed more than 300 rescuers from all walks of life. Not only did she tell the story of rescuers, but as a psychologist, she dug deeper into their psyches to explore the reasons they risked their lives and those of their families to hide people they sometimes didn't even know.[16] Fogelman discovered that rescuers who were part of her interviews had a common background that included the following traits:

1) Deep inner values of tolerance and acceptance of others, as well as religious and moral certainty;
2) A loving and supportive family;
3) A creative mind that allowed them to solve difficult problems; and
4) The ability to see situations where they were able to do something to help another or others.

When individuals witnessed the horror all around them, most had no intention of becoming "the rescuer." Many gave in to an impulse to help that arose from an immediate situation; others made their decision to help as the result of a continuous chain of events. The point at which a decision was made to help someone during the Holocaust transformed a person into what Fogelman calls "The Rescuer Self." These individuals who helped often had to lead a double life: one that was a "normal" life of the time, and another that lied, stole, and even killed. All of this demanded a kind of sacrifice and selflessness on the part of the rescuer. Studying about the selflessness of rescuers has become Dr. Eva Fogelman's defining role in the study of the Holocaust. It is also her great contribution to the study of the Holocaust.[18]

Fogelman's research on the rescuers has brought many new topics to light that had previously been in the shadows of Holocaust studies. When speaking of the Holocaust, we immediately think of Adolf Hitler and his massacre of the Jewish population. However, hearing the stories of the rescuers, thinking about the parents who gave up their children to the care of total strangers even as they themselves were being sent off to die, even thinking about Jews who were on the run and praying that they would make it another day without being caught – all of this is part of studying about the Holocaust.

Personal Note

In completing this final paper, the only statement I can make is that Eva Fogelman was and continues to be a G-d-send to all rescuers and those rescued during the Holocaust. Her conviction in uncovering the stories of their courage and heroic natures is a blessing in many ways to many people. Fogelman's book, *Conscience and Courage: The Rescuers of Jews during the Holocaust* gives recognition where recognition is due — to survivors of a horrendous reign of terror who helped other people. In my opinion, they are true heroes.

Reading Fogelman's book, *Conscience and Courage*, has made me think deeply about my life and my own struggles. Reading about what individuals – victims and rescuers – were faced with on a daily basis reminds me how insignificant my struggles are today. This class pushed me to think about my own values and morals, to question whether or not I would lay my life down to protect another. Could I protect someone who showed up on my doorstep, even going against my own religious, moral, and personal values to do so? When looking for answers to these questions, many of us think we know the answers; we are sure we would help our fellow men and women. But would we really? Would we sacrifice our lives and those of our family to protect someone else? These are difficult questions to ponder, but they are questions we need to think about often. I am grateful that Dr. Eva Fogelman has given us examples of men and women, even young people, who risked their lives for others. These Righteous Gentiles are examples for us all as we live our lives in difficult times.

Questions

1. *Who is Eva Fogelman and what motivated her to become involved in her research?*

2. *What is meant by the term "hidden child" or "hidden children" when it comes to the Holocaust? In what way were their experiences different, even "unique," as compared to other survivors of the Holocaust?*

3. *Eva Fogelman's book,* Conscience and Courage, *focuses on rescuers of Jews during the Holocaust. What motivated some of the rescuers she writes about to risk their lives, and sometimes even the lives of their families, to help Jews?*

4. *If you were faced with having to risk your life for another person, do you think you could do it? Explain. Suppose it also meant putting the lives of your family at risk; do you think you would do it? Explain.*

Bibliography

Blumenthal, David R. "Book Review: Eva Fogelman, *Conscience and Courage: Rescuers of Jews during the Holocaust.*" *Journal of Psychology and Theology*, 23 (1994): 62-63. Available at http://www.js.emory.edu/BLUMENTHAL/Fogelman.html.

Dwork, Deborah, ed. *Voices and Views: A History of the Holocaust*. Madison, WI: University of Wisconsin Press, 2005.

Fogelman, Eva. *Conscience and Courage: The Rescuers of the Jews during the Holocaust.* New York: Anchor Books, 1994.

Fogelman, Eva. "The Rescuer Self." *The Holocaust and History: The Known, the Unknown, the Disputed, and the Reexamined.* Eds. Michael Berenbaum and Abraham J. Peck. Bloomington and Indianapolis: Indiana University Press, 1998: 663-77.

Harris, Mark Jonathan and Deborah Oppenheimer, eds. *Into the Arms of Strangers: Stories of the Kindertransport.* New York: Bloomsbury Publishing, 2000.

Hidden Child Foundation, Anti-Defamation League. "Between Two Religions." 2013. Available at http://www.adl.org/hidden/between_religions/between_religions_toc.asp.

Marks, Jane. *The Hidden Children: The Secret Survivors of the Holocaust.* New York: Fawcett Columbine, 1993.

Rosenberg, Maxine B. *Hiding to Survive: Stories of Jewish Children Rescued from the Holocaust.* New York: Clarion Books, 1994.

United States Holocaust Memorial Museum (no date). "Life in the Shadows: Hidden Children of the Holocaust," http://www.ushmm.org/museum/exhibit/online/hiddenchildren/index/.

Notes

1. Wikipedia. "Dr. Eva Fogelman." 2012. Accessed at: http://en.wikipedia.org/wiki/Eva_Fogelman.
2. Ibid.
3. Ibid.
4. Jewish Foundation for the Righteous (JFR). "History." Accessed at: http://www.jfr.org/pages/about-jfr.
5. JFR. "Rescuer Support Program." Accessed at: http://www.jfr.org/pages/rescuer-support/rescuer-support-program.
6. Ibid.
7. JFR. "Education: Teaching the History." Accessed at: http://www.jfr.org/pages/education/education.
8. JFR. "Holocaust Centers of Excellence Program." Accessed at: http://www.jfr.org/pages/education/for-teachers/holocaust-centers-of-excellence-program.
9. JFR. "For Teachers." Accessed at: http://www.jfr.org/pages/education/for-teachers.
10. JFR. "Speakers Bureau." Accessed at: http://www.jfr.org/pages/education/for-teachers/speakers-bureau.
11. JFR. "For Students." Accessed at: http://www.jfr.org/pages/education/for-students.
12. JFR. "Bar/Bat Mitzvah Program." Accessed at: http://www.jfr.org/bar/bat-mitzvah-program.
13. Hidden Child Foundation (HCF), Anti-Defamation League (ADL). "What is the Hidden Child Foundation?" Accessed at: http://www.adl.org/hidden/default.asp.
14. HCF-ADL. "What the Hidden Child Does." Accessed at: http://www.adl.org/hidden/what_we_do.asp.
15. "What is the Hidden Child Foundation?"
16. Wikipedia.
17. Ibid.
18. Ibid.

Tribute to Ethel LeFrak

▪ ▪ ▪ ▪ ▪ ▪ ▪ ▪ ▪ ▪

Gemma Del Duca S.C.

Co-Director (Israel), The National Catholic Center for Holocaust Education,
Seton Hill University, Greensburg, PA

In 2008, Ethel LeFrak endowed the triennial Holocaust Conference of Seton Hill University's National Catholic Center for Holocaust Education. Henceforth, this conference will be known as *The Ethel LeFrak Holocaust Education Conference*.

In October 2009, Ethel LeFrak conveyed a message to those who were participating in the Holocaust conference that year, expressing her hopes for them and for the world:

> Simply to think of the Holocaust and all genocides sends shivers down one's spine. It is inconceivable that during the twentieth century these horrors occurred. Nevertheless, it is now up to us to continue the fight against bigotry and ignorance by inspiring worldwide understanding and tolerance, by educating the educators to probe and dissect, to publish and disseminate the reasons behind the Holocaust and all genocide, so that abominations like that will never happen again, at any time, to anyone.

When World War II broke out, devastating and destroying the lives of so many, Ethel LeFrak was a young student at Barnard College in New York City. The memory of those years stayed with her. It was during this time that she met and later married Samuel J. LeFrak, the founder of one of the largest private building firms in the world. Ethel LeFrak, loving wife and devoted mother of four, became, along with her husband, a distinguished philanthropist, dedicating her time and resources to cultural, educational, and medical institutions. She served as a trustee of the Cardozo Law School and of the Albert Einstein Medical College, as well as a member of the Council of the Salk Institute, vice-president of the Little Orchestra Society, and patron of the Asia Society. A member of the Metropolitan Opera's "Golden Horseshoe" and "Opera Club," Ethel LeFrak was also a patron of Lincoln Center in New York City.

In her efforts to reach out to as many fellow New Yorkers as possible, she became a conservator of the New York Public Library. Her interest in international affairs moved her to become a member of the Board of the United Nations International Hospitality Committee. Ethel LeFrak's good works through this Committee were acknowledged in 1994 when she and her husband received the United Nations "Distinguished Citizens of the World" Award. The LeFraks co-edited and published two books on their family art collection: *Masters of the Modern Tradition* (New York: LeFrak Organization, 1988; catalogue by Diane Kelder) and *A Passion for Art* (New York: Rizzoli, 1994; text by Diane Kelder). In 1996, Ethel LeFrak was awarded a Doctor of Humane Letters, *honoris causa*, by Seton Hill University.

A well-deserved tribute and award came to Ethel LeFrak in October 2009. Seton Hill University and the National Catholic Center for Holocaust Education presented her with the Saint Elizabeth Ann Seton Woman of Courage Award acknowledging her commitment to the work of the University's Holocaust Center and her noble efforts to foster friendship, peace, and reconciliation among people of different backgrounds. Nobel Prize Laureate Elie Wiesel, commenting on Ethel LeFrak's life's work, said, "You have done so much for so many people of different faiths that all of us, your friends, rejoice in this very much merited recognition."

In May 2013, Francine LeFrak sent a personal e-mail to then Seton Hill University President, Dr. JoAnne Boyle, to let her know about "my mother, Ethel LeFrak's passing" on May 14, 2013. Those who knew Ethel LeFrak were filled with sadness, even as they recalled with gratitude all the good she had done during her life. She touched the lives of many people. May her memory continue to be a blessing.

What could one add to Ethel LeFrak's commitment, to her accomplishments, to her generosity? Perhaps only the poetic words of the Book of Proverbs:

> An accomplished woman, who can find her? Her value is beyond pearls,
> She is like the merchant ships; she brings her bread from afar.
> She extends her hands to the poor, and reaches out her hand to the needy.
> She opens her mouth in wisdom and the lesson of kindness is on her
> tongue (*Proverbs* 31: 10, 14, 20, 26).

Seton Hill University and the National Catholic Center for Holocaust Education will continue to celebrate the life of Dr. Ethel LeFrak and to acknowledge with deep gratitude her commitment to preparing educators to mend the world through understanding and dialogue, learning and teaching in the present for the sake of the future.

Ethel LeFrak
Photo by Gregory Partanio © ManhattanSociety.com

Under a Blue Sky, *2001 by Samuel Bak*
Image Courtesy of Pucker Gallery

ACKNOWLEDGEMENTS

During the weeks we worked on ***Holocaust Education: Challenges for the Future***, we were very conscious of Seton Hill University's long-time, recently retired president, Dr. JoAnne Boyle. News of her death on November 1, 2013, the Feast of All Saints, brought sadness but also enormous gratitude for all the support and encouragement she always extended to everyone, particularly those of us who try to fulfill the mission of the National Catholic Center for Holocaust Education (NCCHE). Dr. Boyle, as much as anyone, even after her retirement, gave her support in many ways so that these conference proceedings could be published. We are very grateful to her.

In addition, we want to thank the NCCHE Advisory Board and its Steering Committee for its help. We also want to thank Sister Gemma Del Duca, S.C., Ph.D., NCCHE Co-Director (Israel), and Wilda Kaylor, NCCHE Associate Director, for their help and support as we worked on this volume.

Thanks also are due to Sister Lois Sculco, S.C., Ph.D., Vice President for Institutional Identity, Mission and Student Life at Seton Hill University, and the many Seton Hill University administrators, faculty, professional staff, employees, and students who supported this endeavor in so many ways.

We also thank Glen Powell, our graphics artist who contributed so much to our book; and Laurel Valley Graphics, our printer, who helped to bring this publishing project to a successful completion.

To Bernie Pucker, Owner and President of Pucker Gallery, thank you for drawing our attention to the imaginative works of Holocaust Survivor Samuel Bak over the years and for connecting us with the Facing History and Ourselves® exhibit. Liz Burgess, Associate Director of Operations at Pucker Gallery, has our special thanks for responding so promptly to all of our requests.

We thank as well The Wolfsonian-Florida International University, Miami Beach, FL for permission to use an image of the poster, *Der ewige Jude* [The Eternal Jew] from The Mitchell Wolfson, Jr. Collection. Likewise, we thank People for the Ethical Treatment of Animals (PETA) for permission to use the image of the PETA ad featuring Pamela Anderson.

We are grateful also to Judi Bohn, Facing History and Ourselves® Special Projects Coordinator, for arranging the loan of *Illuminations: The Art of Samuel Bak at Facing History and Ourselves®*, a gift of Samuel and Josée Bak and Bernie and Sue Pucker, for exhibit at Seton Hill University's Harlan Gallery as part of the Conference.

Finally, we thank all of the contributors to ***Holocaust Education: Challenges for the Future***. They met their deadlines, made their corrections, and generously helped us to meet our deadlines. They made our task so much easier. We thank them and everyone who contributed in any way, large or small, to the conference and to this publication, ***Holocaust Education: Challenges for the Future***.

Carol Rittner, R.S.M., Editor
Tara Ronda, Managing Editor

Index